# THE LIGHT OF LOVE:
## "MY ANGEL SHALL
## GO BEFORE THEE"

# THE LIGHT OF LOVE:
## "MY ANGEL SHALL
## GO BEFORE THEE"

Compiled By
*Patricia M. Devlin*

Queenship Publishing Company
P.O Box 42028
Santa Barbara, CA 93140-2028
(800) 647-9882  Fax: (805) 957-1631

# Declaration

The decree of the Congregation for the Propagation of the Faith, A.A.S. 58, 1186 (approved by Pope Paul VI on October 14, 1966) states that the *Nihil Obstat* and *Imprimatur* are no longer required on publications that deal with private revelations, provided they contain nothing contrary to the faith and morals.

The author wishes to manifest her unconditional submission to the final and official judgement of the Magisterium of the Church.

Cover art: J. Schaefer McGrath

©1995 Queenship Publishing

Library of Congress Number 95-68111

ISBN: 1-882972-53-8

Published by:
    Queenship Publishing
    P.O. Box 42028
    Santa Barbara, CA 93140-2028
    (800) 647-9882 • (805) 957-4893 • FAX: (805) 957-1631

Printed in the United States of America

Printing History:
    *First Printing - March 1995*
    *Second Printing - August 1995*
    *Third Printing - May 1996*

# DEDICATION

To Father Lawrence Mann,
    who wondered if anyone was listening to his homilies;

To Mother Teresa,
    who first gave me the hope that I too might be allowed to serve;

And to Sister Miriam Ferry, O.S.F.,
    whose whole life is a prayer of love.

# Publisher's Note

This book is made up of thoughts from the author, messages from Angels and, most importantly, messages from Our Lord and Our Blessed Mother.

We have not edited the text of this book to avoid the chance of changing the true thrust of the messages.

We want to acknowledge Fr. John Walch's contribution to this book. In addition to being Patricia's spiritual advisor, he is an accomplished artist. Father is shown below putting the finishing touches on the sketch for the cover of this book. Inquiries for Pat Devlin should be addressed ℅ Queenship Publishing at the address shown on the title page.

# TABLE OF CONTENTS

# FOREWORD

by Father John L. Walch,
Father Francis E. Butler, S.S.J.
Father William Vouk, III, STL, JCL

Father John Walch, Patricia Devlin's spiritual director, says he is allegedly a retired parish priest, yet he is busier now than ever before. He writes:

Rarely in a Catholic priest's career is he asked to serve as spiritual guide for a privileged soul — one favored by God with special gifts far beyond the ordinary and who, in addition, is a victim soul.

In summer 1988, after moving from Minnesota to Lubbock, Texas, Patricia Devlin, for the first time, heard the voice of her Guardian Angel. To say the least, this was shocking. But the kindness, care and love he expressed in his voice put her at ease. He taught her how to test spirits to determine if they are good or evil; and the test he gave is one approved by the Church, which you will find in this book. Once, in the beginning, Pat forgot to test, and what she heard was gobbledygook. Her angel reproved her, "You forgot to test. You <u>must</u> test every time!" This was a very valuable lesson.

The God–given name for Pat's angel — which she rarely divulges — consists of six words. When I became her spiritual director she told me the name, but I found it difficult to remember. So I gave her Guardian Angel the name "Glorification" which he accepted with good grace. Today everyone — including Pat — calls him "Glorification." One lesson I learned in dealing with him is that he and all the angels have a very good sense of humor.

For instance, once while speaking with Pat I made reference to "Glorification"; later, in the conversation, I referred to him as "Glory", and still later as "Glo". He said, "Tell Father that if he keeps abbreviating my name, soon he will abbreviate me right out of existence!" Only an angel with a marvelous sense of humor could say that. Personally, I find it very comforting to know that those in the Heavenly realm have a keen sense of humor.

After Glorification's initial talk with Pat, he gradually began to speak at greater length and today, five years later, he speaks freely, giving her warnings when necessary, advising her, and guiding her with words of wisdom. But lest the readers think that a continuous conversation takes place between them, they should know that Glorification speaks only when he deems it wise — with God's permission. Weeks may pass without a single word. If Pat attempts to initiate conversation, she prays first, asking Our Lord's permission to allow Glorification to speak. This prayer may be answered, and again it may not. So he does not "speak on demand," as so many think. It is entirely at Our Lord's time and discretion.

Several times Glorification has spoken to me through Pat, giving me advice or instructions. The first time he joined in our conversation, to say the least I was startled; but today I am rather accustomed to it. When he dictates to Pat, he considerately allows time for her to repeat his words so that I can write them down. So does Our Lord and Our Lady, both of whom have spoken to her. Glorification told her, "You must be totally obedient to your spiritual director and both of you ultimately to the Church."

When Glorification makes his presence known to Pat, a beautiful light precedes him, which Pat, although blind since birth and at present totally without eyes, can see in some mysterious way. It reminds us of Revelations 22:4–5 "They will look upon His face, and his name will be on their foreheads. Night will be no more, nor will they need light from lamp or sun, for the Lord God shall give them light, and they shall reign forever and ever." Sometimes she sees the angels' light for several hours, but no conversation ensues. All angels emit this wondrous light in varying degrees.

In addition to their special light, angels sing in chorus. Pat describes their singing as exquisitely beautiful, ethereal choral music sung in harmony in an unearthly language she cannot understand, but which elicits her highest enjoyment and praise.

On one occasion Pat assumed a rhapsodic expression. I inquired what was happening. She replied, "The angels are processing through this room, singing beautifully." Since I could not hear them, I said, "Please tell them to turn up the volume." Then she said they broke into peals of laughter, just as we humans do.

At the outset, Glorification forbade her to *read any books about angels*, or any *theological* books. She may read the Bible and other spiritual books. Shortly after our first meeting, I commented, "For a person who has never studied theology you are the straightest theologian I have ever met." With an Irish smile she replied, "I have had the best of teachers."

My work with Pat has given me a whole new vision of and appreciation for angels, one not usually taught this way in seminaries. I hope you will find as much pleasure in this book as I have. These beautiful spirits God has given us as constant companions here on earth, and for all eternity, *love us* with a great and everlasting love. May they and we together adore the Most Blessed Trinity and honor Mary, Queen of all Angels and Saints in the heavenly kingdom.

Father John L. Walch,
Spiritual Director

Father Francis E. Butler, S.S.J., has been a guest speaker on Mother Angelica's EWTN. He is currently the pastor of a little church in the inner city of Montgomery, Alabama. With the help of God and generous hearts, he feeds and assists 150 street people a day. He writes:

The book that you are holding in your hand is the Journal of a special soul — a soul, I believe, has a special mission to help spread devotion to the Holy Angels.

Each one of us comes from the loving hand of God and each of us has a purpose for being here on earth — but few are given a task as interesting and as challenging as the one the author of this fascinating book has received. Being blind from birth makes God's selection of Pat Devlin for this task even more amazing, unusual and unlikely. God's ways of doing things are definitely not man's ways of doing things. No discrediting of the abilities of blind people is meant here. Pat herself has said that the thought of writing a descriptive book in which presumably the ability to see might be useful was a daunting one, especially since her sensitivity and acute touch in being able to minutely feel many of the gifts of God's blessings to her could easily be questioned by people who believe sight is the authoritative sense.

I first met Pat in 1988 while on a trip to Lubbock, Texas, with a group of about 70 pilgrims from New Orleans (where I happened to be assigned at the time.) While in Lubbock we were told about a blind lady who had been privileged to speak with her Guardian Angel. So, of course, we were very much interested in listening to her story — and what a tremendous story it was and continues to be! She very simply, humbly and honestly shared with us all that which God was doing in her soul. I was quite impressed with her positive humor, realistically seeing herself and her unusual situation and finding joy and amusement in her own reactions to it. I found all she shared quite believable.

By definition, angels are pure, created spirits. Some angels are sent by God as messengers to humans, as was the case, for instance, with the Archangel Gabriel announcing the Incarnation to the Blessed Mother of Our Lord or the Archangel Raphael healing the eyes of the blinded Tobit. Angels, being pure spirit, of course have no body and do not therefore depend on matter for their activity and existence. The Bible tells us that the number of angels constitute a vast multitude, beyond human reckoning.

One author explains guardian angels as celestial spirits assigned by God to watch over each individual during life. This general doctrine of the angels' care for each person is part of the Church's constant tradition, based on Sacred Scripture and the teachings of the Fathers of the Church. The role of our guardian angels is both to guide and to guard us; to guide each of us as a messenger of God's will to our minds, and to guard us by being an instrument of God's goodness in protecting us from evil. This protection from evil is mainly a safeguard against the evil of sin and the malice of the devil. But the angels also protect us from physical evil insofar as this is useful or necessary to guard our souls from spiritual harm.

A feast honoring our guardian angels has been celebrated in October, throughout the Universal Church founded by Jesus Christ, since the 17th century. We celebrate it now on October 2. After reading this book, you may find that the feast of your guardian angel has a much more important significance for you, and now you can celebrate too!

The existence of angels has been twice defined by the Church at the Fourth Lateran Council and the first Vatican Council. But for some strange reason, belief in angels in recent years has declined. Not only are they not appreciated but in many circles — even some Catholic ones — they are ignored. This is truly unfortunate! As any honest observer of the contemporary scene recognizes, these are trying times in which we live, times of moral and doctrinal confusion. Many people appear to have lost the sense of sin. On a spiritual level, Satan seems to be having a field day as he goes about "seeking the ruin of souls."

But if this were the end of the story, it would be a bleak future indeed. Periodically, however, God, in His infinite goodness and wisdom, selects certain souls to bring a word of comfort. Pat Devlin's mission appears to be that of reminding us that while the power of Satan is strong, that of the good angels, especially our guardian angels through the love of God, is stronger and that we should turn to them as special friends.

Beginning in 1988 and lasting for about four years, I had the privilege of being a spiritual director (though at a distance) for Pat. Not only was I privy to her experiences with angels, but I watched the unfolding of events as Pat was called to an understanding of a deeper faith and love through suffering. As an observer, one easily gets the impression that Pat's whole being is slowly being renewed, shaped and transformed in the crucible of suffering — in union with Jesus as all human suffering can be — and what an extraordinary privilege she considers that to be!

I find the whole thing amazing. Yet, when one considers the age in which we live — an age that views all suffering as useless and without any redeeming qualities; something to be avoided at all costs, the idea to us in this modern time that there might be something everlastingly useful in suffering is, to say the least, unique. Given the current mentality in our hedonistic age, it really is not surprising to see those who see only negatives in suffering spawning organizations and industries which promote death as a final exit out of needless and valueless pain. But even putting aside for a moment the Christian belief in the spiritual value of suffering and sacrificing for others, when has real spiritual growth and maturity ever come without pain? The lack of understanding of this fact and the wish to avoid the immediate pain rather than sacrifice for a greater good afterwards is what makes the Doctor Kavorkians with their death machines so attractive to our benumbed age.

Ironically, all of this is promoted in the name of mercy, compassion and love! However, through her suffering in union with Christ, as all human suffering can be, Pat views suffering as a pathway to holiness, a pathway to life. Suffering is, of course, no guarantee to a life of greater holiness because everyone suffers. Suffering is an opportunity to develop a greater spiritual maturity. Pat has come to view all of life, including pain and perhaps especially pain, as a great opportunity for sanctity. After all, trying to achieve sanctity is what we are supposed to be doing here on earth. Anything else in the scheme of God's Eternal Kingdom would be a foolish waste of precious time.

Father Francis E. Butler, S.S.J.
Pastor, St. John the Baptist Catholic Church
Montgomery, AL

The following was written by Pat's friend of fifteen years, Father William Vouk. Father Vouk is the pastor of a parish in a northern Minnesota town, and the tribunal judge for the Saint Cloud Diocese.

It was our loving God who brought me into contact with Patricia Devlin. Of this I am sure: only He could arrange an event which would bring so much blessing to me! In 1978, I was a college freshman in my first year in the seminary in Saint Paul, Minnesota (a state which is much more pleasant and generally much less cold than Pat has perceived it to be), and Pat was living near the campus. She had run a request in our bulletin for "readers," and I responded; and so soon found myself sitting in her living room, reading a statistics textbook into a tape recorder. Can you imagine the difficulty I had trying to describe the statistical graphs which appeared on nearly every page? Far greater, no doubt, was Pat's difficulty in understanding the descriptions, but she must have understood well enough, because she completed her masters in psychology and went on to doctoral studies.

At this point, I could proceed to relate how determined Pat is, about the strength she has shown in moving toward goals even when there were many obstacles to overcome. But somehow, "determined" is not the first word that comes to mind when I think of Pat, nor what struck me most about her when I first met her. Instead, when I think of Patricia Devlin, I am first reminded of the great spiritual profundity and richness that she possesses, a depth of soul that attracted me and, as it were, enveloped me, from the moment I met her. I remember how, that first day, I had no idea what to expect from this lady, then a stranger to me; I thought I would just go and read some text and then leave.

Instead, I ended up talking with Pat at length, and came to learn about how she had come to Minnesota, and what the Lord had done in her life up to that point. As the weeks went by, it became clear to me that God had given me a very good friend in Pat Devlin.

Since then, no matter where Pat or I have moved, and no matter how infrequent our correspondence has been, I have never felt far away from her. On the contrary, I feel in many ways closer to her now than ever before. Her love for Jesus, her trust in the Church, her care for her daughters and for all the other people who have entered her life, have become more and more evident to me as the years have gone by. When she told me about how she had started to receive the extraordinary visions and locutions which she describes in this book, there was no question in my mind that she was telling the truth. I say this first of all because I know Pat to be an exceedingly trustworthy woman. Aside from this, however, I have examined her reports and find in them no indication of anything even remotely at odds with the teaching of Christ and His Church. My qualifications for saying so are admittedly not as well established as those of others, but I am certain that even the most respected Catholic theologians would agree with me on this point. And not only this, but I am sure they, as I, would find the events and messages which Pat reports to be positively helpful to Catholic spirituality.

I wish everyone could read these notes of hers! I am convinced that the reader who accepts her words with an open heart will experience the fulfillment of the hopes Pat has for him or her: that each would know more deeply the infinite love of God for each individual, and that each would come to love the Sacred Scriptures which the Lord has given to us.

Father William Vouk III, STL, JCL
June, 1993

# INTRODUCTION

By Patricia M. Devlin

[Note: I have been told by several readers that they understood the following introduction more clearly after reading the main text first, and then reading the introduction as a postscript. You may wish to do this.]

I have never read a theology book in my life. Though I have loved reading the Scriptures since I was a little girl, the idea that I might ever have anything to do with compiling a book about God would have terrified me five years ago. I am still deeply awed at the prospect. Yet my own heart and the orders of the priest who is much more than my spiritual director but also my guide to the will of Jesus for me, Father John Walch of Oklahoma City, compel me to offer this book, praying that it will be seen as I have compiled it: as a song of wondering joy to "the Lord of light and love": God the Father, God the Son, and God the Holy Spirit.

As I have spoken of the events recorded in this book, people have said to me, "You seem to be a sincere and sane person, but what you say is so unbelievable, so extraordinary." Yes. What is written here is unbelievable and extraordinary because the love of God for each one of us is unbelievable and extraordinary in everyday human terms. That God should have become a human being "like us in all ways but sin", should have taught us that Divine Love can exist on earth and be given to us through Him and through us to each other, that He should have suffered horribly and died for us, and that He calls us to the Pascal Supper of His new covenant every time we receive Him in the Holy Eucharist—all of this is extraordinary and unbelievable. The wondrous events recorded here are as nothing when compared to these mysteries. But it is as if He says through the events recorded in this book, "I am still with you. I still love you. I have never and will never stop loving you."

I have wondered if you, the reader of this book, could believe its contents. The experiences of God's love with which I have been blessed are, to say the least, extraordinary. One night I wailed to my spiritual director, Father John Walch, "You and I know it's all true, but so many people won't believe a word of it! I am going to tell the world that I talk to angels — and that sometimes they answer me!"

"Don't worry," he told me in his down–to–earth, calm way, "you couldn't have written those conversations, and anyone who thinks you did is paying you a very undeserved compliment. So either you will be believed, or you will be paid a very undeserved compliment."

People have asked me, "Did you have a devotion to your guardian angel before all these events occurred?" Yes, I probably did have a greater awareness of my Guardian Angel than do most other people, though I would scarcely call my awareness "devotion." Over my lifetime, several incidents have taken place of which I am aware and which, until four and a half years ago, would have made me say I was quite sure I had a very active guardian angel. Now, of course, I have no doubts of angelic help.

One of these incidents occurred when my twin daughters were about three years old. I am totally blind. In 1987 I met my guide dog Gia at GUIDE DOGS FOR THE BLIND in California.

Before this, I used a long white cane to assist me in traveling. On a day in 1976, I was walking down University Avenue in Honolulu towards King Street during rush hour. As anyone familiar with Honolulu rush hour traffic knows, on the main thoroughfares the cars whiz by with little or no break. I was walking down to King Street to my daughters' preschool to go pick them up and get a ride home from the preschool with a neighbor.

Believing that a driver stopped at a freeway exit had seen me, I stepped off the curb and began walking across the exit. The driver had not seen me. He drove forward, knocking me over. To avoid his wheels I had to roll away from him into the oncoming heavy traffic. For that crucial moment and that moment alone, no cars were coming. I was badly bruised and went into shock, but otherwise was unhurt. "It surely must have been my Guardian Angel who, by the grace of God, gave me that empty space in the traffic; enough to get out of the way," I thought later.

Another time a few years later, I was walking to an appointment in downtown Minneapolis. The light for a crossing was in my favor. I stepped off the curb and was one pace into the street when a voice shouted in my head, "Stop!!" I froze. In that second, a car came tearing around the corner towards which I was walking and whizzed by me so closely that it brushed me, almost knocking me over. The driver was going so fast I'm not even sure he saw me. I would have been right in his path had it not been for the warning.

From these and other incidents, I had a strong feeling that I must have a Guardian Angel — and that if I did have one as I believed I did, I was sure he worked very hard to keep me alive. But honestly, I did not think much about it. Needless to say, that has all changed now.

Besides being about angels, this book is about the usefulness of pain. I can well imagine you, the reader, rereading those last three words, "usefulness of pain," just to make sure you originally read correctly. But yes, you did read those words correctly. I have been through a great deal of emotional and physical pain in my life, and the idea that pain in and of itself could ever be useful would have been a bewildering one to me before slowly experiencing the events recorded in this book. It has been a joy beyond telling for me to be shown that my pain, offered as prayers in union with the Passion of Jesus Christ, can be and is used to bring life and joy to others through my prayers and offerings, to bring them closer to Our Almighty God. To know that pain can be used for good, that suffering is not wasted or at least does not have to be wasted, has given me hope that I want very much to share.

I no longer have to grit my teeth and bear the pain, as if it were something to get through, something without meaning. Though the pain of physical and emotional suffering still hurts as much as it ever did, it has become my most treasured possession when it is unavoidable because it becomes the vehicle through which I, too, can serve.

In 2 Timothy 2: 11-12 Saint Paul writes, "If we die with Christ, we shall live with Him, if we suffer with Christ we shall reign with Him." The beautiful call of Christ to His followers to "pick up your cross and follow every day in my footsteps" is a call to the sacrificing of oneself, and the sacrificing of self cannot occur without suffering. It is impossible to love without suffering. And so when suffering is used wisely and lovingly, it becomes the wondrous vehicle through which we learn to love more and more deeply, and through which we become obedient to Love Himself.

For thousands of years, probably since human beings could think, people have equated suffering with evil. "Rabbi, who sinned, this man or his parents, that he was born blind?" Jesus's disciples asked him (John 9: 1-4) of a man blind since birth.

"Neither he nor his parents sinned," Jesus answered them, "it is so that the works of God might be made visible through him. ..."

Not only does Our Blessed Lord heal the man, but the newly cured man engages the Pharisees in a battle of wits as he makes fools of them and refuses to belittle or deny the miracle of mercy done for him by God.

It is not only cruel to suppose that suffering and handicaps are punishments from God, it is blatantly un-Christian as shown in the Scriptures. But the practice of blaming the sufferer is far from outdated. A friend of mine (also totally blind) was told by the members of her religious lay community that she was not being healed of her blindness because of her lack of faith. This was both directly and indirectly communicated to her, and it took many years for her to get over the feeling that she is somehow being punished, somehow is at fault. Only great love can be an antidote for such cruelty clothed in tawdry piety. What ideas about God do such people have? To whom do they pray? It is certainly not to the suffering Lord of the universe who died ignominiously on a cross for an unaware and, for the most part, uncaring humanity. It is to this God in agony that those broken in heart, body and spirit can say, "You understand. You know how it feels. I will trust You."

One of the difficulties many people have had, both Protestants and Catholics, is with the understanding as old as the Church that, as Saint Paul says in Colossians 1: 24, "I rejoice in my sufferings for your sake, and in my flesh I complete what is lacking in Christ's afflictions for the sake of His body, the Church." It would seem that Saint Paul is first saying that there is something lacking in Christ's sufferings. How could this ever be? Of course, there is nothing lacking in Christ's sufferings. It would also seem that Saint Paul is saying he, through his suffering, will make up "what is lacking in Christ's afflictions." But in what Our Blessed Lord did for us there is nothing lacking.

However, as I have learned, in what we do or do not do in response to the infinite love of Jesus as shown in His sacrifice — therein lies the lack. "I am the Vine, you are the branches," Jesus tells us. The Vine cannot bear good fruit without the branches, nor bad for that matter. Christ shares His Life with us truly by making us active participants in producing it, for ourselves and others — always through Him and in Him.

In other words, He loves us so much that he reproduces His life in us if we are willing, including His saving life. If we respond in love, we can, as Saint Paul says, "be crucified with Him" for the sake of others. He raises our ordinary human suffering to the level of His own because of His great love for us. He gives our suffering a meaning it has never had before if we respond to His love.

But to force a reaction from us and to make us participate in His work of salvation, either by sharing with others directly or indirectly, would be a violation of our free will. But our free will, as the angels have taught me again and again, is inviolate. Jesus will never force us. It is in our free response to Him that we show our love for Him, and grow in love in all ways. If we remain observers to our own Salvation and to the salvation of others, then no effort on Christ's part can make up this lack brought about by our negligence. We cannot applaud Him in His agony and simply say, "thank You very much, now let's get on with the party." If we are truly "members of His body", we suffer with Him, in Him and for Him, not just for the sake of our own purification but for the sake of others, for the salvaging of their souls as well as our own. Saints Paul and Peter write of this constantly.

How can we say we are members of Christ's Body, one with Him, if we do not suffer with Him for the purpose for which He suffered and died — the redemption of the souls which are immeasurably precious to Him, and therefore to us? It is also wonderfully true that no suffering, evil or difficulty is greater than the love of God for us, and therefore is subject to His love and can be and is used by Him to bring about good. It is BECAUSE He suffered, died and rose for our sake that our salvation becomes possible if we follow Him, and the redemption of others becomes possible through His Passion of love and our offerings of love in union with Him.

In his apostolic letter on the Christian meaning of human suffering: SALVIFICI DOLORIS, His Holiness Pope John-Paul II expresses all this far better than I can. He writes:

"The sufferings of Christ created the good of the world's redemption. This good in itself is inexhaustible and infinite. No man can add anything to it. But at the same time in the mystery of the Church as His body, Christ has, in a sense, opened His own redemptive suffering to all human suffering. Insofar as man becomes a sharer in Christ's sufferings in any part of the world and at any time in history, to that extent he, in his own way, completes the suffering through which Christ accomplished the redemption of the world.

Does this mean that the redemption achieved by Christ is not complete? No. It only means that the redemption accomplished through satisfactory love remains always open to all love expressed in human suffering. In this dimension, the dimension of love, the redemption which has already been completely accomplished is, in a certain sense, constantly being accomplished. Christ achieved the redemption completely and to the very limit. But, at the same time, He did not bring it to a close. In this redemptive suffering through which the redemption of the world was accomplished, Christ opened Himself from the beginning to every human suffering and constantly does so. Yes, it seems to be part of the very essence of Christ's redemptive suffering that this suffering requires to be unceasingly completed. Thus, with this openness to every human suffering, Christ has accomplished the world's redemption through His own suffering. For, at the same time, this redemption even though it was completely achieved by Christ's suffering, lives on and in its own special way develops in the history of man. It lives and develops as the Body of Christ, the Church, and in this dimension every human suffering, by reason of the loving union with Christ, completes the suffering of Christ. It completes that suffering just as the Church completes the redemptive work of Christ."

I remember hearing about a picture of Our Blessed Lord's crucifixion. Saint John, Mary of Clopas, His Mother Mary and Mary of Magdala stood at the foot of the cross in spiritual agony with Him. The four people standing beside the Cross of Jesus suffered their own spiritual crucifixion BECAUSE OF THEIR LOVE FOR HIM, especially did His Mother suffer the pure suffering of a mortal woman who could, because she is full of God's grace, carry God in her womb for nine months and raise Him as her little boy, never losing sight of who He is. But especially could she be His Mother and suffer her own spiritual crucifixion in union with Him because of her love and obedience to the will of the Father (Mark 3: 34). That is the yardstick of our closeness to Him also, our willingness to submit ourselves to the rigors of truly loving. He is at the right–hand of the Father, reigning in glory. But His glorified body bears the marks of His Passion (Rev. 5: 5–6). As members of the Body of Christ, how much do we suffer with Him?

To the degree we love Him, what matters to Him matters to us; and what matters most to Him is us: that He have us with Him in His Kingdom forever and ever. So the little pains we suffer may be joined with His great Passion, both His physical suffering and spiritual agony as he took on the sins of the world. Our little offerings, then, through love of

Him and because of His grace, join with Him in a great union of love for the redemption of our souls and the souls of others. As it is written in Scripture, "Rejoice to the degree that you SHARE IN CHRIST'S SUFFERINGS." We are to rejoice in our sufferings with Christ, the more we share with Him in them, because of the closer union we have with Him through our sufferings, and because of the benefits to others we can bring as offerings to God through our pains.

The horror of the scene in the picture of the crucifixion was vividly portrayed. Under the picture were the words "wait three days." The agony of Our Blessed Lord's Passion and Death became the most powerful prayer of all. It opened the doors of Heaven to us, if we wish to enter. We are never forced, and we can at any time change our minds either way. That is His gift of love to us: we are free to love Him, or free to go our own way. The freedom to choose our own destiny at any moment, whether to belong to Jesus or not, has been taught by the Church for two thousand years. Though He knows what our final choice will be, we are free to make it.

An understanding of all this came to me slowly. This view of suffering has been taught by the Church for two thousand years and only recently has become "unfashionable" because of our society's wish, not only to see no ultimate use or good in suffering, but also out of a compulsion never to be aware of suffering unless it is forced upon us. But we do suffer, and unless we take glorious advantage of the gift Jesus gave us in allowing our suffering to have a precious meaning with His, a life of pain is inevitably a hopeless one.

When suffering is offered to God and the obstacle to prayer becomes your prayer, then your brokenness becomes a treasure to God. He wants wholeness and health, but He is more interested in the wholeness and health which lasts forever, the wholeness of the spirit. It is foolish of us not to share this concern. To put it in secular terms, it isn't good business to think only in the short–term. If we are not vitally concerned with eternity, for ourselves and those we love (as well as for others), we are foolish short–term planners.

To me, one of the most lovely things about God is that He uses those things which seem to oppose good to manifest His goodness. If God in His mercy did not do this, how easy it would be to despair. All of our lives, every aspect of them as offered to God, is precious to Him. Because of His love for us, most precious of all are our offerings of suffering, the aspects of our lives which are the most difficult for us. Our pain is precious to Him because it is our most difficult gift, the part of our lives which seems most irreconcilable with wholeness. But, as Saint Paul writes, it is in our weakness that His glory can most shine forth.

What suffering offered for the salvation of others can do, Jesus showed us on Golgotha. He opened the doors of Heaven, but we can assist others there. He not only shares His life with us, He also shares His Salvific work with us. When Jesus gives His criteria for being a follower of His, He says, "Whoever wishes to come after Me must deny himself, take up his cross, and follow Me. For whoever wishes to save his life will lose it, but whoever loses his life for My sake and that of the Gospel will save it (Mark 8: 34–35)." This is scarcely the description of a one– payment installment plan Faith. The only way one can refuse to follow in the path of Christ's suffering for the sake of others and still claim to be a Christian is to say, "O, He didn't mean I have to imitate Him. I'm home free." But just how serious Our Blessed Lord was in setting an example for us is shown by His own agonizing free choice of a willing and selfless death for the sake of those He loves. The work of salvation is completed by Jesus, but is not yet finished in us. Out of respect for our free will and because of His wish to share the work of completed salvation with us, our response of love is sought.

Reading the Holy Father's letter on suffering helped me understand more clearly what I, and all Christians in some way or other, are asked to do. He writes, "Down through the centuries and generations, it has been seen that in suffering there is concealed a particular power that draws a person interiorly close to Christ, a special grace. To this grace many saints such as Saint Francis of Assissi, Saint Ignatius of Loyola and many others, owe their profound conversion. A result of such a conversion is not only that the individual discovers the salvific meaning of suffering but above all that he becomes a completely new person. He discovers a new dimension, as it were, of his entire life and vocation.

"This discovery is a particular confirmation of the spiritual greatness which in man surpasses the body in a way that is completely beyond compare. When this body is gravely ill, totally incapacitated and the person is almost incapable of living and acting, all the more do interior maturity and spiritual greatness become evident; constituting a touching lesson to those who are healthy and normal.

"This interior maturity and spiritual greatness in suffering are certainly the result of a particular conversion and cooperation with the grace of the crucified Redeemer. It is He Himself who acts at the heart of human suffering through His Spirit of Truth, through the consoling Spirit. It is He who transforms, in a certain sense, the very substance of the spiritual life indicating for the person who suffers a place close to Himself. It is He, as the interior Master and Guide, who reveals to the suffering brother and sister this wonderful interchange situated at the very heart of the mystery of the redemption. Suffering is in itself an experience of evil, but Christ has made suffering the firmest basis of the definitive good — namely, the good of eternal salvation. ...

"It is suffering, more than anything else, which clears the way for the grace which transforms human souls. Suffering, more than anything else, makes present in the history of humanity the powers of the Redemption. In that cosmic struggle between the spiritual powers of good and evil spoken of in the letter to the Ephesians, human sufferings, united in the Redemptive suffering of Christ, constitute a special support for the powers of good and open the way to the victory of these salvific powers."

As I have been told, "no sin is greater than the love of God for you." No evil is greater than the love of God, and so even that evil can be and is used by God to bring about His good purposes for those who trust Him, those who will let Him work. The fact that God can and does use pain to bring us back to Himself, does everything He can to lead us home without violating our free will, — this is my great delight in Him. Only a God of Infinite Love could do this.

As I have recorded these mystical experiences, one of my major concerns is that the reader may incorrectly infer from them that one may live a sinful life, doing as one pleases, and then be saved by "choosing God" at the end. Nothing can be further from the truth! We cannot consistently and in full consciousness choose sin and not be forming ourselves. Each choice for sin and against good is a choice against God and His Laws of Love. Every time we disobey God's commandments, we make it easier for ourselves to sin in the future. We make it harder and harder for ourselves to receive the grace Our Blessed Lord wishes to give us. When we choose evil, when we choose against God's Law, we choose against God Himself. God alone knows the individual cases in which sin is not freely chosen, or when some other extenuating circumstance is present.

My hopes for this book are twofold. If at least in one reader's heart these purposes come to fruition, then the deep vulnerability I give you in knowing me in these pages as I cast aside the privacy which I value so dearly is worth every risk. If one heart rejoices in the love and mercy of God, if one soul longs more fervently than before to know its Creator, then all risks taken will be well worthwhile. If one of you closes this book after coming to its end knowing a little more and trusting a little more in the deeply involved, warmly personal, and infinitely kind love of God for each of His precious souls, then the ridicule I have been promised will come to me, because of this writing, will be sweet.

If even just one person reads the Holy Scriptures with a new joy, knowing more surely that the words of Our Lord Jesus Christ in the Gospels are love letters straight to you and it is because of reading the pages of this book that this is so, then I accept whatever personal consequences may come from the sharing of these experiences with you with great joy. Many pains of this life and discomforts of heart and spirit can be put in perspective by a moment's contemplation of eternity. What does a moment's pain here matter if it can be useful to bringing one's soul closer to the everlasting joy of Christ's eternal Kingdom, and how valuable is that pain if it can be used, as a precious gift from God, to help another soul towards everlasting joy in the full presence of Our Blessed Lord?

This life here, then, is infinitely precious to us because it is here that we can get ready for eternity, hopefully eternity in the Kingdom of Our Almighty Lord. It is here also that we can share with others the "good news" that God has not abandoned us. We are not forsaken. We are precious beyond anything we could imagine, not because we are innately precious in ourselves, but because the love of God, which is fully ours, is infinite; and so we are infinitely precious.

The sharing of this infinite joy of God's love is our trust as Christians. Our Lord's love is not something to be forced on anyone. It is a gift which, when seen for what it is, is refused, I would like to believe, only by the hardest of hearts. Let us pray that ours are not among those hardest of hearts. This is my constant personal prayer, that no pain or unhappiness, ridicule by others, sin of my own or anything in the universe will separate me from the love of my Lord, Jesus Christ. Saint Paul's promise in Romans Chapter 8 is my consolation.

May Our Lord in His great mercy bless each of you always, and may you and I finally stand before Him in Heaven. Let us pray for each other until the fulfillment of that eternal joy for both of us.

Patricia M. Devlin,
December, 1994

# Chronology

March 12, 1953:
  Patricia Devlin was born in Honolulu.
March 12, 1959:
  News that Hawaii would become the 50th state was received.
September, 1959 — June, 1965:
  Pat attended Diamond Head School, which is now Hawaii
  School for the Deaf and Blind (elementary).
September, 1965 — June, 1968:
  Pat attended Washington Intermediate School.
September, 1968 — May, 1971:
  Pat attended McKinley High School.
June, 1971 — August, 1978:
  Pat attended the University of Hawaii, Manoa,
  receiving a B.A. in English and a minor in History.
August 12, 1973:
  Pat's twin daughters, Miriam and Eileen, were born.
1974:
  Pat's right eye was removed because of glaucoma.
January, 1978:
  Pat's left eye was removed because of glaucoma, and a malignant
  was tumor found.
June, 1978:
  Exploratory surgery showed no more cancer.
September, 1978 — June, 1988:
  Pat and the girls lived in Saint Paul, Minnesota. Pat received a
  Masters in Psychology and worked.
February, 1980:
  Catholic Church granted a full annulment from short abusive
  marriage.
Summer, 1985:
  Pat's twin daughters', Miriam and Eileen, last names were
  legally changed to Devlin.
June, 1988:
  Pat moved to Lubbock, Texas, with the girls following.
August 15, 1988:
  The appearance of Our Lady occurred on the Feast of the Assumption at
  Saint John Neumann Church, Lubbock, Texas.
December 14, 1988:
  Patricia Devlin had tumor surgery.

# PART I
# **TRIALS AND WONDERS**
## (1953–1988)

# Chapter 1
# BEGINNINGS

At the request of Father Francis E. Butler, S.S.J., of Montgomery, Alabama, and Father John Walch of Oklahoma City, I am writing down and collecting journal entries concerning the extraordinary experiences with which I have been blessed by Our Lord. I have been a journal keeper since I was a young girl. Almost as soon as I learned to write Braille on a Perkins brailler in elementary school and then was taught the use of a slate and stylus, I have been writing notes, journals and poems. In the last two years I have learned to use computer equipment.

As the events recorded here occurred, it was natural for me to write them down. Later, I was requested by my spiritual directors to keep careful notes and journal entries. I have previously written about the events at Saint John Neumann's Catholic Church in Lubbock, Texas, which initiated the events recorded here. I am not, nor ever have been, a "Lubbock messenger," one of the people responsible for delivering the messages at the Church which drew close to thirty thousand people there on Our Lady's Assumption, the Feast of 1988 on August 15. What I record here is an outpouring of God's grace to me which began on that day.

I will share with you a little of the background of my life in order that you may have a better understanding of the events which follow. My parents are mainlanders who met in Hawaii in 1951 and were married in Honolulu. I was born in Honolulu on March 12, 1953. I was born three months prematurely, and my mother had been in labor with me for 55 hours, God bless her. My heart beat had not been heard since before she went into labor, and the doctors were sure I would be stillborn. After I was born I was not expected to live and was baptized within the hour of my birth. I weighed three pounds at birth, and quickly went down to two pounds.

It was not known at this time that high concentrations of oxygen cause retinal and other eye damage to premature babies' eyes. There are many of us born in this time period who are totally or partially blind because of this lack of medical knowledge. Within a few days of my birth, eye damage was already apparent. My physical condition had become so critical that one night my father and mother were told to go home and rest. There was nothing more to be done. I would not make it through the night. My father was asked to sign autopsy papers in order that the doctors might continue attempting to discover the cause for the eye damage in us little preemies.

I battled pneumonia and, despite everything, pulled through. The fact that I was born at all and survived was my Lord's second gift to me, after His first gift of life itself. I was three months in the incubator, and was finally allowed to go home with rather strenuous conditions set by the doctors for my care.

I have a brother, born ten months after my birth. He has made the army his career, and done well.

When I was about the age of three my grandmother, who taught me my prayers, told me about the Blessed Mother and Our Lord Jesus. At the mention of the Blessed Mother, my heart leaped up. Later when I fell away from the Church as a young adult because of deep feelings of unworthiness and shame, I still loved her. I could never explain these feelings of closeness.

In one of the conversations which I will relate in more detail later, our dear Blessed Lady told me that Our Lord God had allowed her to come to me during the three months I was in the incubator as a newborn. At that time, medical staff did not in anyway touch or hold seriously ill and premature little ones. I am told this is no longer true today, now that the great need to be held and cuddled is more clearly understood.

Our Blessed Mother told me with such love and tenderness that I can never convey that she had been allowed by Our Lord to come to me in the incubator, hold me, and sing to me. She had also come to my home to do this. She is truly my Mother, given to me by God.

My mother and father's sorrow over my blindness was great, but I think it was especially hard for my mother. She had dreams for me as all mothers do, and it probably seemed to her impossible they would ever be fulfilled. But Our Lord has bigger dreams for us than we can conceive, and what a relief that is. I, if somebody had asked me, would have said then what I say now, "It's great to be here, and I thank God for the chance to live this earthly life."

As a young child, I had light perception but no concept of actual sight. I did not see things, but only some light and occasional sensations of color without being able in any way to identify objects. I remember my parents holding up a child's beach ball in the sun, turning it, and asking me to name the colors as they did so. But by the age of seven, my color perception was gone. For years afterwards and even now, I do what I call my "color review", naming colors to myself and remembering what they look like as best I can. In the events which I will relate later when I began to see colors for which I had no name, could not ask others about, and had absolutely no mental ability to create, I knew this was something entirely from the outside, something my own brain could not have fabricated, because I had no previous mental concept of the colors I had never seen naturally, but would see supernaturally. For example, it would be like telling you to imagine a sixth sense that you had never experienced. You couldn't begin to construct what it would be like to have another sense.

I went through an elementary school for blind children in Honolulu. I was an active little participant in life right from the beginning. Most sighted people would suppose that a blind child would be cautious and careful because of not fully knowing what was around her, as children with vision do. My philosophy apparently was, "Since I don't know what's out there, how can I be afraid of it?"

Every three or four months during my first years in elementary school, I would reenact a personal tradition of running hard into poles and trees because I was going too fast to stop and was so intent on playing. "Patti hit her head again," was a common statement among other pupils and teachers.

One memory I have from first or second grade causes me a great deal of amusement now. I was riding with other younger children on a merry-go-round, one of those large, round, metal merry-go-rounds with handles for children to hang onto while others run around in circles on the outside, turning it. Older blind children were doing just that. I felt sicker and sicker, more dizzy by the moment. I hung on valiantly telling myself, "Don't let go! Don't let go!"

But the inevitable happened. I went flying off the merry-go-round and because the older kids could not see that I was in their path on the ground, as I jokingly put it: they trampled me to death. It is thanks to the fact that my parents did not unduly overly protect me from life that I have these and other precious memories.

I then went to secondary and high schools with "normal" children. This, along with other life experiences, has given me a deep appreciation for people, things, and experiences which are out of the norm, and a curiosity about other cultures, other ways of thinking, and different ways of doing things.

This gift of a lack of rigidity along with a deep sense of responsibility and a wish to be a human being whom God would be happy He had created was helpful to me when, at the age of twenty, my twin daughters were born. The circumstances around this event were traumatic. I was briefly "married." The "marriage" was declared null by the Church in later years. I have been a single parent since my children were babies and, of course, it has not been easy. But my daughters, Miriam and Eileen, are my true blessings from God.

During these years, I fell away from the Church out of a sense of unworthiness. But I had a hunger for my Lord that no scholastic explanations of the world or emphasis on status and achievement could satisfy. In school, I always carried a little card with me which said, "The purpose of all learning is to know more of God, and, through that learning, to serve Him." My heart quietly yearned to know more about God and I felt inwardly sad because I felt sure I would probably never be able to serve Him. I did not know at this time of His tender love for each of us, His unending kindness.

When my children were two and a half years old, I returned to the Church after a direct experience of love from my Lord which changed my life. That is another story.

In my children's early years, the glaucoma from which I had suffered since the age of eleven became much worse. I was on prescribed narcotics for years to try to cope with the pain. This suffering, along with nightmares of past physical abuse I had endured during my "marriage", began to form and shape my soul into a deeper understanding of Christ's Passion and compassion for others than I never could have experienced had life been easier.

My grandparents had lived with us between the years I was four and eleven years of age. My grandfather never went to church. He had been born a Lutheran, but had permitted his three daughters to be raised as Catholics. When, as a little girl, I asked him why he didn't go to church with us he said, "The church would fall down if I went into it." He was however, one of the most deeply religious people I have ever known. His religion was very personal. He read the Bible everyday. He was a quiet man who loved to go fishing and watch the stars.

Grandpa implanted in me a deep love for the Scriptures. He read the Bible and many other books, including some of the famous classics, to me for hours at a time. One Holy Week, he read the story of Our Blessed Lord's Passion to me. I think I was about seven years of age. I cried and cried at the descriptions of Jesus's torment. Most adults would have stopped reading, thinking it was too much for a young child. Grandpa, to my eternal gratitude, continued quietly reading on through to the marvelous account of our Blessed Lord's resurrection. Without realizing it at the time, this implanted in me a deep love for Jesus in His Passion, and a belief that no matter how difficult or horrible life might be, there would always somehow be a resurrection for me and all who wanted it through Jesus's love.

One evening when I was about eight years old, I went out into our front yard where grandpa was looking at the sky through his telescope. We were quiet for a long time and then he said to me, "Sweetheart, I don't understand how it is possible for anyone not to believe in God, especially anyone who has ever looked at the stars." Though I knew next to nothing about the Catholic Church or the Bible and my parents rarely went to church during my teen years, this memory and others made me aware of God as a great and powerful being. Only in time would I begin to learn of Him as not only great and powerful but as One who loves me more than any other can love, and has a tenderness and mercy, a sensitivity beyond words and a humorous kindness for His beloved children.

Though my actual blindness was caused by the condition resulting from premature birth and placement in an incubator with exposure to high concentrations of oxygen, I can't remember a time when I didn't have some trouble with my eyes. The glaucoma caused me great pain, and by the time I was 25 I had reluctantly agreed to have both eyes removed. During the operation to remove my left eye, a cancerous tumor was found. A following operation showed all the cancer had been removed and I was clear of it.

Because of personal circumstances, we left Hawaii shortly after my twins had turned five years old. I had just received my B.A. in English from the University of Hawaii, and later would receive a degree in psychology from the University of Minnesota.

We went to Saint Paul, Minnesota, mainly because I had relatives there and I wanted to get a masters degree in counseling at the University of Minnesota. We had never experienced snow before, and the shock of three foot drifts and 40 and 50 F temperatures below zero with wind chill sometimes below that is something I will leave to your imagination. We were like little birds of paradise set adrift on a floating iceberg.

The next years were very lonely for me. I deeply wished for an adult companion to share my life — for a marriage centered in our Lord. If someone had told me at this time that my fervent prayers for this would not be answered and that within ten years of this time I would be thanking God even more fervently for refusing me this favor, I would have found it incomprehensible and unbelievable.

But I have always been blessed by my Lord with loving and lasting friendships, and by the time we left Minnesota I had a close circle of loving friends.

In 1980, I began to have the first symptoms of Meniere's disease. I thought the dizziness, ringing in my ears, and general instability and sometimes severe vertigo had something to do with my eyes. It was not until 1982 that the disease was properly diagnosed. It was all very strange. I would feel so terribly ill with motion sickness, hardly able to raise my head because of the sensation of spinning, and yet within a few hours after the fluids in my inner ears had properly drained, I would feel weak but perfectly balanced. Though I was put on medication which mitigated the severity of the disease somewhat, Meniere's disease was more debilitating to me than blindness has ever been.

Despite setbacks, I finally received my masters in counseling student personnel psychology from the University of Minnesota in 1986. I worked for two years but was not able to get a full time position in the area which I love most and in which I am most qualified to work — as a marriage and family therapist.

I was sitting in a doctor's office one day in late 1987, and the wait had been long. Suddenly I thought, "I'm going to go and get a doctorate in marriage and family therapy." Great decisions happen at odd moments. It was, I'm sure, a rather foolish decision to make in some ways. From the standpoint of becoming better employed it was an excellent move, but at the time I was steadily losing my hearing because of Meniere's disease. I did not know how much longer I might have before becoming totally deaf. Would it be a few years or a lifetime? I will relate the events of our move to Texas in another book, and the subsequent miraculous events at Saint John Neumann Church, including my complete cure from Meniere's disease. Over six years after the Feast of the Assumption in 1988, I am still free of this disease. Glory, glory be to God.

I often recall the days and nights of roaring in my ears, sometimes becoming so dizzy that I felt as if I were on a gigantic wheel, spinning and spinning around in an unending horrible ride. I kept a container next to me for nausea, and prayed that if there were a fire or other emergency someone would drag me out of the house since I was unable to stand. I relate this in detail because I want to share the magnitude of the cure I received on the Feast of the Assumption in 1988. I have had no symptoms of Meniere's since that day. I had not asked for a miracle, it had not occurred to me to do so. It was a gift given gratuitously, a gift of pure love and compassion I will never forget.

But, ironically, along with this physical cure, I have also gained a sense of how unimportant physical healings are. They are manifestations of what our Lord wishes to do in our souls, a dim mirror of the healing and loving He wishes for us in order that we may do and be what truly matters — His people. I am no less grateful for this and the other physical healings I received that day, but these are not at all the most important gifts I have received.

When I was little and my eyes were deteriorating, I would sometimes see bright lights of different colors. It was my brain trying to stimulate the area having to do with sight. The lights were small and they would move around in front of me and to the sides. I would sometimes become afraid of them and my father, in his love and kindness for his little girl, comforted me by telling me they were good fairies come to visit me. When I put my hands over my face, the lights would still be behind them as one would expect since they were being produced by my brain. By the time I was seven years old, there were no more lights.

# Chapter 2
# WONDERS

A few days after the Feast of the Assumption at Saint John Neumann Church in 1988, I began to see bright lights. These lights were different. They were large and bright and beautiful and further away from me, not tiny, close and small as the lights of my childhood had been. Also, when I put my hands over my face, I blocked them out. "What is my brain doing?" I asked myself many times. "Even though it is different from my childhood I must be imagining this." It was amazing to me because, of course, I had not seen light for years. As totally blind people we are not, as is widely supposed, in total darkness. Because cells around eyes are sensitive to light, even I (with both eyes surgically removed) was not in total darkness. I and others who are totally blind experience a dim sense of difference between total darkness when our eyelids are down, versus when they are not. I have a difficult time describing this because I have little with which to contrast what I have experienced to actually being able to see.

The lights I began to see right after the Feast of the Assumption were of hues, intensities and feelings I did not have the vocabulary or ability to describe.

The light was particularly bright at Saint John Neumann Church. It played over the waters of the fountain in the church courtyard in a beautiful way. During the Transubstantiation* it was so bright I often had to cover my face. During these times there was not one, or two or three different sources for the light, but the room or the church or wherever I was would be filled with light. I began to see a glow around some people and often one near them as well. I was disturbed by all of this, not knowing what to think.

"If I am crazy," I thought, "at least the rest of my life seems to be going well." I was carrying a heavy graduate school schedule with re-

---

[Note: The Transubstantiation is the moment during Mass when the bread and wine become the Body of Christ, when He is present fully: Body, Blood, Soul and Divinity.]

search, working with clients, going to classes, hiring and organizing readers, and trying to do assigned readings on top of everything else, plus attend to my responsibilities to my children. It was overwhelming at times, but I was very happy doing it. I look back on these months as some of the happiest of my life up to that time. I was finally free to work and enjoy it without fear of a Meniere's attack and without the deep, quietly ever–present fear of steadily going deaf.

Then one night as I sat praying in my living room and the light became bright near me, I saw reflected in the light the color of my guide dog Gia's coat. I had never seen that color. I had no concept of what that lovely red-gold-brown color might be. I knew this was not my imagination. I could not have named the color unless others had already told me what it is. I cannot prove that I saw it, but I know I did. Despite this, I still struggled in bewilderment. What was happening? I did not know.

When I occasionally began to hear voices out of the lights, I really started to worry. As a professional counselor, I am very well aware of what society firmly believes to be the situation with those hearing voices of beings not physically present — with the exception of radio and television since they are explainable.

These voices are directional. They come from the outside, just as a voice of another human being would. They come from the same direction from which I see the light, and they are unique — each one beautiful and different. I cannot control what they say to me as one would control one's thoughts, but they do not in any way take over or try to control me or my separateness as a human being. The best way I can describe what happens is this: It is a conversation like any other except that I hear what is being said to me with all of my being, rather than just my ears but also including my ears.

When I first began hearing the voices out of the light I thought, "Now you're hearing voices that other people can't hear as well as seeing lights other people can't see. Hmmm. It may be time to go for a little help at a psychiatrist's office, Patricia." But the voices were gentle and kind. They wished me "peace" or "the peace of our Lord be with you." I decided to wait. I would praise God for His kindness and love for us, for giving us His Son, for allowing the Blessed Mother to come to us here, and the light would become brighter. Once I heard a beautiful choir singing with many tones of voices with a music that flowed in beautiful individual harmonies so lovely I got tears in my eyes.

One night I had a particularly difficult session at our clinic in the Marriage and Family Therapy Department. The father of a family I had just seen seemed so hard and indifferent, insensitive to the pain and confusion of his children, indifferent and cold towards his wife. As I stood waiting for a ride to go home, suddenly the light became bright and a loving voice I would come to know well as my Guardian Angel's said to me, "I am going to show you how this man feels all the time."

For the next minute or so I physically felt a sense of such deep stress and fear that I could hardly breathe. I felt trapped. I felt completely alone, with no chance of being helped or understood.

"Please try to help this man," the gentle voice continued. "Now that you know." This little incident which was not really little at all changed the entire way I worked with this family.

One Monday night in October something happened as I went up to receive the Holy Eucharist. This incident perhaps more than others opened my heart to the love of God in a totally unexpected way. As I stood in front of the person distributing the Host, I suddenly saw light moving toward me. It seems incredible that I should use the word "saw", considering that both of my eyes have been surgically removed, but that is the only word I can think of to use. I did not see the person in front of me. What I did see was a disk of light coming toward me which had rays of light emanating from its edges. I put out my hand and the beautifully glowing disk of light was placed in my palm. How can I tell you what it was like with my head bowed, looking down at the disk of light in my hand? "This must be what people mean when they talk about seeing shape and form," I thought rather incongruously.

I did not know at this time that it is not proper to dip the Host in the Communion cup and then consume it. I did this rather than drink straight from the cup because of my fear of an accident occurring, and the spilling of the Precious Blood of our Lord. This had happened to me several years ago, and I was deeply concerned that it never happen again. As I stood with the Host in my hand in front of the person holding the Communion cup, toward me came a beautiful, liquid golden light. I did not see the cup. The light rippled and played. I described it to myself later in the terms I know, "It looked to me the way rippling water on a stream feels under my hand." I dipped the Host in the Communion cup, and stepped to the side shaking. As a Catholic, I have believed that I am receiving the Body and Blood of our Lord Jesus Christ in the full sense of those words. I receive Him physically, spiritually, and emotionally. I don't believe this anymore. I know it. I know it.

I stood shaking and then went down on my knees on the hard floor, not caring what anyone thought. I cannot now receive my Lord in the Holy Eucharist without remembering this incident and other times I have seen this. I would go up to Communion on my face if I could. How could anyone ever turn away from our Lord in the Holy Eucharist, knowing what I know? That the God of the universe would come to me in the form of Bread and Wine so that I might receive His love which is beyond my understanding is the greatest miracle of all. No one could leave the Church, turning his or her back on Our Blessed Lord, present fully under the appearance of bread and wine, to "find Jesus" somewhere else, knowing what I know. I did believe before, but now! What a gift to be shown.

I had begun to suspect that the light I was seeing might be the light from the angels, and this was confirmed one night by a gentle word from my Guardian Angel. During these months, I was going through agonies of uncertainty and turmoil. How could this be happening to me? If it wasn't really happening, what would that say? If it was, what did it mean? What did our Lord want from me, of all people? Who would believe me? Did I believe myself? What would it be like if I finally stood before our Blessed Lord and was told, "O, yes, you are the one who thought angels talked to her." If this was not from God and I were to speak about it, I might be responsible for leading others astray. If it were from God and I did not speak of it, God help me then. I tried to confirm some of the things I had been told, but was unsuccessful. "Be patient," my guardian angel told me.

I began to see extremely painful and terrible pictures in the light, scenes I will not write about here except that I was told they were happening to real people. "Why am I being shown these things?" I asked. "Because no one is praying for them," came the reply. "Please pray for them."

---

[Note: Later my Guardian angel would tell me that other sorts of fasts are pleasing to God. "Try fasting from saying one hurtful word to or about another person," he said. "Try denying yourself the gluttony of impatience, of rudeness, of unnecessary chatter." These fasts are often much harder than other forms of abstinence.]

Our family had begun to take fasting and praying together much more seriously before the Feast of the Assumption, but now we made more efforts to do so. I had never liked the idea of fasting. It seemed to me to be detrimental to health and not very beneficial to praying more deeply. I found as we tried to follow the Blessed Mother's requests here that fasting was beneficial to prayer and could be managed, with prayers for grace to do so, if we ate well and completely on the five days we did not fast. I just learned recently that Wednesdays and Fridays, the days we have been asked to fast, are traditional days of fasting in the Church. We had not known this. We found it was a good idea to begin fasting after Tuesday evening supper and break our fast for dinner on Wednesday evening, doing the same for Thursday evening and Friday.

Here are several excerpts from my journal:

August 31, 1988

As I sit here in the study carrel at the Commission for the Blind on the third floor of the Tech Library, the light around me is incredible. I checked the light switch, and of course turning it on or off makes no difference to me — I can't tell whether it is on or off except by position. The lovely light is still there. Glory be to God!

September 1, 1988

I am quite tired these days with such long hours. We had been planning to go to church but when I got home, Miriam and Eileen were still over at a friend's house. I began getting ready and right before they were due to arrive, the weather changed suddenly from a bright beautiful day to a torrential downpour. It reminded me of the lovely rain we received on the Feast of the Assumption which dried within minutes, and my heart rejoiced. I have always loved rain. But now I think of it, as Bishop Fulton J. Sheen wrote in a little story, rain is holy water from Heaven.

When friends arrived with my daughters, the girls came rushing into the house. "We don't have any clothes for school! We have to stay home and do our laundry! Is that okay?"

"Yes." Then into the drenching rain, and loving every minute of it.

The light I could see in the church was so distracting and beautiful that I had a hard time concentrating. It was especially bright where most of the people were sitting, but extended to the altar as well. At the time of the Consecration, the light on the altar was so bright I thought I would not be able to bear much more brightness. I have a hard time believing that I, a totally blind person with both eyes removed, could be writing this in all seriousness. But it is true, gloriously true. And when the people came up to me to wish me peace, I saw lights moving next to them. Are these the lights from their guardian angels?

September 13

It would be easier to be crazy than to be experiencing this, I suppose. I would know what to do. I would go to a psychiatrist, get medicated, probably lie on a couch somewhere for a year or two and my family receive a good deal of sympathy. But what if this is truly happening and I am not imagining anything? I have a great imagination which has always been a delight to me, a great amusement, but I am clear about what I am imagining versus what is happening.

So I say in confusion to my Lord, "You know what you are working with, my God. I am confused. I am uncertain. I don't have a strong faith sometimes, despite all the blessings you have poured out, because I really don't know why I should be blessed at all in what seems to me to be a way in which others have not. And yet it is You who are Lord, You who are weaving the fabric of our lives. Please do whatever You wish with me, and give me grace to love and serve You. Please be patient with me."

My Guardian Angel and others wish me peace and tell me of God's love and care for me and all others. I am afraid when it happens, but it is not the kind of fear one has for oneself when one is in danger. I don't feel in any danger at all, but I do feel an immense awe. I am infinitely aware of my smallness. It is as though a loving Goliath has turned to speak to and caress an ant — and I am the ant.

My Guardian Angel has told me that I will receive proof that what is happening to me is not my imagination.

I finally did what I had thought I should do all along but had been hoping to avoid. I made an appointment with my academic advisor. "I may be needing you to quietly recommend some professional counseling for me," I told him. He sat quietly listening to me. He asked me several questions about my family life and our move down to Lubbock, my adjustment in the program, etc. I sensed he was thinking of what he knew of me as a person. Then he said,

"You are a Catholic. I assume you believe your faith was spread by people who were not crazy, who had extraordinary experiences which a lot of people now might think of as possibilities for DSM3* classification?"

I thought of Mary of Magdala going back from the empty tomb to tell the apostles that Jesus, whom they had lain in the sepulchre 40 hours before as a mutilated corpse, was alive now—and that she had seen Him and spoken to Him. I thought of the over five hundred people who, once convinced of Jesus's resurrection and divinity, would (and many did) die rather than recant. Most importantly, I thought of my Lord Jesus Christ, the founder of my Church. "Yes, but ..." I stammered.

"We can't explain everything, Pat, and we're fooling ourselves if we think we can," my advisor said kindly. He said it almost comfortingly, as one might attempt to comfort someone younger than oneself who is in the process of discovering that she knows so much less about the world and its wonders than she could have imagined. I have thought about this since. Perhaps our belief that we can ultimately explain everything, and always through the scientific method of empirical validation or concrete observation, is a symptom of our wish to control life.

"But what should I do, then?" I asked.

"Look," he said. "you're no more crazy than I am. Of course, that may not be saying much. But these voices wish you 'peace' and 'peace of God.' That sounds all right to me. Just wait to find out more what is happening, and keep me informed. Don't discriminate against any way of knowing." How many others would have been so wise?

"Well," I thought later, "now the only thing I can do is wait, just as I have been wisely advised to do. I have been rigid because of my scholastic background in discounting what I don't understand. How arrogant of me. But what if angels are really talking to me? There are no mores as to what one does in that case." But I was at peace.

---

[NOTE: The DSM3 is a system of categorizing mental illness which has been developed by the American Psychological Association.]

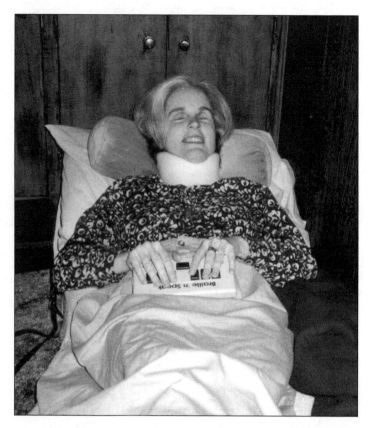

*Patricia with her "Braille and Speak." The bulk of the book was written using this method.*

# Chapter 3
# THE REQUEST

On the night of Wednesday, November 2, 1988, I was in my room helping my daughter Miriam with her homework. The light became very bright near the door of the room as we talked. It was not that I had become used to this — far from it — but most often when this happened, the lovely beings that were surrounded by this light either simply wished me peace (or "May the peace of Our Lord be with you") or simply stayed quietly in the room for a while. So I murmured a greeting in my heart and continued helping Miriam. When she left the room, I continued puttering, doing what I had been doing before she came in. But I had the feeling that whoever was there was patiently waiting for me to pay attention.

I said a prayer and went down on my knees. "My beloved daughter," Our Lady said. It was not just these words that let me know it was she. It was a recognition deeper than any taught reverence, church doctrine, or story. It was the kind of glad recognition you feel when you have been parted from someone; someone you love dearly and know loves you, despite time, distance or difficulties.

"You have struggled with all this long enough, sweetheart," she told me. "Our Lord uses whom He wills."

I did not physically see our dear Mother, but the light from her being was so bright yet gentle that I could tell where she was standing from the direction of the light, and from her voice. The light filled the entire room. One of the things that amazed me most about this visit and Our Lady's two subsequent visits to me was my deep sense of her presence. She is a Queen beyond all other queens, pure and stately, and if this were all that she is it would seem impossible that I or anyone else here on earth could be in her presence. But, at the same time, she is warm and loving with a tenderness and compassion for the deepest secrets and hurts of our souls. I knew that she looked straight into me and saw everything that I am. But from her there was only love for me and the burning desire that I turn my life over entirely to her Son. There was no reproach, yet at the same time she was uncompromising in her wish for me to do only the will of God. This combination of compassion and tenderness with an iron will that Our Lord's wishes should be fulfilled in all things is very hard to explain.

"In order that you will not doubt quite so much later that I have spoken to you," she said, "I tell you now that my public messages at Saint John Neumann Church will be over by Christmas." I asked her if I should make this public.

"No," she told me, "that is for my messengers to do. I am telling you this only so that when it happens you will know that I have been with you and am with you. It is not to be made public by you."

She told me several other things of a personal nature which were prophetic. Some of these things have caused a great deal of uncertainty in my heart since then because I still don't understand them. But I am learning to trust my Lord and the wisdom of His Mother.

Then she told me something which has greatly healed my heart of one of its deepest sorrows, something I had never discussed with anyone. She made me a personal promise, saying she had prayed for a special gift for me and that gift had been granted by her Son. The fulfillment of this promise for my personal life would not only bring great joy to me but would also glorify Our Lord. This, and her other promises, are secret.

She told me I could ask her anything I wished. If you are ever in a similar position, believe me, all the profound questions you have wondered about will completely slip your mind and it will be the everyday worries of your life you will ask about. You will ask as a child would ask, which is what I did. I was gently reassured and given words of insight I never could have come to myself. She promised that my daughters would be protected and would be guided by Our Lord and would give Him glory.

She showed me the road of the rest of my life. On one side of my path were deep ruts of pain. On the other side of my path were deep ruts of joy. They were running side by side. She showed me that I would not live to be a very old woman, and I was filled with joy at this because, even at that very moment, I wanted so very much for her to take me with her, not to leave me on earth. I forgot all my earthly worries and responsibilities in her presence, and wanted only to be with her and my Blessed Lord in Heaven..

I wrote a letter to my friends and family about these events, but I did not include what I will write here because of a fear of being disrespectful to Our Lady. But I can only restate what she told me, and let others much wiser than me decide. She told me that our human hearts could be as sacred as the Tabernacle of her holy womb in holding her Son, Jesus Christ. She said that if we allowed Our Blessed Lord Jesus to enter into our hearts completely, He would walk the earth again indeed. She did not say that it would be as if He walked the earth again, she said that He would walk the earth again in us. She said that a constant humility of spirit on our parts would have to exist before this could happen. She wished me her peace and the peace of God and was gone.

From what the Blessed Mother told me, I know I am not nor ever will be one of her "messengers." The visits with which she blessed me were private ones, paid by a loving Mother to her daughter. Those who are her messengers have a responsibility to relay her messages to the world. We who are visited simply out of the tenderness of her heart can share the beauty of that love of a Mother for every single one of her children.

Early the next morning, I was praying in my living room before leaving for the Tech campus. The light became bright, and Our Lady was there in the room with me.

She blessed me and told me she wanted me to write down what she had to say this time. "Go get your brailler," she said smilingly, "I'll wait for you."

What wonderful laughs I have had over this since. "Go get your brailler. I'll wait for you." Just as a mother would tell her daughter. Please understand that I mean no irreverence in recording this. She was entirely human and completely loving with me, showing me a warmth of motherly love which was very natural and sincere. She let me know by this that I had nothing to fear. I was in awe, but how could I be afraid of my Mother?

When I returned, she began to dictate,

"Glory to God, glory. My dearest children, all the angels and saints in Heaven are praying for you, that you may open your hearts during this time before Christmas — open your hearts so that my Son may enter into them and be reborn into your world through you.

You are more precious to Our Heavenly Father than you can understand, but please let your hearts open in faith to believe.

Our Father has entrusted a great work to your families through your lowly and blessed Church.

Let your hearts sing praise to Our Father wherever you are, and do not be afraid. All that concerns you is of concern to us.

My dearest children, speak lovingly and gently to each other in your homes and in your everyday actions. It is through these little acts of kindness and understanding that you will be particularly blessed.

Open your hearts and your homes to those who come here. You will serve them, but they will bless you in ways beyond counting.

My peace and my love are with you always."

One sentence in this dictation stayed in my heart for weeks afterwards. "You are more precious to Our Heavenly Father than you can understand, but please let your hearts open in faith to believe."

On Thursday, November 10, I had been at the noon rosary at Saint John Neumann Church. I waited for the ride I had arranged for in order to get back to the University. It did not come. John Hart, one of the parishioners, kindly offered to take me where I needed to go. I decided to go home since I had no more appointments that day and did have plenty of work waiting for me at home.

As John and I sat in my living room talking for a few minutes before he was to leave, the light became bright. It was Our Blessed Mother. She had apparently wanted John there for what turned out to be her last full visit to me.

"You struggle way too much," she said to me gently, "and sometimes you have to be in great pain before you stop struggling. You must ask for the peace you need in order to rest in God. It's very important that you ask for God's peace because the Holy Spirit wishes to work through you. The Holy Spirit will be working through you all your life if you are open. This is the last time I will visit with you in this way. The next time I visit you so closely will be when I hold you in my arms in Heaven."

I was in deep pain over this. I wanted her to take me right then. I had begun to cry. She comforted me, saying that when that time came, when she held me in her arms in Heaven, I would look back on this moment here on earth, and the time between this moment and the moment in Heaven when she held me would seem "Like the blink of an eyelid."

She told me that life here is extremely transitory, that when I come to the end of my life here and look back, it will seem so very short. "Eternity is forever," she said.

She went on to tell me something that made me cry even harder, but for joy and surprise this time. "You are very much loved and respected in Heaven because, though you have sinned and will sin, God sees the desires of your heart and the desires of your heart are constant. The desires that you have, whether you fail or succeed, are what you will take into eternity with you, not your successes or failures."

I thought of this a great deal later and realized it could never be used as an excuse for wrongdoing. I found and still find such joy and comfort in it.

She spent a few minutes talking to me about things which are deeply personal.

The Blessed Mother spoke words of love and kindness to John through me and asked him to do several things for her. He could not see the light or hear her, but he had a deep sense of her presence.

She continued speaking to me but it also seemed she was speaking to others of us as well, all of us. "...from Heaven I will hear your songs of praise to Our Lord; and your songs of sorrow. I will see your hearts. I will hear your crying. I am a Mother who hears her children crying in the night and comes. I hear your outward lamentations and your inward weeping," she said gently.

She asked that we think of the rose, how beautiful it is and how it brings joy, and that is its purpose. It fades only after giving quiet glory to God. "Look at the rose as an example of how to live your lives. It opens, gives itself perfectly, and is just there, giving its beauty and joy."

She asked that a collection be taken up to decorate the altar and the Church of Saint John Neumann for Christmas Eve Mass. She preferred roses, but other flowers were also fine. "Please give each person one to take home as long as they last. These flowers are little signs of the love of God for you. The great signs will fade from memory, but the little signs will be given to you constantly to speak to you about the love of God. Open your hearts to these little signs because they will not fade from your hearts."

Our Lady told me without words that I would not be at that Christmas Eve Mass. Later, I was sure I must have misunderstood her. Where else would I be on Christmas Eve except with my family at Holy Mass?

The dearest Lady told me that I would suffer physical and emotional pain in the near future, and later — ridicule. I will never forget as long as I live that SHE pleaded with ME, the Mother of God pleaded with me, asking that when this suffering happened would I please offer the pain as prayers "for those souls which in the normal course of things, will not stand before our God." I promised I would do this.

She told me that she knew her leaving suddenly would be painful for me, so she would leave gently and slowly. That day was a Thursday. I had not eaten properly. She began to gently but firmly scold me.

"Today is not a fast day, Pat," she said. "I want you to eat properly on non-fast days. You are to take care of yourself. You have not eaten well today. Go, get out the soup in your refrigerator for yourself, and maybe John would like some coffee."

These are the last words she said to me in this visit in which she was fully present, and I laugh now as I remember. I went into the kitchen to heat the soup and make the coffee. She left slowly and gently as she had said she would, but her love is always in my heart.

*Patricia holding the Crucifix with the corpus that moves.*

# Chapter 4
# PAINFUL PROOF

"What kind of pain would you experience in the near future?" I was asked by friends.

"I have no idea," I answered. Despite these incredible happenings, I still suffered from deep doubts. How could this really be happening to me? I'm no mystic or saint. I'm just myself, Patricia Margaret Devlin. I prayed for the peace the Blessed Mother had told me I must ask for, but I still asked Our Lord for proof.

It saddens me to think now that I would have asked for such proof after so many blessings had been given to me, but I realize that this is probably quite understandable, considering my cultural and educational background.

On Saturday November 12, I sat pondering everything. The light grew bright. My Guardian Angel told me again that I would receive proof I was not imagining these events. Two days later, he told me to go get "head x-rays."

I procrastinated in going for a CT-Scan. I had never felt better in my life. I also had to find a reason to ask for the CT-Scan. I didn't think it would be too good an idea to go to a doctor and say my Guardian Angel had told me to go get head x-rays. I might get more than head x-rays. So I decided to go to my eye doctor and tell him I had been having headaches behind my eyes. I always have these headaches, but when I am under stress I have them more frequently.

My seventeen and eighteen hour days at Tech probably had something to do with the fact that, though I was feeling very strong and well, I had had a few more of these headaches than was usual. I also used the fact that I had had a cancerous tumour removed from behind my eyes in 1978 as leverage in asking for a CT-Scan.

"I don't expect to find anything wrong," my eye doctor said.

"Nor do I," I said cheerfully.

"We'll call you to let you know everything is all right," he said. Instead, I was called for an appointment.

I found out about the tumor on November 22. "It's in a very critical area," my doctor told me. "I want you to go to a neurologist right away." He recommended a neurologist and I was in his office within the hour. The neurologist was adamant. He told me the tumor was probably benign, that he couldn't be sure how fast it was growing, but that it was in a critical area — at a place in the lower left side of my head where a great many things came together. Within a few months he believed it would be inoperable. By the time I would have had any symptoms, it would have been too late.

"What would have happened then?" I asked him.

"Your balance would have been affected. You would have become paralyzed on the left side and eventually you would have died. Oh, and you probably would have lost the ability to speak fairly soon in all that."

He told me he was sure I was already deaf in my left ear. "You couldn't still hear and have that tumor where it is."

"But I can still hear."

"You only think you can because your left side nerves are so damaged. Your right side is compensating."

He believed I never had had Meniere's, that the symptoms were due to the tumor and the reason I felt better after the Feast of the Assumption was because the nerves in that area had been destroyed and so were no longer sending damaged messages to my brain.

Another neurologist disagreed. "Your symptoms and your sensitivity to salt point to Meniere's. There is no known medical cure for Meniere's. You'll probably get it back."

"Oh, no, I won't," I thought. "Whatever else is going on with me I don't have Meniere's any more."

Hearing tests showed that not only did I have normal hearing in both ears, but that I tested high normal in both ears! My doctor could not believe it, also considering that my previous hearing tests done in Minnesota showed that I barely made it into the normal range of hearing in both ears, and this was progressively getting worse. So this downward progression had not only stopped at the time of the Feast of the Assumption at Saint John Neumann Church, but I had regained my hearing fully. I was told this is medically impossible.

At first I told only a few people in my department about the tumor. I wanted to get through that Thanksgiving which was coming up on

Thursday before telling my children. As is our custom, we went to Mass on Thanksgiving morning. We were invited to express our thanks to God during the petitions part of the Mass, and the outpouring of love and gratitude from the people of Saint John Neumann parish is one of my cherished memories. Even through my own quiet agony of spirit, their love for God and their sincere thanks and trust reached me.

After Mass was over, a group of us stayed to pray the rosary. I took out a treasured set of rosary beads, one given to me by a friend in Hawaii. They are made of Job's tears. They were made by a priest who was dying of cancer in about the year 1976.

As I held the crucifix of the rosary in my hands, I don't doubt that most of the people heard my gasp. The little figure of Our Lord on the cross had been straight, arms even with each other, head up. The head was now bent entirely away from the cross, lowered to the right. The whole body was off to one side. The left shoulder was at a twisted angle in relation to the rest of the body. The arm was still nailed to the cross, but the shoulder itself was pushed outward, drawing     t h e whole arm away from the cross beam. Later when my daughter Eileen had a dislocated shoulder from swimming, the position of the shoulder of the little figure of Our Lord on the cross reminded me of how her shoulder felt. His right shoulder was in a normal, straight position. This is still markedly visible on this crucifix as of this writing.

I have written about the changing of my crosses in the previous text about the Feast of the Assumption at Saint John Neumann Church and subsequent events. If this were all that they are, a mere changing of metal, they would be nothing but curiosities. But for me, each sign is an indication of the deepest and most personal love imaginable; no, far deeper than anyone could ever imagine. Feeling the change in the little figure on that cross that morning and knowing beyond any doubt that it had changed because of my sensitive fingers and my intimate knowledge of all my crucifixes, I quietly cried. My Lord could not have shown me more clearly, more concretely than He did, that He was and ever is with me. By its change, that little figure of my Lord said to me, "I know what pain is. Believe me, sweetheart, I know. I am with you in yours." This crucifix and the others, but especially this one, remind me of this in a tactile, physical, and to me indisputable way even to this day.

I am told that welding marks are visible on this crucifix, as they are also on some of my other crucifixes which have changed. These marks are not just visible to some, but to all of you with keen eyes.

It is not so important to me that you believe what I say, though what I say is true, but I wish you could feel the love of my Lord as I did that Thanksgiving morning. Having the physical, tactile proofs of His tenderness for me are greater miracles than many other things most people would consider much more remarkable. I do not need others to believe, though I and they are blessed when they do if it brings them closer to my Lord.

When Eileen and Miriam heard about the tumor, of course they were worried. But Miriam said to me, "Mom, I know it's awful. I love you. But Mom, if you did die, just think where you would be! I would know you were having the most wonderful adventures." What she had experienced on the Feast of the Assumption at Saint John Neumann Church over three months ago had given her a certainty of God's love and a sense of eternal life that many never feel. She had no doubts.

# Chapter 5
# "THERE IS NO SOUL ON EARTH WHO DOES NOT HAVE A GUARDIAN ANGEL."

Excerpt from Journal Entry:

Monday, December 12, 1988

I am in a better frame of mind to try to write about all of this. I attempted to do so on Thursday, but I felt as if all of it were so unreal, as if I were enclosed in a bubble, and everything I tried to write about or do involved someone else. I am out of the bubble now, and am being given a joy and a peace I did not know were possible under these circumstances.

On Halloween night we were at Saint John Neumann Church, and during the Mass I had such a feeling of joy. It was a regular Monday night rosary but, being Halloween, I thought it was particularly important that we be at the church. Faintly, as we prayed, I could hear others praising the other side, the other one, the darkness,—evil itself. There were many more of them, but we drowned them out as we sang our joy. I feel a little like that now, as if there are many more reasons to be heartbroken and fearful, but I am being allowed and given the strength to sing my joy.

I remember the Blessed Mother's beautiful words to me, "You are very much loved and respected in Heaven because, though you have sinned and will sin, God sees the desires of your heart; and the desires of your heart are constant. The desires that you have, whether you fail or succeed, are what you will take into eternity—not your successes or failures." When she said this to me, I imagined myself standing before God with the desires of my heart laid bare when this life is passed.

I think of Our Lord Jesus Christ who said to those He cured, "What may I do for you?" He asked them. I imagined myself being asked that question by my Lord. What would I say if I had that incredible opportunity? What is the true and honest desire of my heart? I would say, "Please, Lord, even though I am so small and imperfect and have done some very wrong things in my life, please, by Your grace and Your love, let me serve you." If I serve God at all as a blind person, would I serve Him better as a sighted one? If the answer to that question is yes, then I would want very much to see, whatever that might mean. It might be quite difficult for me.

But I had prayed not to receive my sight unless it would give greater glory to God to restore it to me because I have truly organized my life around being blind. By this I mean that for me being blind is normal, I live with it as completely natural to me. The adjustment to sight for a totally blind person who has never seen is something that most people who have seen and do see now cannot begin to understand. Perhaps this is a grace that might be given to me as it was given to those Jesus cured. Restoring physical sight does not mean restoring an ability to see. Jesus performed a double miracle, a miracle modern science cannot replicate in the case of a person who has been blind since birth. As stated in the Gospels, several of the people Jesus cured were blind. At least one of these people had been blind since birth. Jesus gave those He cured the physical ability to see, but also gave them the gift of being able to interpret what a congenitally blind person would experience as frightening chaos. It takes seven to ten years for a person who has never seen and then is medically given sight to adjust, and these are traumatic years. One has to "learn" to see a chair, another human face, everything. I don't want to waste that much time, unless it is my Lord's will.

Of course, Our Blessed Lord could give me the same sort of miracle He gave to those others in the Gospel. But would that bring me closer to Him, or help me serve Him better? Would it help others have more love for Him or grow in their faith?

I wonder, too, what would I say to those who had not received such a miracle? I don't think I would feel unworthy, but I wonder what difference it would make in eternity? A miracle like this would hit the national news, "Blind Woman With Surgically Removed Eyes Sees Miraculously, Totally Unexplainable To Medical Science." So what? Then what? It would be a "wonder for three days." Now I have a right to comfort others and to say that it will be better because of my own pain. There is a unity with others who are disabled, who suffer. It is a unity which opens one's heart to love, to give it and receive it. If the gift is used wisely, it makes it more difficult to be hard. It is easier to be compassionate if self–centeredness does not get in the way.

But I'm so happy I don't have to do that with Meniere's!! The pain of the prejudice I face as a blind person and the difficulties in just coping sometimes are often heavy loads to bear, but I am used to them now. There is also a challenge to me in living this life, and a joy of sharing my unique world with those sighted friends and acquaintances with open and interested hearts.

I asked the Blessed Mother about my eyes, and was told to be patient. I was given no other answer. Charismatic communities tend to be rather obsessed with "healing." I think this is true of Christians in general now. Where is the understanding of the necessity of brokenness? Jesus was "broken for our sake." I begin to understand that it is through brokenness, through the openness of pain which makes humility more possible, that Our Lord can work. It is through the prayers offered in this state of openness that abundant grace can most freely flow.

Where is the understanding of the great call of discipleship, of offering, in order to "pick up one's cross and follow Christ?" I think that, on the whole, when we concentrate too much on physical healing we start to believe that God is a magician with whom we need to plead to pull some magic trick out of a hat for us. If we cannot look further than physical healing, we lose an opportunity to get our priorities in order, to have a marvelous glimpse into eternity.

I have been deeply grateful for the cure of Meniere's Disease. I have thanked God every morning and evening, and often in between, that I will not be called upon to adjust to life as a totally blind and totally deaf person, ready to be struck at any moment with severe dizziness and debilitation. But I wonder now: How does this healing of my body affect my spirit, which is where anything permanent must be reflected, anything which is to last for eternity? The physical healing is a gift I will thank my Lord for forever, but now what? How can I grow closer to Him through this miracle of healing?

I have thought a great deal about all of these things since finding out about the tumor. It is a challenge. How can I praise Him now, in such pain of spirit and constant worry? It is one thing to say "I trust" when things are going well. But now, what if I should have to live as a multiple handicapped person in a body which has become a prison, possibly isolating me completely?

The tumor is located at the base of my skull, on my left side. With all my heart, I thank God that the area of my brain which it effects has nothing to do with my ability to think or with my emotions and mental stability. The prognosis after surgery may be very serious. My doctor has told me not to be afraid if I wake up on a respirator. "The nerves affecting your lungs are probably far enough away from the tumor site so that even if they are damaged, they will probably rejuvenate and you will most likely be able to eventually to breathe again on your own," he says.

He tells me I have a 99.99 percent chance of losing all the hearing in my left ear. He says that I must just make up my mind to understand that this will happen. He says my left side will probably be weakened, possibly permanently. He tells me to be prepared for the possibility that my face might fall on the left side, leaving very little muscle control.

He is anxious for many blood donors. He says he hopes to get at least forty. The response from people to give me their blood has overwhelmed me beautifully with love.

So now, in the face of all of this, do I still insist that there is a place for pain? Not now. Not right now, anyway.

One night I sat praying, pleading with God. I said, "I am no Helen Keller. Others can face living life as a multiple handicapped person. I have had to be strong in many ways, but I can't face this. Please don't ask me to face this." It was truly my Gethsemane, and I was given the grace to at last be able to say, "But not what I want, but what You will."

Suddenly the light became bright on my right side. The gentle voice, yet incredibly strong, which I have come to know as my dear Guardian Angel's spoke to me. "Pray for what it is you truly want," he said.

I thought for a long time about this. "All right," I said, "what I really want is to have all my senses, except sight of course, up until the moment I die. That's what I really want." But I also knew I wanted God's will above this, if it were in contradiction to my prayer.

I rather hesitantly began to pray for this, and in the process realized that my dear Lord wants me and others to truly ask Him for the bonanza, the true wish of our hearts. It is His prerogative, and mercifully His great wisdom, whether or not to grant us our requests — but I knew then that He wants us to ask without reservation or hesitancy. I can ask, ask, and ask again, and leave it up to the wisdom and mercy of my Lord to decide.

I have just come out of about two weeks of emotional immobility. I did not have the strength to reach out even to the people closest to me, those who love me dearly.

Right around the time of the Feast of the Immaculate Conception, December 8, my Guardian Angel said to me, "Please become consecrated to me."*

"What does this mean?" I asked. I have never heard of such a thing. What does being consecrated to my guardian angel mean? Is it some sort of ceremony, or do I do it privately? What changes afterwards?" My guardian angel did not reply.

On Saturday, December 10, I was asked to speak to a lovely group of people, pilgrims from New Orleans. I think I have met one of the best friends of my life among them — Debbie Cordes.

Also among them was Father Francis Butler. He is so filled with love for others, enthusiasm for his priesthood, and a wisdom that gives me great joy. He also has a wonderful sense of humor. He knew about consecrating oneself to one's guardian angel!

Surgery was scheduled for December 14. The love and support I received from the people of Saint John Neumann and from the instructors and fellow students of my department was phenomenal. It would take pages to talk about it. All I can say is I will do my best for them to help them if I ever can, and they will have my continuous prayers. I will never forget their kindness, and I beg God not to forget it either.

Gia was taken in by Karen Nelson, the secretary at The Commission for the Blind on the Texas Tech University campus, and my daughters were adopted for a month by the Cochrans. "Thank you for asking me," Anne said when I hesitantly requested her help. "I want to help, but most of the time I don't know what to do and I end up not doing anything. Thank you."

---

[Note: Consecration to one's Guardian Angel is no longer permitted by the Church. It is preferable to call a close relationship to one's guardian angel a "dedication," as my guardian angel has said. See chapter 49 on Opus Angelorum.]

It gave me a strange and empty feeling to be making a will assigning the guardianship of my dear girls...just in case.

"I still have to face the ridicule the Blessed Mother talked about," I said to myself, "so I suppose I will live through the operation. But I was in the deepest despair. I went through the motions of living. When I could pray, I asked to be taken if any more of my senses would be lost during the surgery. I wanted to crawl into a little shell and never come out. I could not reach out to other people. I avoided the love and help I most needed. But isn't that the way it is so often?

On the night of Friday, December 2, I had sat for several hours (I think it was several hours, I didn't have much of a sense of time) immobile, not thinking or caring about anything. I was in complete despair and sorrow.

Suddenly the light became so bright that I could SEE IT THROUGH MY HANDS. The voice I had come to know as that of my Guardian Angel began to speak quietly and gently to me.

He told me first, which surprised me, that he was in sadness now because he did not have a body. He felt my pain and wanted very much to reach out to me and comfort me. He said that we as human beings have the incredible gift to be able to reach out to each other. We can touch each other, hold each other, express things through touching each other that are very hard to communicate otherwise. He loves me so much, and seeing me in that kind of despair made him want to reach out to me in every way possible to comfort me.

He told me that God the Son, Our Lord Jesus Christ, and human beings suffer in a way that angels cannot suffer. This suffering is a means to spiritual growth and a deepening of love. I do not understand how this applies to God, if it does, and this is a question I may have the opportunity to ask my Guardian Angel at another time. At any rate, it certainly does apply to us. He said that angels cannot suffer as we do but they suffer because of their love for us. They love us because God loves us and created us with the flame of His Spirit within us. They suffer as they see how we suffer, how we hurt each other, how people who sin suffer because of their sin and how there are consequences and suffering for those their sin touches. This suffering of the angels is a pain we cannot know yet.

He did not tell me about the crucifix I have around my neck (the formerly silver one), but he did tell me that he had been allowed to touch the crucifixes in our house and on my rosaries to remind me and my family of the love of God for us. I will write about the crosses changing and other events in another account, the text about the occurrences having to do with the Feast of the Assumption in 1988 here in Lubbock.

I was surprised at his talking about angels growing through suffering. I have always believed that angels were created by God and more or less stayed as they were created, but he said no. "All creation must grow toward God or die," he said. I don't understand how this would pertain to hell, since hell is not growing toward God, but perhaps this, too, is a question for another time.

"I don't mean to ask a question I should not," I said, "so please forgive me if I should not ask this question and this is none of my business, but there is something I have often wondered. When I and other people die and go to wherever we're going, do you and other guardian angels get sort of 'reassigned' to other souls?"

"No. We go through a rigorous training, long and hard. Some angels do not finish it. It is a deep training in love and in discipline. Our love is deepened in order that we may be with you through all facets of your lives and be devoted to you. Our discipline is deepened because as we love the souls more and more over whom we are given guardianship, it would be so very easy for us to do things which would make life easier for them, which would on the surface seem to help them towards Our Lord. But we must not do anything apart from the will of God, and we must not interfere with you or your world. We must leave you free to make your own choices. Our greatest duty is to protect your right to make the last choice. This choice is the choice between good and evil, love and indifference, hate and kindness. It is directly related to your openness to God and to whether you will stand before God or

---

[Note: My Guardian Angel explained later to me that angels often do, always with the permission of God, have a direct influence on our physical and spiritual well being. My guardian angel was talking here only about the interference which might contradict our free will.]

not. You must be free to make this choice, however you make it, and this is what we try to guard most for you."

"When a soul chooses damnation, the grief of that soul's guardian angel is terrible. It is a grief so terrible that it cannot be imagined here. The angel is shattered into little fragments (so to speak) because of not being able to bring his ward to God. Each soul is so precious to God that we are given only one soul each for all eternity, and this soul is an infinite treasure to God and to us.

There is no soul on earth which is not given the gift of a guardian angel by God, and when a Guardian Angel cannot bring this treasure which is a priceless human soul to God, that angel's suffering destroys that angel. There is a special healing and loving that must take place in Heaven for the guardian angel of a lost soul in order that the angel may be made whole once more."

My Guardian Angel would later explain to me in answer to my questions that, though angels and saints are in perfect joy because of being in the full presence of God, they also at the same time can and do experience great sorrow because of still being linked to us. They are not immune to our suffering and sinfulness, and this affects them deeply. It is possible for them to be in perfect joy in the presence of God and yet also to be in deep sorrow over us. The Blessed Mother in her appearances often weeps in sorrow over us, but her complete joy in God remains intact. How it is possible for those in Our Lord's Kingdom to experience perfect joy while at the same time experiencing sorrow over us is something the angels told me later we cannot understand until it is our time to experience it ourselves.

Because my spiritual director and other priests wished more clarification on this point, Our Gracious Lord allowed my Angel to tell us more. My Guardian Angel said, "When I said that a guardian angel is shattered when that angel's ward chooses hell, over many decisions of a lifetime and or because of a great sin, I did not mean that the angel itself is shattered. Remember, we are pure spirit. You think in terms of a creature breaking or a vessel shattering. No. But do not in any way underestimate the grief of an angel whose ward chooses hell. Remember, we are given charge of each of you by God Almighty, and for us each soul is an infinite trust, an infinite responsibility, an infinite heartache, an infinite joy.

"There is no such thing as consolation of an ordinary sort for us when one of you chooses hell because to the angel whose beloved charge has chosen hell, it is as if all of humanity, all of creation is lost for that angel. As it is with God, each one of you is as precious and loved as all of the members of the human race. A soul is not just one soul among many. It is infinitely, immeasurably precious, beyond price, beyond measure, beyond recompense. And so when it is lost by the angel Our Blessed Lord has placed over it to guard and protect it, you cannot comprehend the devastation of the angel. That devastation comes because of the soul's loss but also because the angel, as well as bearing its own heartbreak (a human word I must use), also suffers, knowing the great grief of the Lord whose beloved one that individual soul is.

"Our Blessed Lord has tried to express His love for you in images of the tenderest kind: of a shepherd losing one of his lambs, of a mother losing one of her children, of a dove losing one of her fledglings. But the loss of a soul is beyond human imagery, beyond human understanding. Please simply understand that each of you is beyond price, beyond value. This is because you are loved by the Lord God, whose love is infinite. If you are loved infinitely, then to the One who loves you you are beyond price. Only He Himself could have offered the infinite sacrifice for you.

"We angels who are your guardians, though we love you with our entire beings, love you only imperfectly and impartially. But remember, our love for you is rooted in our love for Him to whom we have given our whole beings, our whole existences, our whole service. So when you reject God, we mourn your loss, His grief, and our own desire and dream of bringing your souls safely, after your earthly lives, into His Love forever.

"Yes, we are in need of great consolation and love from the Lord of all Consolation when you choose hell, though we understand it is your free choice and beyond anything we could have prevented. But we love you. Can you please try to understand this love just a little beyond what you comprehend as love? When love truly exists, the fate of the one loved is so dear to the one loving that more than just feeling is shared. Though we part on the brink of hell from the souls who have chosen hell, we suffer our own agonies because of our love for you and it is because of the great and perfect love of Our Beloved Lord that we are healed of these agonies. Do not doubt that we are always in perfect bliss and deepest joy because we are in the presence of God. But remember, love is never aloof, never uninvolved, never apart from the sufferings of those who are loved. The Lord of all that is holy and good has clearly shown you this. We, the holy angels, are not exempt from the involvement of love."

In the conversation my Dear Angel had with me during that difficult time in December of 1988 before my surgery, he wanted to tell me of some of the things which would happen in the future including what would happen with the operation, but at that time I could not bear even to listen, I was so afraid. I asked to be told later, if that would be all right.

"I'll try to handle it now if that is for the best," I said, "but if I could hear these things later, I would very much appreciate that. I am so overwhelmed."

He said that would be all right. Strange that I could not be reassured or comforted about the operation. I know now that he wanted to reassure me and give me good news, but I was too afraid to hear any sort of news at all — good or bad. I have always believed I could handle things better knowing the worst rather than being kept in the dark. Apparently, that is not always true with me.

He did tell me, however, that Our Lord and Our Blessed Mother would be there "during the entire time of the operation" and that "the room will be filled with angels." Filled with angels!

# Chapter 6
# LEARNING TO OFFER

I thought I was to enter the hospital on December 13, Tuesday, but on Monday afternoon about one o'clock the phone rang as I was rushing around, washing clothes, cleaning and trying to get ready to leave. "The doctor wants you in right now!" the nurse told me.

My father was flying in from Honolulu within a few hours. I had hoped to have an evening with him before entering the hospital. "Well, I thought," I still will have the evening, but it will be a little different from what we had planned."

I knew the prognosis for fully recovering the use of my vocal cords was questionable. I love to sing. As I continued packing I thought "I would like to sing a song of praise and thanks to God for letting me know about the tumor and for all the other blessings I have received." I started to sing, but broke down, crying. What if this were the last song I would ever sing — here on earth anyway? "Dearest Lord," I prayed, "You gave me my voice as a gift when you first created me. Please give it to me as a gift a second time, and every song I ever sing, whether religious or secular, will be dedicated to You in thanks."

Immediately after checking in and being taken to my room, my prayers began to be answered. I had prayed that, IF AND ONLY IF, my pain offered as prayers could be of service to the souls Our Lady had asked me to pray for—if this pain could be of some use, would Our Lord please give me as much pain as I could stand without permanent repercussions. Ordinary tests went awry. Needles did not go in properly. Again and again my veins collapsed as a young woman attempted to insert an I.V. needle. I had black and blue marks on my arm for months afterwards. I have never had any reactions to medication, but my body seemed to be super sensitive to everything.

This was all strangely comforting, though I hesitate to tell you since I could so easily be labeled a masochist. But I was comforted because I knew that my wish to do as my dear Heavenly Mother had asked was being respected.

## THE LIGHT OF LOVE

Excerpt from Journal Entry:

Tuesday, December 13, 1988

I am very glad that my angiogram, a rather long and painful process of getting a dye into a large artery in my groin so that pictures may be taken to show the doctors where the blood vessels around the tumor are, has been postponed. I can write now using my Perkins brailler propped on my hospital table and a pile of paper beside me.

I have received an outpouring of love that is unbelievable. I think over and over again to myself that God surely must have given me a special gift at my conception, "and she shall have friends."

Last night my Guardian Angel spoke to me briefly again. He told me that each soul, according to its needs, weaknesses, and mission, is given special gifts. Weakness itself may be a gift as well.

These gifts are given at the time of each soul's creation by God. These are not the same gifts as the "gifts of the Holy Spirit" listed in the New Testament but are gifts given to each soul gratuitously. He explained that it is rather like Christmas when these special gifts are given to a newly created soul. Certain gifts are given, but there is a special big gift that is different for each soul. Most souls are not consciously aware of their particular gift. Many souls become bitter because of their suffering, believing themselves to be deserted, unloved. Because of their pain, they shut themselves off, wishing to minimize their hurt.

But, he told me, a wise use of suffering will show us more clearly what our particular gift is. The idea of suffering and weakness as gifts is one I have thought of before, but to have it verified by my Guardian Angel causes me to ponder it more seriously now.

I can't help but think continually of the blessings I have received. An acquaintance and I had planned to get together to pray the rosary at noon on the Feast of the Immaculate Conception, but she came to my house on Wednesday with her husband and little boy. They gave me some beautiful flowers and a card.*

---

[Note: The names of some of the people in this account have been omitted, either at their own request or because of my desire to preserve their privacy.]

I had to go to Saint Mary's Imaging Center for an MRI, a more advanced test using magnets to try to pinpoint the location of the tumor, and they offered to drop me off there. Before this, they wanted to go to Saint John Neumann. I have not been able to be around the church these days, or around people in general — I have felt so raw. But I was glad to be going with them to spend a little time praying.

It has become a treasured ritual of mine to go down into the courtyard, to pass the fountain going toward the church, to stop at the fountain, make the sign of the cross, and pray a short prayer. Mary Constancio, one of the Lubbock messengers, has told us that the Blessed Mother blesses the waters of the fountain continually and will always do so.

I blessed myself with the waters of the fountain on that day as usual. It was very cold, and I had to break a sheet of ice to get to the water.

We were at the church about 45 minutes praying. We were in the side chapel which is connected to the church. I looked up, and saw with amazement that the statue of the Blessed Mother was bathed in a beautiful, golden light. I know where the statue is in the chapel, and we were right in front of it. Contrary to what people may think, I never get used to this. It is a miracle each time for me. I suppose this is because, though I am very well aware of the supernatural source of the light, I also haven't seen a great deal of light in my life anyway, so light itself is a miracle to me.

We went out into the courtyard, and went towards their car. It had grown even colder in the 45 minutes since we had entered the church.

As we came out of the church I jokingly said out loud, "Well, Lord, and Blessed Mother, there have been some very wonderful things happening around here lately. Suppose you heat the waters of the fountain?"

My acquaintance and her husband were worried that their little boy might get sick again. He has had some serious bouts with illness lately, poor little tyke. So his mother hurried ahead with him to get into the car. His dad and I came along further behind. This is what happened from my perspective.

As we passed the fountain, my companion stuck his fingers into the water and touched me on the forehead in blessing. I had not wanted to stop to bless myself this time because I was so very cold.

As we hurried toward the stairs I said, "That was very nice of you! I usually stop to bless myself and say a prayer, but I didn't want to stop this time. It's so cold. All I could think of is getting warm. Thanks for doing it for me."

"Well," he said, "you blessed yourself coming down."

"And you blessed me going back up," I said.

"No, I didn't."

I was angry at first, thinking he was playing tricks on me for fun. But he is not like that at all, and would not have been that familiar with me. "Don't do this to me. I can't take it right now."

"What are you talking about?" he asked in rising irritation.

"Didn't you just dip your fingers in the water of the fountain and touch my forehead in blessing?" The hand had been a real hand, a calloused hand, a workman's hand.

"No, I didn't!"

His tone made it clear that he would never even think of doing such a thing to me—and probably not to anyone else either.

"Is there anyone else around?"

"No, there isn't. We're the only ones here."

"A very human hand just dipped its fingers in the fountain as we went by and blessed me. See, the water is still on my forehead. I felt the fingers, and there was nothing unusual about them. It was a kind hand blessing me."

He saw the water there on my forehead and exclaimed. A few moments later, his wife saw it also and we were all amazed.

When I was in the MRI tube, I began to get claustrophobic. To make matters worst, I could hear Gia out in the main room whining in distress at all the strange noises and lights and at my disappearance. The technician was trying to comfort her.

Then I remembered the beautiful blessing I had just received and I thought about something my Guardian Angel had told me when I inquired about a painful situation, "Our Lord knows about it," he had said. (I would hear this gentle, comforting phrase from the angels many times in the future when praying about a difficult or painful situation, "Our Lord knows about it." That was enough to guarantee its outcome of good and love, Our Lord knows about it.) "I am sure there are several angels in here with me, as well as Our Lord too. No wonder we're so crowded in here in the MRI tube," I thought. But I'm surely glad of the company." I felt comforted.

That night we had guests, and after everyone had left our home, I prayed deeply. I asked my Guardian Angel if I might know who it was that had blessed me. It had been a man's hand, roughened by work. That was why I had been sure it was the man with me and, of course, he was the only person there in the ordinary, physical sense. I thought it might be my Guardian Angel, but when he spoke to me he said no. He showed me the image of Christ on the cross. I heard my Guardian Angel's voice saying to me, "And He suffered and died for you also."

"Was it Jesus Himself, then, who blessed me at the fountain?" I asked in astonishment. I had not had the audacity to think it might have been, though it would have been logical to believe so, considering the roughened yet gentle hand. I could not have imagined He would do that to comfort me, the smallest of His people.

"It was Christ Himself," was the reply from my Angel. I got the impression that my Angel was saying to me also by his tone (though he did not speak these words), "If He would die so horribly on a cross for you, do you think He would not give you a blessing when you were in such need of one?"

As I sit in my hospital room writing this, my dear Guardian Angel has just let me know, as the light gets brighter, that this angiogram will hurt quite a lot. I cried tears of fear and asked him to hold my hand and he promises he will do so. He tells me so lovingly that he will be there, and to please offer the pain for the souls. I promise again to do so, and ask for the grace to do so. Please help me, Lord. I am so very afraid.

My Dad came in yesterday, and I saw him for the first time in two and a half years. I pray for him, and I love him so very much. He is amazed about what I have told him concerning the tumor and how it happened that I went for a CT–scan at all, and about the blessed angels, but he trusts my word and my sanity and the fact remains for him also: I would not be here in the hospital waiting for an operation necessary to save my life if I had not been told to go for those head x-rays. There is no way I would have known naturally.

My mother, despite ill health, went to Mass for me. She also brought tears to my eyes when she sent a little Miraculous Medal I had worn as a tiny newborn baby struggling for life.

My dear girls came into the room last night with their youth group leaders and some of the kids from the youth group. It was a pleasant visit, and the other kids' presence helped my girls.

Miriam told me in some astonishment today that when I prayed out loud, thanking God for bringing dad safely to me during this difficult time all the way from Honolulu, he was fighting tears. It means more than I can say that he is here.

I may not be able to write for a long time now. I had hoped to be able to write after the angiogram, but I have just been told this may be difficult or impossible to do. My doctor told me last night that he now believes I have a meningioma rather than an acoustic neuroma. I may need more blood than we had thought.

Father James was here earlier. He gave me Holy Communion and "The Anointing of the Sick." Thank God it is no longer called "the Last Rites." "Just in case" sounds so much better than "Good-bye."*

My Guardian Angel asked me to offer the pain of the operation for one of the people who was here. It is a blessing to me to offer the pain as prayers for him; to know the identity of one of the people I am to offer for.

Wednesday, December 14

I am surprised to have the chance to write more. Surgery has been postponed until noon, rather than early in the morning as we previously thought.

So very many people have been flooding in to see me, and a crowd down in the hospital's chapel is praying the rosary for the surgery to go well. I have a peace I could not have dreamed of, and we had good news last night. With the added information from the angiogram, the tumor appears to be a meningioma rather than an acoustic neuroma. The nerves to my ears are not as close as was thought, so the chances now are 50-50, rather than 99.99% that I will lose the hearing in my left ear! Glory, glory be to God!

---

[Note: The Sacrament of the Roman Catholic Church commanded in the Book of James for the anointing of the sick was previously called "the Last Rites" or "Extreme Unction."]

My Guardian Angel has told me that he has been given special permission to talk to me, indefinite permission. When I asked if this would be for the rest of my life he said he didn't know, but it was indefinite. This gives me great comfort and has made him quite joyous. He says it is very rare that such permission is granted, and we are both honored by it and blessed by God.

"You are not a messenger," he told me. "You are a chronicler."

"A blind chronicler?" I asked very skeptically.

"You will write what you see," he said with lovely amusement.

I am almost afraid to write this, it seems so incredible. He tells me that Our Lord has special work for me to do. I am to bring souls to Him. He says I will be traveling on Our Lord's business. He tells me I will even leave the country on this business. I am afraid to write this down because it seems so incredible. Me? And from a hospital bed facing this serious operation?

My Guardian Angel asked me a little earlier to "please become consecrated to me, and to all the angels." I don't understand the phrase, "and to all the angels." From Father Butler I understand there is a consecration ceremony in which one dedicates oneself to one's guardian angel, but what is this "and to all the angels?" I don't have any knowledge or background to explain any of this.

I am so filled with awe and wonder, anxiety, and great fear over the coming operation. But I do believe, despite myself — I do believe, and I am comforted. Surely, if my Lord and the angels have all these plans for me it must mean I will be able to function after this operation. It does mean that, doesn't it? Please...

Later. At first as I continued to see the lights, I began to see images in them. These images, as I have said, were deeply disturbing and painful. Many of them involved great pain to innocent people — great suffering. One scene I saw haunted my dreams. It was a mother casually putting the lighted end of a cigarette against her baby's arm. She did it not in anger, but almost thoughtlessly, automatically. It was horrible.

---

[Note: My Guardian Angel would later explain that the word "dedication" would be more appropriate to describe what we are doing rather than would the word "consecration." See entries of July 1 and July 20, 1992.]

The baby screamed, of course. The mother did not react to the scream at all. She seemed to be in her own little world, oblivious to the child. How often have I been oblivious?

Another scene I saw was a barren room. A man, at first seeming to be quite old, lay on the floor on an old sheet. There was only a broken wooden chair in the dirty room. He was injecting himself with something. I looked closer and saw that he was actually young.

"Why do I keep seeing things like this?" I asked my Guardian Angel.

"Because nobody is praying for them. Please, please pray for them," came the same answer I had heard previously.

By October 2, I was having a hard time bearing these scenes. I asked in prayer to be given a rest, but before that I asked to be shown a joyful scene.

At first I thought that "God's crew," as Eileen calls them, had not heard me correctly. What I saw was a tumbled down two-room little hut made of boards, cardboard and possibly tin cans and God knows what else stuck together with mud and sticks and some sort of matted weaving. The house was full of about 12 to 14 people of all ages. They were dressed very poorly. Outside, a woman was cooking something in a pot over an open fire. The pot was suspended from the branch of a tree over the fire. I could not see what was in the pot, but whatever it was did not fill the pot, certainly was not enough to feed all those hungry people jammed into the house.

But as I looked closely, I saw how very happy the people were. They were laughing and talking, playing with the children in a warm and deeply loving way, telling each other about their working day, and making jokes about their hardships. The love between them was so very obvious it brought tears to my eyes. Out in back I could hear a woman singing.

These lovely people were expecting an honored guest who would be eating with them. There was, as I have said, hardly enough food for anyone, but they were deeply joyous that this guest, whom they knew and loved, would be sharing their meal.

So on the surface of things, it was just one more tragic scene. But God could see their hearts, and those in Heaven could see their hearts. This to them was truly a joyous scene and they showed it to me as such.

And as I too saw their joy and their love for each other, it became a joyous scene for me also, and I began to cry.

I have seen none of these visions since. Whether or not I am being given a rest and they will resume, or whether they have ceased because it has been decided they are too hard for me to bear, I don't know. It grieves me to think that it may be that I am too weak, but God knows best.

The medicine is beginning to make me feel drowsy in preparation for the big operation and some of the people I most love, the girls, my Dad, Anne Cochran — are here. I will stop now to spend time with them.

Please bless me, all of you who love me on earth, all of my friends in Heaven, all you blessed angels and saints, my dear Guardian Angel and Saint Joseph in particular, my beloved Blessed Mother, God the Son, who is my dear Jesus whom I am beginning to know more each day, God the Father who is the great Creator and lover of all, and God the Holy Spirit whom I began to know and love first.

Blessings on all, and please love and protect me. Amen.

# THE LIGHT OF LOVE

# Chapter 7
# PAIN AND HEALING

Even over four years later, at the time of this writing, I have not been able to record in my journal the events in the hospital following the tumor operation. I believe that this is because, though everything went amazingly well with no serious lasting repercussions except migraine type headaches, I have not wanted to relive the pain I endured in these months.

I was unconscious after the surgery for only a short time. In fact, I regained consciousness briefly that very night and was able to squeeze the hands of my Father and daughters and the others who were allowed briefly into intensive care to see me. I remember only about a minute of consciousness, but even in that minute I felt as though my spirit was trying to tell the rest of me and those I love, "I'm still here. I'm still in the running."

I was fully conscious by late afternoon of Thursday, the very next day. My neck muscles had been cut during the surgery in order to go underneath my skull to get to the tumor that way, as well as the removal of bones right above. The pain of these cut muscles was worse than the tumor incision itself. I did not sleep for about eleven days because of this pain, though I lay quietly with my eyes closed most of this time.

By Sunday, I was begging to get out of intensive care. The intensive care staff were noisy and rude, yelling at each other, using profanity, and at times treating me as if I were just a piece of unthinking and unfeeling meat. I knew I would receive more consideration and tenderness from the people who had cared for me before the operation, the regular nursing staff.

On Friday I had begun to feel as though I would like to eat some soup. A dish of sticky, butterscotch pudding was brought to me. How nourishing.

"I can't eat this," I protested weakly.

"Oh, yes," the ICU staff told me. "it will be good for you." I retched for 24 hours after the second spoonful.

"Don't heave!" my doctor told me. "those neck muscles...everything ... don't heave!"

When I was finally out of intensive care, one of the most loving incidents I experienced occurred. My whole body rebelled with spasms of sickness to a drug used to keep an injured brain from swelling, a drug which made me very sick but which I had to be given.

"I can't decrease the amount," my doctor told me worriedly as I heaved and struggled in agony over my neck muscles.

A nurse who rarely spoke came in after that regularly to give me the drug intraveneously. She would slowly drip it into the I.V. The moment I started to react, she would stop. Drop by tiny drop, she gave it to me. Sometimes she sat patiently giving me infinitesimal drops every five minutes. She could be there as long as half an hour. Though I still reacted, because of this patience and love I no longer wretched. This gentle patience and consideration is a kindness I will remember always.

My doctor did not prescribe a strong painkiller for me because of the fear prevalent at the time of addiction. The painkiller which he did prescribe for me is one I still take for my severe headaches. It is not a narcotic. I want to make this clear, because I had experiences in the hospital which might be attributed to a chemical reaction via drugs. This was not at all the case. I have to admit here that the pain became so severe at times that I would have given a great deal to have been given strong drugs. Warring with my physical weakness and desire for respite from pain was my unceasing wish to fulfill my dear Mother's request that I offer pain for the souls so treasured by her Son, Jesus Christ. Yet I also knew I could take pain killers, as this is one of the things she had told me I might do.

Friends told me later that they had been distressed for me, seeing me in such pain. I would tell them, "This martyr stuff is enough, I've had it. I've really had enough." Despite this, I felt desperately sad. I felt inadequate. I had been asked, no pleaded with, by the Blessed Mother of God herself to offer this pain as a margin of grace for the souls who could not repent for themselves. And there I was, taking pain killers as fast as they were given to me and wishing they could be ten times stronger.

"If only she could know how much I want to offer this, even though I'm not doing very well with it." I cried tears of frustration and sorrow over my inability and weakness.

Many of the people from Saint John Neumann and from my department visited me. Among them were Mary Constancio and Mike Slate, two of the Lubbock messengers. I felt comfortable and happy with them, though they were not at this time the close friends they later became. Mike's quietness especially touched me. I could feel his sympathy and tenderness toward me as he saw my pain. It is a compassion he has for everyone in pain.

"I asked the Blessed Mother if you couldn't please have less pain," he told me on one of his visits.

"What did she say?"

"Well," he told me slowly and reluctantly, "she said no." Mike thought he was giving me bad news. "She said no, because she said, 'that is not what she wants.'"

My heart leapt for joy. Despite my weakness, she knew I wanted to do what she had asked me to do. Mike had known nothing about this, but she knew. Please try to imagine how relieved and happy this made me feel.

Despite my continuous pain, I felt a joyousness because I knew that this was an answer to my prayers that I be allowed to offer as much pain as I could handle. The nursing staff on the regular patient ward were wonderful to me. "You're hurting so much," they told me, "but you're always smiling, thanking us, and joking with us. We argue over who will come in to help you when there's a choice about it."

"It's easier for me to bear the pain when you laugh with me," I told them.

In the afternoon of December 23rd I began to have excruciating pains in my legs. By the wee hours of the morning of the 24th I was crying and screaming in pain. I couldn't move without stabs of pain, and to lie still wasn't much better. "O, God," I prayed, "I want to offer this, but please just give me a little bit of a respite. Just a little relief, and then I'll go back to offering again. Please."

A nurse who had been distressed at my pain came into my room. "Your doctor ordered pain medication for you for right after your surgery," she told me. "You never took it. I might get in trouble for this, but I'm going to give it to you now." Because of her compassion and the love of God, I was given five hours of blessed relief. I understand now that the fear of people "getting addicted" has recently been dispelled by the finding that small doses of pain medication administered by the patient when needed does a good job of controlling pain without negative repercussions. It is ironic to me that if this had been known at the time of my surgery, I would not have offered as much for the souls for whom Our Lady wished prayers. But to that lovely, compassionate nurse, "thank you with all my heart."

The agony continued through the 24th. On Christmas Eve, I had another unexpected brief respite. My Guardian Angel gently told me to come with him. He took me out of my body and we traveled to several different places, visiting people that I knew and others whom I did not know. If they were praying, we prayed with them. If they were not praying, we prayed for them and for their intentions. There was nothing dreamlike about this experience. I knew that I was out of my body, and I did not feel frightened or strange. I had all of my faculties: my memory, my entire personhood, my entire self. I felt perfectly natural. The presence of my Guardian Angel reassured me that everything would be all right.

Then my Guardian Angel took me to a very beautiful place. People were celebrating with great joy. No one was excluded. No one was left out. The great and beautiful Host of the ongoing banquet was totally dedicated to bringing joy to His guests. It was a celebration of true thanksgiving. We were there for only a short time. I believe I was given a glimpse of Heaven on this painful and yet joyous Christmas Eve.

"It's time to go back," my Guardian Angel told me. I returned to my body as naturally as I had left it. A few minutes later, I was put on a gurney cart and taken down to receive angiograms in my feet. The doctors were worried that my severe leg pains might be caused by blood clots.

The pain of being moved, of having little or no support for my neck, added to the pain in my legs gave me more to offer. I remember lying on the cold, hard table, my neck and my legs hurting terribly. Again and again and again the doctor in charge attempted to inject the dye into the veins of my feet. My veins kept collapsing. Each needle prick caused excruciating pain. I lost control of myself and writhed, flinging the covers off. There was nothing for me now but the pain.

A nurse held my hand on the right side. The doctor and his assistant worked at my feet. There was no one to my left.

"O, my Lord," I screamed within myself, "this is nothing in comparison to what You endured, but I'm hurting, Lord, I'm hurting!"

I had removed the chain holding my special Crucifix from around my neck. I was clenching the Crucifix in my left hand. Suddenly there was someone to my left holding my hand with the crucifix in it. I could feel the warm hand holding mine. His gentle voice said to me, "It's everything to Me that you should do this." There was such a tenderness and gentleness in His words that it is impossible for me to describe it to you.

"Lord," I said, "please let this pain be granted as grace to even just one soul. Let one soul be given this pain as if it had repented. Just one, Lord, just one."

"Many more than one, dearest," He said to me.

Finally the dye was injected into my left foot. Then the same thing happened to my right foot. Again and again, my veins collapsed. "Couldn't we just inject the dye in her ankles?" the assistant pleaded with the doctor.

"No," he said sadly, "a clot may be in her feet and we would miss it." I wanted to comfort them, strangely enough. I wanted to tell them what had just happened. I wanted to tell them that God in His kindness was allowing me to offer this inevitable pain so that many souls would eventually be able to enter Heaven. He was giving me the gift of being allowed to share in the salvation He had completed on the Cross. But I was in too much pain to tell them, and I think I had the presence of mind to realize I wouldn't have been able to explain it and they probably wouldn't have understood anyway. It was certainly not the time for explanations.

When I was finally taken back to my room, I unclenched my hand from around my Crucifix. This is the Crucifix which had turned gold on the Feast of the Assumption, which had physically changed, and which I now wear around my neck at all times. The position of the Corpus had entirely changed on the Cross. It was twisted in agony.

It has since straightened and still moves, but I knew by this that my Lord had suffered with me every step of the way.

Through the explanations and teaching of my Guardian Angel, I have come to understand that Almighty God does not demand suffering from us as some sort of recompense because of the sins of others.

He is not a blood thirsty Lord. Our sins and the sins of others cause an imbalance in our world, an imbalance caused by our hurtful, immature acts committed through our own free will. Our Lord will not interfere with our free will, but wants to bring as many souls to Himself as possible despite the consequences of our free will. Our offering of pain is given as if it were felt by another soul as the pain of repentance for his or her sin. It is, therefore, Our Lord's need of help from us, not because He needs our help as He is all powerful, but because He chooses to give us a share in His Kingdom, which includes love for others through sacrifice, to redress the imbalance of sin that causes the necessity for the offering of suffering. Our Lord will not interfere with our free will, but neither can He bear to lose any soul because of the consequences of our free will unless this is inevitable.

If a soul cannot be saved without interference with its free will, Our Lord will do nothing out of respect for the soul's freedom to choose. In other words, the soul will damn itself to hell. But for those souls needing help to repent, He gives His grace. Often that grace comes through the intercession of ordinary people, the offering of their lives, their prayers, their pain. Our whole lives can be offered as prayers, and our pain offered to God is an especially powerful prayer of love.

So, through His love and mercy and, I would almost go so far as to say, His vulnerability because of His love for us, He needs our help because He chooses to make us participants in His love. Because of His love and respect for us, our all–powerful Lord (who needs nothing from us) chooses to make our little love, our little offerings, necessary. He loves us so much that our prayers and offerings of love, small as they are, really DO make a great difference in the universe. Our love through our prayers matters so much to God that the effect of our love, the outcome of our love, is magnified by His grace into a result far greater than we can conceive.

We are, therefore truly joined in the redemptive passion of Our Beloved Lord, Jesus Christ. This too is a gift — this joining in love. If chastisements come, it will be because there is no other alternative to redress as much as possible the imbalance caused by blatant sin which is no longer even acknowledged for the evil it is, not even justified, but defended as a right and "an alternative lifestyle."

Our pain must never be induced by ourselves, unless we have been clearly requested to induce it and are under the direction of a wise priest. All pain to be offered comes naturally, or by Our Lord's own request to us to bear super–natural pain. To bring about pain for ourselves in order to be offered only starts us on the road to craziness. Our Lord must remain in charge.

This picture only later became clear to me over time as I was given more experiences by the angels and more explanations, and as I diligently studied the Scriptures. It was amazing to me how many other Christians have offered their pain, their joy, — all of their lives — to Christ as a prayer, as a "living sacrifice."

I give these thoughts here out of chronological order in order to clarify for you what only later became known to me. At the time of my surgery and the subsequent pain, I offered my suffering without understanding why, simply because I had been asked to do so. I did not have any sort of background that would have made this a familiar or acceptable thing to do. I had not been raised at all with the phrase "offer it up."

The pain in my legs abated and was finally almost entirely gone by the wee hours of the morning of the 26th. A day or two later I was taken for further testing. I wanted very much to try to sit up in a wheel chair because I had been promised the journey would be a fast one. After the tests were completed, one of the hospital staff came for me. Half way to my room he suddenly said, "I'm going to put your chair right on the side here and someone else will get you in a minute." He then walked away. I sat for a few minutes but then began to feel terribly sick to my stomach and dizzy. I started to heave. I waved my arms and cried out for help. I was in an unfrequented area in the hospital. A woman working at a desk about twenty feet away began to call for help for me. I became weaker and weaker and the heaving was overpowering me. My neck muscles felt as if they were about ready to tear my head off. I knew I would fall any minute. I slowly crawled out of the chair and lay on the floor, hoping I would be less likely to be hurt doing this. Within three minutes hospital staff had picked me up on a litter and carried me back to my room.

I thought a great deal that day about how abandoned my Lord, Jesus must have felt. He was totally helpless as I had been, but He had been in a situation in which there had been no help, and in which those around Him had as their goal His brutal murder. Though I had been the victim of negligence, at least no harm had been intended.

Many of the people of Saint John Neumann told me that, over Christmas especially, they had smelled "Our Lady's roses." Perhaps, I thought, they were smelling some sort of perfume, or scented candles. But one night in the hospital, over the scent of chemicals and some cinnamon herbs someone had given me, I smelled the scent of fresh, living roses so beautifully that it was unmistakable. It was there strongly for a few minutes, and then completely gone.

The Mother of God loves roses so much because He, her Son, is the Rose, the full flowering of God's new covenant with us. The beautiful words of the old carol with its lovely old tune ran in my mind that night:

Lo, how a Rose e'er blooming
From tender shoot hath sprung.
Of Jesse's lineage coming,
As men of old hath sung.
It came, a flow'ret bright,
Amid the cold of winter
When half spent was the night.

Isaiah 'twas foretold it,
The Rose I have in mind.
With Mary we behold it,
The Virgin Mother kind.
To show God's love aright
She bore to men a Savior
When half spent was the night.

We pray you, Mary, Mother,
The world's fair rose of grace,
That by your Christ Child's Passion
We too may see His face.
So, may He help us all,
To offer us His treasure
Our hearts His dwelling place.

I was determined to get out of the hospital as soon as possible, sooner hopefully, because my dear friend of many years, D., was coming from Hawaii to be with me after my surgery. She was using up precious vacation time to come all the way to Lubbock, Texas, to be with me immediately after my release. She arrived on January 5th. My doctor had told me he would not allow me out of the hospital until I could walk at least four steps without a walker. I made myself do it. Every fiber of my being went into doing it. I was not going to lie in a hospital bed while one of my dearest friends in the whole world waited for me in my empty house.

My dear Gia, my guide dog, was returned to me, a little uncertain about what would happen next. She had gravitated between wild playfulness and depression while with Karen Nelson and her family. She had been allowed to visit me once in the hospital. I was afraid she would jump up on the bed and possibly hurt me, but she came to me gently and licked my nose. She was uncharacteristically very quiet.

When she finally arrived home, Karen said she had tried to leap out of the car before it stopped. When Karen was ready to leave, Gia was unsure as to what she was to do. For days afterwards, she was reluctant to let me out of her sight even for a moment.

A few weeks after my return home, I began to write a letter which I subsequently xeroxed and sent to my family and friends about the events of the Feast of the Assumption at Saint John Neumann Church and the following events in my own and my family's life. Sometimes I wrote only a paragraph a day.

------

[Note: LO, HOW A ROSE E'ER BLOOMING, is a twelfth century carol.]

# THE LIGHT OF LOVE

# PART II:
# THE SPECIAL GIFT
## (1989)

*Gia —Patricia's constant companion.*

# Chapter 8
# THE TEST OF AUTHENTICITY

On February 10th, 1989, my Guardian Angel spoke to me at length for the first time since December 2nd. I did not write what he said down verbatim, but within a few minutes after the conversation, I wrote it down as closely as I could remember.

He started by talking about the difficulties we were having at Saint John Neumann. He said these difficulties would increase and were being allowed to strengthen us, but that we would be given special graces to bear them.

Then he began talking more generally. He said (paraphrased):

"The time is coming when there will be many deceptions and many will be deceived, some of them our Lord's people. It will appear that those who are, in actual fact, truly serving the prince of darkness are serving the Lord of Light and Love. They will be servants of the evil one, but will appear to be servants of God. Things will appear to be wonderful, and many will be taken in and believe. Many of those who will be deceived are sincere and good people.

There is a way by which you will be able to untangle this confusion. There are many things about which Lucifer can deceive you, but one thing he cannot pretend. He has not, nor will he ever, be willing to suffer for his people. People are expendable to him. His followers will not be willing to suffer for one another or extend themselves for each other or anyone else. Our Lord Christ has suffered and died for you and continues to suffer because of your pain, and because of the pain you inflict on each other. You are His followers to the degree that you love and extend yourselves for one another."

He said we were to pray deeply and ask two questions:

1) Are the people who seem so wonderful or their leader(s) willing to suffer for each other or anyone else?

2) Is even one person expendable "to achieve a greater good?"

This reminded me of a poem quoted by Bishop Fulton J. Sheen. Bishop Sheen did not give the author. The poem makes clear that being a follower of Christ means the willingness, perhaps the certainty, of suffering for the sake of others' souls. Here is the poem:

"Hast thou no scar,
No hidden scar
On foot, or side, or hand?
I hear thee sung as mighty in the land,
I hear them hail thy ascendent star.
Hast thou no scar?
Hast thou no wound?
Yet I was wounded
By the archer's bent,
Leaned Me against a tree to die
And rent by ravening beasts that compassed Me
I swooned.
Hast thou no wound?
No wound?
No scar?
Yet as the Master
Shall the servant be,
And pierced are the feet
That follow Me.
But thine are whole.
Can he have followed far
Who hast no wound or scar?"

My Blessed Angel told me that not one human soul is expendable to God, but that Lucifer throws anything and everything away which does not serve his purposes, or discards what has finished serving his purposes.

My Angel said we are to pray deeply for guidance and clarity. Many good people will be taken in by deceptions. When they realize they have been misled, they will struggle against this evil, but will not prevail against it. We are not to despise or reject them because they have been misled. As followers of Christ, we are to imitate Him in loving. God does not throw anything good away. What is good and loving belongs to Him. Though these people will be unsuccessful in resisting this future evil and will suffer greatly for their efforts, they will be redeemed by Our Lord in time. We are to love them.

My Dear Angel showed me large crowds being deceived, as well as individuals. He also explained that those who would be disregarded or "sacrificed" for a "greater good" are not those who are disruptive or harmful to others, but are innocent and precious souls who are not seeking power and who are, in fact, only cogs in a great machine of evil and deceit.

My Angel told me that a test for those saying they are followers of Jesus Christ is this: Are they willing to live lives of sacrifice for others, suffer for others and, if necessary, die for others, and for their Lord and His Faith?

The willingness to sacrifice oneself out of love is the true test of the authenticity of a follower of Christ. This self–sacrifice is not a grand gesture. It may be the only alternative for one who wishes to remain faithful. It may be a lifetime of quiet self-giving. A life of sacrifice, whether it be martyrdom or a day to day giving in love through personal sacrifice, is considered the ultimate in foolishness by those who worship themselves.

## TESTING OF THE SPIRITS

It was around this time that I was instructed concerning testing what happens to me in a spiritual sense. I was taught by my Guardian Angel that when anything extraordinary is happening, I am to say, "If you are of my Lord Jesus Christ who loves and created all things, then you are welcome in the name of the Father, and of the Son, and of the Holy Spirit (making the sign of the cross.) If you (or this) is not of my Lord jesus Christ, then by His holy wounds, His agonizing Passion, His cruel death, and His glorious rising you are to be gone now in the name of the Father, and of the Son, and of the Holy Spirit (making the sign of the cross.) Amen." I was told later by my Guardian Angel that this is a manner of testing which has been approved by the Church, and we found it to be so. It is, of course, based on the test given in the Scriptures that Jesus Christ must be acknowledged as Lord and Savior. My Guardian Angel told me that, in order not to be conspicuous, one might test very quietly, even making the sign of the cross mentally in order that the attention of others present might not be drawn to the tester. I have also added after the test I was taught that whoever is speaking to me must repeat after me, "Our Lord Jesus Christ is true God and true man and is Lord of all." When I ask them to repeat this after me before I will listen to them, the angels are quietly pleased. One angel, joyfully added after repeating my words, "Our Lord Jesus Christ is true God and true man, and is Lord of all, Alleluia!"

One night, I became so excited when the light became bright that I did not test the presence. I grabbed a piece of paper and got ready to write, but what was said was full of ridicule and gibberish. I knew it was very wrong. I tested the presence as I had been taught in the words above, and immediately whatever it was was gone. I was sternly warned never to forget again, never to be afraid of testing. "Strong evil can masquerade as good, sometimes for a long time," I was told. "Always test." I do test now always, and will not forget again.

# Chapter 9
# NO GREATER LOVE

On the night of Thursday, February 23rd, an acquaintance of mine came to visit us with her husband and little boy. I was happy to see them as I had not seen them since getting out of the hospital. They had been kind to me during this time.

We tried to pray a family rosary at eight every Thursday evening and then we read from the Scriptures. As we sat visiting, it was getting late so I told our guests about our custom and asked if they would care to join us. They were glad to do so.

We were praying the Sorrowful Mysteries, using a Scriptural rosary book so that a passage from Scriptures was read in between each of the prayers. We were on the last decade commemorating the Crucifixion of Our Lord. I was holding the Crucifix of my rosary in my right hand and the beads in my left, when suddenly the right arm of the little figure on the Cross gave way beneath my fingers.

"Oh," I thought, "I've broken it!" I checked the arm and it was all right. "I'll bet it's the nail," I thought, "it's probably loose." I checked it. It was all right. Then the little figure began WRITHING UNDER MY FINGERS.

I screamed out that the figure on my Crucifix was moving. I don't know who took my rosary from me. My girls and our guests watched as the body on the Cross tried to push itself up, the arms moved, the head changed position. The horror and the terrible beauty of it went on for about ten minutes.

How can I ever express what we felt? I think we were all crying. I know I was. I reached out several times during these ten minutes to feel the figure moving and then couldn't reach out again for turmoil and joy. I imagined what horror it would have been if it had been life size. But I was there in my heart, nevertheless.

I thought of all the times I have closed my heart to the love of Our Lord and the love of other people because of my fear of being hurt yet again, how I have made of prayer a commonplace, what a temper I have sometimes, how thoughtlessly words about other people can spill from me, words that would never be spoken if that person were standing right next to me, and on and on. Of all these, my closing of my heart to loving and being loved seemed the worst. "Let ten thousand hurts not make any difference, Lord, because You have done this," I cried in my heart. "Please help me to be strong." It was this series of thoughts and feelings that came to me as the unbelievable became a touchable and seeable reality for us.

The light I see filled the room and a voice which went straight to my heart, and seemed to echo around the world to every other heart, said words I had heard once before:

"I love you. I love you. I love you. Don't ever doubt that I love you. I love you."

We cried.

After about ten minutes, the figure stopped moving. It is now in the same position of all the figures of each of the crosses in our home, with the head of Our Lord's figure down on the right shoulder, but this one is much more forward. There is no part of the body on this Crucifix which touches the cross except where the poor hands and feet are nailed.

The body truly hangs. I don't think I will ever be able to touch a Crucifix again without my fingers remembering that little moving figure under them. May I never forget that love.

I knew strongly that we should continue with the rosary though we were hardly able to do so. One of our guests brought a moment of relief to us when he said, "Does this sort of thing happen to you people every time you say the rosary? ... No, I can see by your faces that it doesn't."

This may seem flippant to you, but believe me it was not. There is, after all, only so much our limited human hearts can stand and we had gotten close to being shattered.

We continued. We came to the reading in which Our Lord says from the Cross to His Mother, "Woman, this is your son," and then to Saint John, (and all of us), "this is your Mother." I was holding the little medal of the rosary on which there is a tiny figure of the Blessed Mother. As these words were spoken, the little figure of the Blessed Mother started moving UNDER MY THUMB.

I cried out again. In my letter I have said that Miriam and Eileen could not look at this. However, they told me after the letter had been composed that they also had seen the little figure of Our Lady moving on the medal.

I have probably heard these words of Jesus to His Mother many times. I felt a deep sadness that I had never really considered how terrible it must have been for Holy Mary to stand there watching the person she loves most in the world suffer so horribly, and knowing who He is.

When I went to bed that night, the little figure on the medal was all the way to one side. It is now back in the middle.

I am acutely aware that what I have written here opens me up to serious allegations, the least troublesome being that I am crazy. Two things occur to me here. The first is that all these signs in and of themselves are only important because of their manifestations in the physical world, that a deep, spiritual response is being requested of me and of others. For whatever reason, my family and I, D. and her children, and the hundred or so other people who have seen my Crucifixes moving in the last six years have been privileged to know through our own senses that Our Lord, Jesus Christ, God, really did live among us. He really did suffer and die for us, and rise in glory. I had taken this on faith. Now I know it. Why I and the others have been blessed with the gift of this certain knowledge, I still do not know. I praise and thank God for it.

The second thing which occurs to me is my own background of study: my love of history, my love of other cultures, my interest in almost everything. This new certainty of our beloved Christian faith now expands me. What does God have in mind that He should have shown Himself to us, such ordinary people? I think of what the Blessed Mother told me, that we could become so unified with Jesus Christ, Our Beloved Lord, that He would walk the earth again in us. Jesus's suffering, death, rising and ascension are completed acts. But if we are Christians, Our Lord's life and love must be reproduced in us. Because I believe in Him and want to love Him totally, my life must follow His pattern, though, of course, with different details. This pattern involves sacrificing for the salvation of others, as well as rising in glory with Him. I love the old Spiritual hymn which contains the line, "If you can't bear the Cross, my brother, you can't wear the crown."

United with Him, I can't just live the good parts. What sort of unity would that be? But how marvelous to know that just as He turned pain and evil, and even His own death, to good in His own life, so will He use everything in mine to His good purposes if I give Him my free will and my love to do so.

When the Mother of James and John tried to obtain top positions for her sons in Our Blessed Lord's Kingdom, He asked, "Can you drink from the cup from which I must drink?" His question was: How perfectly can you imitate Me? Can you suffer and sacrifice for others too? Can you say, "Let it be done unto me according to Thy Word?" When the Blessed Mother said this, I wonder if she was referring to a total obedience to God's Word, her Son.

What a challenge for us who want to take Our Lord seriously. I keep wondering: How can I live every moment imitating Jesus within the circumstances of my everyday life? How can I deepen my willingness to sacrifice myself totally as He did? If it is a true sacrifice, there is no glory or notoriety in it. It probably won't be noticed by anyone but God and His angels. Who else needs to notice?

God's grace is sufficient, but being the true Gentleman He is, Christ will never force me to His way. I must choose Him every moment of my life. In 2 Timothy 2: 10-12 Paul says, "Therefore, I bear with everything for the sake of those who are chosen, so that they too may obtain the salvation that is in Christ Jesus, together with eternal glory." This saying is trustworthy, "If we have died with Him we shall also live with Him; if we persevere, we shall also reign with Him..."*

The Thursday following the first time we had observed the figure of Our Lord moving on the Cross, we were praying the rosary again. It was March 2nd. The house had been filled with light that day, and it was almost as though the angels were all waiting for us to begin the rosary. I, being human (the excuse always available), wondered as we prayed the rosary if the figure on the Crucifix would move again. My Angel firmly but gently told me I had received my sign. I later discovered that Mike Slate had been praying for me the week before, on that wondrous night, just at the time the Crucifix figure had moved.

My Guardian Angel told me on this night of March 2nd that the prayers of our family would be heard in a very special way on Thursdays. Thursday is a day of grace for us and for our descendants. Our prayers may not be answered as we wish, but he promised they will be acted upon in a special way. He commanded me to keep February 23rd as a special day to be honored and celebrated in our family to commemorate the gift we have been given.

I was surprised when the crucifix figure on the cross around my neck moved on my birthday — March 12. I am like a cup, and God's love for me is like the ocean. He pours Himself into me, and when I am full He still keeps pouring.

Journal Excerpt:

Saturday, March 25, 1989

Yesterday was Good Friday. I took Gia out to bathroom her for the first time since my surgery. This involves walking around with her in a circle while she is on leash. She has been trained to know that her great moment has arrived. But walking in circles has made me dizzy up to this point.

It was an incredibly beautiful morning, with the birds singing for joy. The air was crisp and cool before the heat of the day. This is my favorite time of day and it reminds me of home, of those beautiful Hawaiian mornings I will never forget. I felt a deep sorrow pulling at my heart because I am sure it was on such a glorious morning that my Lord, battered and bloody with His back ripped to pieces by the scourging; blood streaming down His face from the crown of thorns pressed into His head, was lead out to be crucified. God has given us such a beautiful world, and what terrible things we have done while surrounded by its beauty. This contrast deeply saddened me.

I sat praying the Medjugorje rosary about three o'clock on this Good Friday. As I prayed, the figure on the cross began to move again. I was entirely alone this time. Oh, God!

The light became bright and I said, "Lord, I thank You with all my heart that You should allow me to know this again. But we are remembering Your terrible Passion and Death today. You died at three in the afternoon, and yet You show me this?"

---

[Note: These thoughts were jotted down over a period of time, as the blessed angels spoke to me.]

"I am never dead to those whom I love and who love Me," He said. Glory be to His kindness and love forever and ever.

It is almost midnight now and Eileen and Miriam have just come home. The Easter Vigil was shorter than we thought it would be. Mass tomorrow begins at ten instead of nine. An extra hour of sleep! Please, God, may I be strong enough to go.

# Chapter 10
# THE BLOOD OF THE
# HOLY INNOCENTS

Journal Excerpts:

Tuesday, April 18, 1989

My dear Guardian Angel reached out to me in love yesterday. He reminded me of the terrible agony I was in spiritually before the surgery, not believing or understanding how things could go well with so many factors against it. He had tried to comfort me then, to let me know everything would be all right. He reminded me of this now. He now wants me to know this again in my new pain. But I ask the eternal human question, "How? How can it be?" And, "Why? Why?" Yet I do find comfort in remembering how impossible it all seemed then too, and how the love of my dear Lord and His Mother and the angels was there for me, as well as beautiful human love. It is all there for me yet again.

My Dear Angel also answered a question I had asked several days ago, and then forgotten I had asked. During the Feast of the Assumption, some of the people saw Jesus as a babe in His Mother's arms. Some saw Him as a young child. Others saw Him as a man. I wondered and asked about this, and received no answer.

But yesterday, my Dear Angel did answer, "Jesus as a man was born at a particular time in history, lived and died and rose at a particular time—just as the Scriptures say. But what God is, is eternal and so Christ as God is eternally a baby, eternally a little boy, eternally a young man, eternally suffers for you, eternally dies—and eternally rises." Yes. "Yesterday, today, and forever." Glory be to God.

Thursday, April 27, 1989

Today is the day of our special graces, and how I know it! Torrents of joy and peace flow through me now, despite the pain, and I know that my unity with God and His will are the source of this joy. Whether I am or am not in union with God I don't know, but it is the deepest desire of my heart to be so. And even though this intense desire will pass, I will never be quite the same again because it is with me now.

I have realized in the last week or so that I can, and indeed do, want to bear with a great deal in my life as long as I can know that what is happening is God's will. But of course very seldom am I sure of God's will, and so my next step in faith may be that I endure on the chance that it is God's will, and on the mere chance that it serves His purposes — just on the chance. "All things work for good for those who love God." That is a promise. That is an act of faith to believe.

I find myself asking during decisions, questions, actions, "What is it my Lord, Jesus would want?" And even if the answer is sometimes not at all clear, the importance of asking the question may be more vital than having the answer.

Mary Constancio asked me one day to ask my Dear Angel why it is we doubt Our Lord after being given so many signs and special gifts. Much of the time, he prefers not to answer. This time, however, he was anxious to do so. "Because," he said, "you do not know truly yet that you are God's children."

"Does God become displeased with us?" Mary asked.

"God knows your limitations. When you know perfectly that you are His children, He experiences great delight in your perfect knowing."

"Do we have to wait to go to Heaven to have this perfect faith?" she asked. He did not answer.

... Because we are His children. What does that mean? If we truly knew we are His children, we would not need these signs, no matter how marvelous and incredible they are. They are a small manifestation,the tiniest expression of Our Lord's love for us. We can handle only the smallest expression of Our Lord's love for us. And these signs — the most important ones — are all around us. They are a fresh morning breeze, dew on the grass, a red cardinal's song, an unexpected kindness with no looked–for return, an act of quiet courage. Most of the important signs are so very quiet. When Jesus was born in the stable, how many people knew? Who were they?

The Blessed Mother came to me briefly last Friday night. I was surprised. I had thought she would not visit me again. But this visit was different. The magnitude and fullness, the closeness and intimacy of her presence was not there as it was before. The light was bright, and I heard almost an echo of her voice. It was not in the full way in which I had heard her voice before.

She was in deep distress over abortion. She had told Mary Constancio that if our country does not repeal the abortion laws, the chastisements Our Lord will bring upon our nation will be more severe than otherwise. She pleaded with me to become actively involved in fighting abortion.

"Put out your hand," she said to me. When I did, I put my hand into a container of warm, sticky blood. I could feel it and smell it. I was very frightened. It was real blood, not an illusion. It was on my hands when I pulled them away. I felt sick in my stomach with revulsion and fear. The revulsion was not so much because of touching the blood, but I think for the first time I actually realized this was human blood and that human lives were being destroyed.

This is not my imagination. Things like this don't happen. But they do, and this did happen to me. I realize I may be thought mad to write of this, but it must be written, nevertheless. It is more important that this incident be recorded, hopefully to bring about a more vivid realization of the horror of the silent murder of millions of innocents; than that the risk be taken by me that my sanity may be questioned. I am well aware of this risk. All I can do is state what I know to be true.

"The blood of these innocent little ones covers your land," Our dear Lady said to me. I can't convey the heartbroken tone in which she said this, an ever present, infinite sadness completely beyond momentary grief. There was nothing maudlin in the way she said it. She spoke with immeasurable sorrow.

I did not learn until later that "the blood of the innocents" is a Scriptural phrase. I promised her that I would become more actively involved in fighting legalized abortion, even if it were only to pray more deeply.

All of this has resulted in a change of heart for me. I had been personally against abortion for years, but I could not bring myself to be a pro-lifer because of my concern. As a nation, we have become accustomed to abortion on demand. What would happen if the laws were repealed? Women would flock to the back alleys, to the abortion clinics which would most certainly spring up everywhere. I thought a massive education campaign to emphasize the value and importance of human life from conception to the grave would be most effective before any attempt at changing the law was made. But no.

I have come to understand that there can always, and have always been, reasons to continue the killing. "If the Jews come back," people in Germany said, "and are re-established, we will lose the business that used to be owned by one of them and then how will we live?"

There is always a good reason to continue something which is wrong. I think of the clearances of the last century when the Irish and Scottish crofters were removed from their lands in order that sheep herding might be established. I think of the justification for slavery in our own country. Yes, there are always very good reasons.

I believe the Blessed Mother showed me the horror of abortion in the way she did because of my blindness. You can look at a film. I have been rather anesthetized by not being able to see. Though my account may seem graphic and it certainly was horrible for me, was this the only way she could show me so that I would understand with my guts, just as you understand when you see? I believe it was.

After this incident, after I had washed the blood away, I still felt for days as if it were there, the memory was so haunting. I began to realize that we all share in responsibility for wrongdoing. Not actively participating does not absolve us if we could have done the smallest thing to prevent it, and did not do whatever we could.

Before the light faded, I heard Our Lady's voice again. "Thank you for the pain you offered during your surgery, my beloved daughter. Thank you for the pain you offer now, and the pain you will offer for the salvation of souls. Would you be willing to accept great pain in the future for this purpose?"

I had a choice. This request was different from the one she had made to me on November 10th of the previous year. She had asked me then to offer pain I would have to bear. Here, she was asking me willingly to accept pain at some unnamed time in the future, and to offer it.

"Yes, I will," I said to her. "but I am concerned. My program has been very good to me. They have given me time to heal. They have been very understanding about all this and wonderfully supportive. But surely I can't expect or ask them to give me any more leeway. If I take on this pain in the future, should I drop out of the program?" "No," she told me. "you should not drop out of your program. You will be given the grace and the strength to do what matters."

I have to say here that my work is one of my greatest concerns. Her statement that I would be given the grace and the strength to do what matters has comforted me, but I also have wondered "what matters" means. I am very impatient with my own slowness, and pray for a greater trust in this also. What if my Lord's definition of "what matters" is not the same as mine?

# THE LIGHT OF LOVE

# Chapter 11
# A PRAYER WHILE IN PAIN

May 29, 1989

S omewhere around this date, or perhaps around June 1st, is the date on which I should have been born — in 1953. It is almost impossible for me to comprehend what life would have been like if I had not been premature. I would not have been put in the incubator, where I had to fight so hard for my life with the oxygen destroying my eyes. I would have been "normal". Or would I? Today I have been thinking about a poem I wrote several years ago. I am not sure why I am thinking about it. Here it is:

IF

If all the world were blind, then who could prove
There are such things as clouds or stars—or blue?
Sight would be a magical childishness,
An unimaginable, unrealistic sense.
If there were those who for vision did yearn,
They would be ridiculed, ostracized, or burned.
And if One could see and dared tell what He saw,
He would be crucified, correctly, under Law.

Perhaps my Lord has been slowly preparing me for all this since He created me. Perhaps this is only one more step to the next adventure.

Father Francis Butler has been in touch with me about becoming consecrated to my Guardian Angel. "But Father," I told him, "how can I study? My Guardian Angel has told me I am not to read anything about angels. I can't even listen to tapes. I suppose I am to find out about them through them, and not get confused with anything else."

---

[Note: See Chapter 49 on Opus Angelorum]

Father believes this is a special situation, and that we should honor my Guardian Angel's request that I be consecrated.

Three pictures have been taken of me which clearly show the light which I see when angels or holy persons are near. The light was not visible to others before the pictures were taken, and people knowing about such things have examined the pictures. They tell me the appearance of the light in the pictures does not occur because of faulty cameras or picture taking. I have copies of only two of these pictures, but in both of them I showed the people to whom I was speaking where the light that I see was visible to me immediately before the picture was taken. It appears in the picture just where I showed them. In one of the pictures, a figure in the light is clearly visible. In another, some people say they see a figure with "kind eyes." For some who look at this picture, the figure is very distinct.*

I had lain down yesterday for a rest. When I awoke, the light was beautiful and bright. I had not seen it this way for several days, and decided to pray the Divine Mercy Chaplet. I love to think of my Lord's Divine Mercy.

As I prayed, the light grew brighter and I had the sense of a presence wishing to speak to me. I tested the presence, and then asked in our Lord, Jesus's name who it was — and was told in that never-forgettable voice I had heard in the hospital that it was my Lord, Himself. I went down on my knees.

He gently told me He knows what He is doing in my life. He told me He would be with me in my grief, and had been especially close to me in the last six weeks.

"Please, Lord," I said, "I am having such a hard time getting back on my feet again. I keep grieving, and I'm not healing as quickly as I could because of it. I'm worried about my work. Please help me."

He dictated a prayer to me which I am to use after each decade of the Divine Mercy Chaplet. It is such a simple prayer, but taken phrase by phrase it touches on everything important to remember when one is in physical or emotional pain. This prayer to help cope with pain is to be shared with others, but I am not sure how or when. It is:

---

[Note: Since this writing, a fourth picture has been taken.]

"I am the beloved daughter (son) of the Lord who made me and who created the whole universe. He has done great things for me, and He is preparing great things for me. Glory be to His Name."

It seems so simple that at first I almost thought "Well, but ..."Then I thought about it phrase by phrase:

1) A reminder to myself of my preciousness to God.

2) A reminder of God's infinite power and wisdom — He created me, and the whole universe.

3) A moment of contemplation of the problems and sorrows of the past, how God has helped me then, answering prayers of the past (though not always as I have wished, they are perfect answers), the love and the effort God has put into helping me in my life.

4) A reassurance of continued love and help for the future and a call to trust in the preparations He is making for me for this future, both here on earth and in the real life to come.

5) Giving Him praise — which is the perfect antidote for a hurting heart. It is a gift to Him, but is more of a gift to me to be able to praise Him because of how it opens and changes my heart.

# THE LIGHT OF LOVE

# Chapter 12
# THE DISCIPLINE
# OF OBEDIENCE

Wednesday, June 7, 1989

I had plans for Sunday of last weekend. But no, I was at a memorial service.

On Saturday morning I awoke early and could not believe how beautiful and bright the light was. It was so bright that I could see the reflection of the colors off my bedspread and sheets.

This is such a beautiful and constant miracle. I will never get used to it. As I write now, the light shines over my hands.

The light that morning was so bright that as I put my hands up to my face, the light shone through them. My hands were there, but they were immaterial. It is our bodies, our world, that is immaterial. It is what we call the "spiritual world" that is the real world. The light is all. Our Lord of Light and Love is all. I have heard the angels call Him this.

I wondered why the light was so bright, and then I remembered that it was the Feast of the Immaculate Heart of Mary — the celebration of the creation by God of the most beautiful and pure fully human heart. She is the only human being who has never known sin, saved by her Son out of love, out of time. Our Lord is both man and God. So she is the ultimate of what we can be as human beings. And to think, she loves me and has spoken to me. She is truly my heavenly Mother.

Saturday is a day I will never forget for another reason. The news of the horrible massacre of the Chinese students in Beijing's Tiananmen Square began coming to us. I felt like a sick, helpless bystander able to do nothing.

The first news we heard was that several hundred may have been killed. Now the estimate is six thousand. The army went in first with machine guns into the packed, unarmed crowd, and then rode over the bodies with tanks.

I have loved China since I was a little girl and have been fascinated by its people and history. Perhaps some of the closeness I feel to China comes from growing up in Hawaii. I have felt so hopeful in these last few months reading about the desire of the students and others to form a democracy and gain political freedom. These young people were the children of the Mao nurseries, the state run day care centers; perhaps they were the most brainwashed people in the world. But they want freedom to think, freedom to elect public officials, perhaps freedom to know Our Lord God as much as it is possible for any of us to know Him. What a triumph of the human spirit. I pray for them, for their friends and relatives, for the future of China. I have not yet been able to pray for those who ordered, and those who executed.

Saturday, July 15, 1989

Father O'Dwyer of Saint Elizabeth's, the Irish priest from Tipperary who has not yet developed a West Texas accent despite being here for quite a few years, has brought tears to my eyes with both the homily I heard tonight and the homily last weekend. One sentence stood out for me tonight, "If one attempts to form a spirituality without mercy, it is very possible that one is attempting to form a spirituality that is an insult to God."

Tuesday, July 25, 1989

Up till now I have not been strong enough to ask people into my home as guests. It is such a joy to have guests in my home again after so long and to know once again that lovely combination of informality and celebration as we eat and talk together.

I have been running a fever all day. I've had a sore throat for several days, am deeply tired, and have a pounding headache. But I am quietly happy. Several nights ago I was bathed in the light of the angels and I felt as if I was wrapped in their arms and held on their wings in love. My dear Guardian Angel has told me that he and the others will not be speaking to me for a while. When he told me this, he also made it clear to me that I am not to talk about what is happening to me to anyone but my confessor and a few close friends. I do not know how long this silence is to continue. It doesn't matter how long it lasts, as long as it is what my Lord wants. I am grateful that I can talk about it to a few close people. I see and understand more clearly that this silence is a discipline, and must be kept until it is lifted.

I have not known much about discipline of this sort. In order to be having these marvelous experiences and not burst out for wonder and joy about them demands that I trust my Lord, that His will becomes that much more important to me than my own. My pride also must diminish, since I acknowledge that He is far wiser than I in everything, and my good and the good of all lies in obedience. Obedience has not been one of my favorite words, nor is it a very popular word in our society. I suspect I will be growing in spirit through the discipline of obedience, and it is exciting to see it in this new light. In Hebrews 5: 8, Saint Paul writes of Christ, "He learned obedience through what He suffered." This startling assertion that Christ had to learn obedience, and through suffering, has caused me much pondering. If Christ, then how much more I?

I have been consecrated now to my Dear Angel, but still must be consecrated to all the angels. I have been very reluctant to do this, not feeling at all worthy. I know nothing. I feel as though I am nothing. I have asked my Lord that if this is truly His will for me, He will arrange it without my raising a finger to bring it about.

My beautiful Guardian Angel tells me that after this period of silence, not my silence but theirs — in which they will not speak to me, he and many other angels will speak to me for the rest of my life. What an honor, but what a responsibility. I would feel bereft at their silence, but they are all around me and their light surrounds me.

# THE LIGHT OF LOVE

# Chapter 13
# A DAY OF BLESSINGS

Sunday, August 6

I have not yet written about my consecration to my dear Angel, so I will do it now. Saturday, June 17th was the big day. I flew down to New Orleans to be with people I now think of as relatives — Debbie and George Cordes, George's parents known to everyone including me as 'Maw' and 'Paw', and Sandra Killeen and many more. There were two other people making the consecration, Rhonda McCullough and Lisa Janusa of New Orleans. It was a beautiful and simple ceremony. With all the blessings I have received, I have to admit I did wish my dear Angel had been able to speak to me. But I am sure he and many other angels were there to bless us.

After the consecration ceremony, Sandra told us that she had looked up on the wall of the church. It is not their regular parish church. She had seen a little niche with a piece of glass over it. In the niche was a little hand holding a rosary. Beneath the niche was a plaque which stated that the rosary had been made by Saint John Neumann in about 1828 and presented to a man named Butler. Father Butler was consecrating me and the others, and we were surprised at the fact that the last names are the same, though it is unlikely they are related. The link with Saint John Neumann lifted my heart.

"By the way," I asked in some embarrassment, "what is the name of this church?"

"It is Saint Mary's Assumption Church," I was told. Again, we were surprised. Bishop Fulton J. Sheen believed there is no such thing as coincidence. Perhaps there cannot be coincidence when God is so close to us, so involved with us, whether we know the beginnings of His love or not.

But something even more special happened to me right before the consecration ceremony. As I came into the entry way of the church, I smelled the scent of roses as I have never smelled the scent of roses before. It was like walking into a garden with hundreds and hundreds of roses growing — early in the morning when they are most fragrant, as the sun is just rising, the dew still on the flowers, fresh and lovely, without a dead or dying flower among them.

I exclaimed to one of the people who was there to greet us, "You must have some wonderfully beautiful roses here!" I did not think in that moment of anything supernatural, it was too real.

I could feel her looking at me strangely. "No," she said, "we have some artificial flowers here, but no roses."

I had been rather skeptical when people at Saint John Neumann told me they smelled roses. I believed them but .... maybe it was perfume. This beautiful smell of roses is not perfume, nor can it be mistaken for a bottled scent. There is no life in the scent of perfume. But this! It is like having someone gently put your whole face into a vibrantly living, never to die bouquet of roses, lovely living roses. Two other people in our group smelled the scent of roses also. The others did not.

The sensitivity of my Lord and my dear Mother in giving me gifts I, as a blind person, can most appreciate—gifts of touch and smell, gifts that say, "I love you"—this sensitivity surprises me continually. I see them more and more as loving family members who say to me, "touch this," "smell this," "learn about this." All of these signs of love are to reassure me for the times ahead, and to give me a foretaste of eternity. I could never have conceived it would be like this — my beloved Creator, and I and all of His creation as His cherished family.

In these experiences, I feel like a little girl, curious but also blind, whose family are saying, "Look!" as they take my hand or in some other way I can know, show me.

Yet as an adult of my times and probably more skeptical than most, I doubt. Lord, please have mercy on this doubter, and yet I thank You for my doubts. I would not dare do otherwise. There are too many possibilities for error and blasphemy. I take such comfort in remembering what my dear Angel told me one night (before he stopped talking to me during this time, of course.) As I struggled with my doubts and fears he said, "Our Lord is pleased with your doubts, because they mean you take Him seriously. But," he said, "the time comes for putting aside doubts when you have enough indication, perhaps not to be absolutely sure or obtain the proof you would like, but enough to believe with good reason. Then you step out in faith."

My Angel has spoken to me about being entirely obedient to "your confessor." No matter what he or the other angels tell me or anyone else tells me, I am to be completely obedient to my confessor. Whoever he is, he is to always have the last and binding word in everything, and no information is to be directly or indirectly withheld from him. These are my orders. I don't have a confessor right now, but from what my Angel told me it sounds as if I will have one soon. I so very much wish that Father Butler were closer to me, that he could be right here in Lubbock. Father Butler is too far away to see regularly, though we do have frequent phone conversations. If I could see him in person, he would be the priest I would ask my Lord to allow to be my confessor. This is another area for trusting God. My Lord got me into this. He will help.*

Later on the day of the consecration, we went to a little "perpetual adoration chapel" in which the Blessed Sacrament is always exposed. People are praying twenty-four hours a day there. It is open to anyone who wishes to come, day or night. How I wish with all my heart that there could be such places in every community. Churches are locked now because of the fear of vandalism and desecration. I and many others have not been able to find a church open when we wished so deeply to pray in one.

So we went there, and I was deeply touched, because the chapel was filled with light. It was a gentle radiance which filled me with serenity.

"The light is particularly bright right here," I told Debbie and Sandra and the others. I pointed. They told me I was pointing straight at the Blessed Sacrament, position and level. I am filled with awe and joy and laughter at my Lord's tender humor. I, who know where nothing is at all when I enter a strange place and usually do not bother to ask

---

*[Note: A priest in the Lubbock diocese did become my spiritual director for a time with advice from Father Butler being welcomed in angelic matters. In May of 1992 after knowing Father John Walch for over a year, he became my spiritual director. I also have a priest here in Lubbock who regularly hears my Confessions.]

because of the effort, and because it is usually not essential. I, who have heard repeatedly throughout my life in kind tones, "I wish you could see this." So I laugh in delight at my Lord's gentle humor in allowing a totally blind person with no eyes to see Him in His full presence in the Holy Eucharist. What more could I wish for? What more could I want to see?

I so enjoy my Lord, and smile at His humor and kindness to me. And then I cry because He loves me.**

I am grateful that my Lord seems to have such patience with my doubting and questioning. But despite my doubts and deep feelings of unworthiness, my joy bursts through. Then there is nothing but joy. There is no more room for doubt, and unworthiness becomes irrelevant.

---

**[Note: I have been in several other unfamiliar churches since this time, and have pointed to where the light was brightest, directly at the monstrance, as verified by the people with me. I do not see this every time I am in a church, but it has occurred at least six times that I have pointed at the monstrance based solely on my perception of the light.]

# Chapter 14
# OUR LOVING MOTHER

Journal Excerpt:

Monday, August 21, 1989

T he Blessed Mother spoke to me gently for a few moments tonight. It is so unexpected when this happens. I miss her terribly, but it never occurs to me that she might speak to me again. I don't even hope for it, and so it is always a surprise. As I have said, she is not there in the deep, personal way in which she was present to me last November. I had forgotten that tonight is the eve of the celebration of her Queenship. Before the Feast of the Assumption of last year, I knew little about the calendar of our special days in the Church. I am trying now to remedy this.

I would have thought she would be in great joy, but she was gently sorrowful. "Please pray for my Immaculate Heart," she said. "My Immaculate Heart is torn and bleeding because of the way you, my dear children, crucify each other." She was more sorrowful than anything else, more grieving and almost matter-of-fact, rather than reproachful. It was painful for me to see this acceptance. She seemed weary in spirit to me.

I got the impression that she was sorrowful, too, because she wanted to do more for us — the children Our Lord has given her to pray for and to love. She comforted me in my personal pain (not to be explained in this writing), and her total acceptance of me and tenderness for me amazed me and made me cry for joy. I am to tell only a few people of this for now, so that they will join with me in praying for her. She seemed weary and, though I am hesitant to record this, it seemed to me that one of the biggest reasons she was asking for prayers was to help her go on in praying for and helping us, to give her strength.

# THE LIGHT OF LOVE

# Chapter 15
# "THERE IS NO KINSHIP IN HELL"

I had quite a few visitors that summer, friends from Minnesota, pilgrims over the Feast of the Assumption, and all the way from Hawaii came my dear Sister Miriam Ferry of the Franciscans. Sister has been close to me, and then close to the girls, since 1972. She knows me and loves me. She has been in religious life since 1926, and says if she had her life to live over, she would do it all again the same way. What an example for today.

At this time also, I began to meet with the priest who, except for a break of a few months because of illness, would be my confessor for the next two years. I use the word "confessor" rather than the modern "spiritual director" because this is the word my Guardian Angel used to describe him when he told me I was to be completely obedient to him — before I met him. I will refer to him simply as "my confessor" in order to preserve his privacy.

On the night of Friday, September 22nd, I recorded the following experience and conversation as it was happening.

I was thinking of something else just now, in deep prayer. The light is gentle and yet bright, as an angel spoke to me and is still here speaking. He says, "You are surrounded and protected by many angels in preparation for your consecration."

"Really!"

"Yes, and you will be protected by more of us afterwards. Satan has not bothered with you much before, but now it is different."

"Why now?"

"He did not hold you to be of much account because to him you are weak and powerless."

"I am still weak and powerless."

"Yes. But you are being called to help in drawing souls away from him."

"Why does Satan value souls so much?"

"He does not value them at all except that Our Lord values them. If Our Lord did not value them and love them, they would be worthless to Satan."

"Why are they of worth now?"

"Because Our Lord loves them. Our Lord and those in His Kingdom are in great distress and sorrow when souls are lost. This fills Lucifer with glee. It is only because of this that you or any other human souls are of use to him. REMEMBER THIS. After a soul is lost, it is like dust in the wind to Lucifer, and is of no further use or account.

"It is Lucifer's disdain and contempt for these souls and his malice and arrogance, his viciousness towards them, that creates and sustains their unspeakable tortures. He is gleeful at their choice of evil, but he disdains them for it. He counts them as fools, but is too arrogant ever to see his own foolishness. He has no loyalty for those who follow him, only contempt of the deepest sort. He laughs at their wish for power, while grasping at it for himself. He sees no contradiction in this.

"Be warned! All of you, be warned. There is no kinship in hell."

The angel stops speaking. I sit here amazed. I have never thought in these terms. Before the Feast of the Assumption of last year, I did not think much of Heaven or Hell, though I did think a lot about God. What has just been dictated to me is not of or from me. Glory be to God that I and others who have dismissed so much of our Tradition as superstition, or at least not taken it very seriously most of the time, should be warned like this.

The light is still bright, and I am being gently comforted by the angel. He is speaking again. "Never, NEVER forget the love and mercy of God. Truly you have been told that there is no sin, no matter how deep or shameful, that, repented of sincerely, cannot be forgiven. You have been told this over and over again, but in their fear of unworthi-

---

[Note: Only one sin, according to Sacred Scripture, is unpardonable. It is the sin against the Holy Spirit. From what the angels have told me, I gather (my own interpretation) that this sin is a complete hardening of heart, a refusal to see the wrong one has done, nor feel any remorse over it. In this case, God can't give His forgiveness to the sinner because the sinner will not receive it. Our free will is always respected, as the angels have told me so many times.]

ness, many do not believe. But no unworthiness is greater than the love of God for you."

The light dimmed. I had been frightened over this conversation, not for myself but because, suddenly, hell is now a reality for me and for others, whether they are aware of it or not. I had often wondered how a loving God could create hell. Now I know He did not. Lucifer himself did, and we put ourselves there.

But the beautiful angel left me with such peace, a calmness of spirit. I felt even more secure in my Lord's love, having a little more understanding of His never-ending mercy and justice.

# THE LIGHT OF LOVE

# Chapter 16
# STEPPING OUT IN FAITH

On Saturday, September 30th, 1989 I was consecrated to all the blessed angels. As I have said, I had reservations about this because of my feelings of unworthiness. But I wanted to do my Lord's will, and the conditions I had asked for to indicate clearly that this should be done, as well as my dear Angels request of course, were met beautifully. My Angel had told me that the purpose for the consecration (or dedication as a better word) was that it would enable me more effectively to serve with the angels in bringing souls to God. The ceremony, at this time, had not been prohibited by the Church as it has been now because of the Church's concern over the possible misunderstanding of the word "consecration." As recorded later, the word "dedication" would be a more apt phrase to clarify the purpose of the ceremony (see Chapter 49 on Opus Angelorum.) We dedicate ourselves to our angels to do all we can to assist them to bringing our souls to God. To bring our souls safely to Heaven is their mission in being our guardians. It is their sacred trust, given to them by our loving God. By becoming more aware of them and working with them (instead of against them) to become the holy souls of God's Kingdom, we bring great joy to them and spiritual growth towards God for ourselves. One can dedicate oneself quietly and privately, just as one would ask Our Lady or a saint for help in reaching sanctification. The Church will, as it should, curb any devotion which appears not to be centered in Christ. The Church will never discourage these devotions as long as they are balanced and completely centered on the Holy Trinity. We ask the saints and angels for their help and prayers, just as we ask friends for their intercessory prayers because "God is a God of the living, not of the dead" and "we are surrounded by a cloud of witnesses" so that physical death does not separate God's family members from one another, nor from the Lord who loves us all.

I flew down to New Orleans, then I and the Cordes Family drove to Sterrett, Alabama, where Father Francis Butler and Father Doyle celebrated an outdoor Mass for several hundred people. It was at this Mass that I and two others were consecrated to all the angels.

On the way to the field, my Dear Angel asked me to do something very difficult. "Please," he said to me, "remove your glasses during the Consecration ceremony." I am self-conscious about my appearance, though I have been told I need not be. Because I do not wear prostheses, it is very obvious that I have no eyes.

"I know this will be hard for you," my Guardian Angel said to me. "But please do this in penance for your own sins, and for the sins of callousness shown to those who suffer disabilities." I didn't want to do it. I wished my confessor were there. I would have asked him if I had to do it. My Guardian Angel had asked me several days before to remove my glasses during the Consecration ceremony, but I had conveniently forgotten about it. It really wasn't intentional, I was just trying to spare myself some pain. But here it was again.

The Consecration ceremony itself was beautiful. As we made our promise, I tried to balance the candle I was holding in one hand with the Braille pages in the other, while with my imaginary third hand I tried to hold a rose I had been given. The wind was blowing, and after about the second sentence of the promise, I had to drop out. I asked Father if I might repeat the promise alone, and this I did.

After the Consecration, several people came up to me separately. "Why do you wear those glasses?" they asked me. "We've never seen you without your glasses. You are very beautiful. Your eyes are so pretty. Why do you hide them?" I was in shock to hear this. These were strangers telling me this.

"I don't have any eyes," I told them. I removed my glasses so they might see. They were surprised. "That's not what I saw," each of them told me. Two of them told me they were close enough to me to be positive that I had eyes, and that this was not just some sort of shadow effect. They said they had seen me looking at members of the crowd. I had very mixed emotions about all this, especially when others told me they saw that I had eyes in the pictures that were taken of the Consecration ceremony. Perhaps this is just a shadow effect, but it is very curious that people both at the Consecration ceremony and later examining the pictures would tell me the same thing. Perhaps no penance is ever as severe as it seems at first.

The fall months were very busy. I attended classes during the day, saw clients in our clinic at night, and studied God knows when. I had the uncomfortable feeling that my family might not remember my name. Once I offhandedly thought, "I wonder why my Dear Angel hardly ever talks to me at school." Suddenly he said to me, "Because you rarely listen to me there."

As I helped conduct a group for seven- and eight-year old children whose parents are undergoing divorce, I felt the presence of the children's guardian angels and saw their lovely lights near each child. Their deep concern for their children and their tenderness with them touched me so. At moments, they pleaded with me to help their children. They do not know the future just as we do not know it, and I was told they feel our suffering indirectly because of their love for us.

I realize it would be wise for me to ask the guardian angels of the people I counsel for guidance in how best to help them, if Our Lord would permit this.

The language I use now in thinking of these things is the language, more and more, that the angels themselves use. I think of Our Lord "permitting" this or that, or allowing something — and that is how the angels talk! They have called Our Lord "the Lord of Life and Love" and sometimes "the Lord of Light and Love." I have written this into a poem.

COMMUNION

My heart pours out like water
To the Lord of Life and Love,
An unreserved libation,
A draining of the cup.

No holding back this time,
No bitter drop remains
To contaminate the new wine
With old fears and pains.

But as I wait with open heart,
With arms stretched fully wide,

With not even vulnerability left
Or misgivings to act as guide;
For the first time I am empty
With no old wounds to bind
And in glad anticipation
I wait for what God has in mind.

In late October, I sat praying one night — actually begging God to help me keep up with my work. The light became bright. I tested the presence.

"Your prayers are so very much needed now," my Guardian Angel said. "Let me show you something."

He asked me to put out my hand. When I did, I felt a tapestry or heavy weaving of some kind. It was large. I stood up to feel it better. It was beautifully embroidered with shapes and forms I could not identify. The weave was rich and beautiful, perhaps of a satin-like material with other fabrics woven into the work.

But down the middle of the tapestry (I don't know what else to call it) there was a rent. The rent went from the top of the weaving to the bottom. It did not quite go all the way through the fabric, but it was jagged. It was not a clean rent. I felt sad that such a beautiful work should have been so vandalized.

The rent effected the whole piece. Of course the damage was worse along it, from the top to the bottom, but there was no place in the weaving that was not loosened or unravelled.

"What is this?" I asked my Angel.

"It is the Church," he told me. He said the Church would be rent as this beautiful weaving was torn, from top to bottom. Many people would fall away, either in confusion or arrogance. "Many people will be like lost, bewildered sheep without a shepherd, frightened and not knowing where to go or what to do."

"There will be three main areas of attack," he told me. "The first attack will come upon the Sacraments. It will be said they are only empty forms. The Eucharist, those in error will say, is not the true body of Our Lord. Baptism is only an initiation, marriage only a social contract."

The second area of attack he said would be on the Resurrection and other Biblical events, but mainly on the Resurrection of Our Lord. It would be said this was merely symbolic. A great false "proof" that the Resurrection of Our Lord Jesus had not happened would be forthcoming. Many Christians, even some devout and faith-filled ones, would believe the falsehood. Those who did not believe it would be considered primitive, back in the middle ages, fools.

The third area is the Church itself. It would be physically and spiritually rent apart as I had felt the fabric. The fabric was shown to me, he said, so that I could better understand what is to come, and pray. He pleaded for my prayers, and the prayers of others.

He said these things could not be avoided, but our prayers could mitigate them.

I felt very sad about all this, especially since I increasingly experienced the love of God through the love of the blessed angels.

I knew that some had already dismissed one of Our Lord's most loving gifts to us — the guardianship and friendship of the angels, as mere superstition. From what my Guardian Angel told me, this was only the beginning of the dismantling process. So I quietly prayed.

# THE LIGHT OF LOVE

# Chapter 17
# THE IMPORTANCE OF OUR PRAYERS TO THE ANGELS

Journal Excerpt:

Wednesday, November 15, 1989

It is nearly five-thirty in the morning and, again, because of my incredibly tight schedule with my seventeen- and eighteen-hour days and going to Tech on Saturdays, I did not write in my journal over the weekend.

A classmate and I are to do our presentation this afternoon for a class, and I have just been praying I will not do too badly.

I had not seen the light from the angels for two days, but the moment I and the girls knelt down to pray this morning, there it was. All glory to God that I should be allowed to see this.

After we had finished praying, the girls jumped up — Eileen to get ready and Miriam to lie in bed until 6:30 or so. Poor love, I doubt that she gets any more real sleep during this time.

As they were leaving, an angel who is not my Guardian Angel began speaking to me. It was that angel's light that I had seen so brightly.

"You do not know what joy your prayers give the angels," he smilingly told me. "We pray before the throne of God asking that we may be allowed to be actually present when you pray because of the joy it gives us." I was amazed and touched by this. That they should "pray before the throne of God" to be allowed to be there when we pray!

"Do you ask my Lord to be there when we pour out our hearts in prayers of pain?" I asked.

"Yes, because even though you do not trust fully, that you bring your petitions before Him at all is trust, and this gives Him and us great joy. There are so many who do not pray at all." This constant appreciation of even our smallest gifts is not the image of God I have had. How He loves us!

My dear Angel asked me to add another of the prayers given at Fatima to the rosary. After the GLORY BE and the Fatima prayer now recited which is, "O my Jesus, forgive us our sins. Save us from the fires of hell. Lead all souls to Heaven, especially those in most need of Thy mercy", my Angel asked me to pray the prayer given to the children at Fatima by the Angel of Peace, "Lord, I believe in Thee, I adore Thee, I hope in Thee, and I love Thee. I beg pardon for all those who do Not believe in Thee, who do not adore Thee, who do not hope in Thee, and who do not love Thee. Amen."

He asked me to pray this prayer with loving thought for the pain of God over those souls to whom He wishes to give His grace who continually reject Him and refuse His love. My Dear Angel told me that if I prayed this prayer with love for the Father, it would greatly console Him. I marvelled that I could give meaningful consolation to the Lord of Lords. I and all people must matter to God far more than we know.

I remember a story I heard at Mass when I was a young girl. It was told by Father Lawrence Mann, one of the priests at the time at Holy Family Church on Oahu around 1968. As I remember it, the story goes that a peasant came in from the fields every evening. On his way home, he would go into his little village church and kneel down for a long time, quietly. One evening, the parish priest asked him what he did in prayer as he was so quiet for such a long time there on his knees. The man said concerning the Lord, "He looks at me, and I look at Him." Sometimes that is my prayer also, that He just looks at me and I look at Him in my heart.

I'm not here to talk, Lord,
I'm not here to ask
For guidance and help
In a situation or task.
I'm not here to explain
Or to give you my view.
If you will permit,
Let me just be with You.

# PART III:
# **CONVERSATIONS**
## (1989–1990)

# THE LIGHT OF LOVE

# Chapter 18
# PROTECTIVENESS AND GENTLENESS OF GOD

In late November, several events occurred which were very difficult for me. On top of these external events, I suffered the first of vicious attacks from Lucifer. I had always been skeptical of these so called diabolical attacks. Perhaps this skepticism is more deeply rooted than simply resulting from my professional background. At any rate, I would like to say here that these internal attacks do not resemble clinical depression or paranoia. It is very hard for me to explain what happens. A tangible, external force of evil does its best to crush any will to continue serving God. It does this in whatever way it can, using whatever particular individual vulnerability of its victim which is at hand. Anything and everything which can potentially crush a human spirit, cloud free will or make one feel worthless is used by the Evil One.

I felt woefully unprepared for anything of this sort, and had to be instructed by the angels as to how to deal with it. First of all, I was told to test all presences in the way I had been taught. Testing is so important that I will repeat it here. If testing is not being done then no matter how beautiful or good supernatural events may seem, they are dangerous. The test is:

"If you are of my Lord Jesus Christ who loves and created all things, then you are welcome in the name of the Father, and of the Son, and of the Holy Spirit (making the sign of the cross). If you are not of my Lord, Jesus Christ, then by His holy wounds, His agonizing Passion, His cruel death, and by His glorious rising you are to be gone now; in the name of the Father, and of the Son, and of the Holy Spirit (making the sign of the cross)."

This test is approved by the Church and is based on the Scriptural injunction that any doubtful spirit must acknowledge Christ as Lord.

I was also to use holy water. All of this was very new to me. Before all of these experiences, I might have thought of this as being quaint, almost medieval. I didn't think this way by the time the angels taught me all of this, and I had lived through external experiences which showed their vivid reality.

Journal Excerpt:

Monday, November 27, 1989

Again, I am writing early in the morning, about ten to six. I have gotten only four hours of sleep because of working into the wee hours of the morning this morning on a paper that is overdue. My headache is gone, but I am very tired. Eileen rushed off this morning without our morning prayers because I woke her up too late. What a grind this is. I pray we can all survive life.

And yet I feel such a joy this morning, a lightening of my spirit. As I sat typing the paper at 12:30 a.m., I realized there had been a beautiful light shining over me on my right side. It had been there for the past few minutes, possibly longer. It was particularly bright and beautiful, and very gentle. I tested the presence as I have been taught and asked if I should stop my work. I was told to continue. I continued working, feeling happy. I came to a good stopping place and was gently told to write down our following conversation. I grabbed some scratch paper. On the scratch paper, I have written only what I said and what the angel said, but as I copy the conversation into this journal I will also write a little of what I was feeling and thinking as the angel spoke to me. He began:

"It is not Our Lord's will that you have suffered in body and mind like this. Some suffering is a pain He permits for good. This suffering should be offered as prayers. But you must learn to protect yourself." He says this with deep concern and gentleness.

"How can I do this?" I ask.

"Constantly call upon the Father, the Son, and the Holy Spirit. Also, ask for help from Saint Michael and all of us. You are dedicated and consecrated to us to help us draw souls away from Lucifer, but you are also under our care and protection."

"Are you scolding me?"

"I am." He is laughing at me and with me. I feel very loved. He is also amused at his own tone towards me, and yet he is very serious about what he is saying to me. The warmth and concern of this angel reaches out to me in such a special way.

"You are not my Guardian Angel. I know the difference."

"No, I am not your guardian angel."

"May I know your name?"

"It is hard to communicate it to you. "PROTECTIVENESS AND GENTLENESS OF GOD" is the best I can do. I am one of those who loves you dearly, and I have been sent to give you strength."

"I've needed it, haven't I?"

"Through your own failing to ask us for help!"

"How can I ask for your help besides calling on the Holy Trinity?"

"So many in your time believe they can protect themselves — by themselves, with themselves — that they can build a wall of protection around themselves. They give it different names: HEALTH, GROWTH, UNDERSTANDING, PSYCHIC POWERS, MATERIAL GOODS. These things look different and they are used by different people, but they are all the same. The one way to protect yourself that never fails is to gird yourself with the sure knowledge that God, Our Lord and Creator, loves you with a love that is unshakable, unconditional, and irreversible. You are created out of His very heart. You are spirit of His spirit. You can never be separated from Him except by your active choosing — and even then there is grace for some if others are praying and suffering for them."

"So I must know clearly that God loves me?"

"Yes. That knowledge, to know you are created out of the very heart of the Lord of all things and that you are precious to Him beyond all things, will protect you and guide you. For you cannot help but cherish those others He has created and given into your care if you truly know this about yourself."

I wondered whom it is that God has given into my care besides my family. Then I thought of the parable of the Good Samaritan told by Our Lord.

"What about those who are evil or who have chosen evil?" I asked. "You will know them by their fruits as Our Lord has told you. You must work actively to protect yourself and others from them as a grower of fruit works to protect his yield. Our Lord's harvest is a treasure to be protected. You are being wise and prudent when you guard yourself against evil and protect yourself and others from it."

"I have had such a hard time doing this. It seems contradictory to being a Christian sometimes."

"The dignity of spirit I have told you about, which comes when you know the love of God for you, will help you do this."

"But doesn't God also love evil doers?"

"He loves them, and it wounds Him and those in His Kingdom that they have chosen evil. But their right to choose, and your right to choose must be protected at all costs. That right of choice is what your Guardian Angels guard most for you, as you have been told. The risk that some will find a joy in causing others suffering and will desire power over becoming servants of Love must be taken, in order that all who serve Love and Truth may be free. It is a high price, but a necessary one."

"But what about the innocent ones who get in the way and suffer because of that price?"

"They are hurt little ones held in Our Lord's arms. He has promised that all will be well with you and with His creation, and that is a trust you must cling to."

"How can I learn to trust more?"

"Open your heart day and night, with each of its beats, to knowing with everything in you that He loves you. This may seem like a simple answer to you but it is not. It is not! You could spend a whole lifetime trying to know this with your heart and only just begin to sense it, this love is so great."

"Why are we not able to fathom Our Lord's love more?"

"You could not remain in your earthly form if you were to know His love too deeply. Your joy would be too great to remain as you are."

"I have felt a bit like that thirteen years ago when I was given my beautiful blessing."

"You chose the Kingdom of Heaven then, Pat, and though you have sinned since then and wandered in your way, your choice has not wavered. Our Lord blesses you and gives you His peace."

I feel such joy at these words. I am in tears. "Thank you. I love my Lord."

"Remember what I have said about calling upon us for help and remembering always the love of God. You must remember these things in the future, and never try to fight these battles alone."

"I didn't mean to be proud. I just didn't know."

"You know now. Please remember. This is very serious. Do not take it lightly."

"Will I have more attacks?"

"You will. But Our Lord will never let go of you."

"I am very glad to know that ... this is also new to me. I don't understand most of it."

"You try to understand everything! Open your heart and let Our Lord Christ and His Mother, the Queen of Heaven, bathe you in their love and in their graces. The source of this love is the Father. Remember that you cannot understand the love of God. You must open your heart to it. Your heart knows."

"Thank you. You have given me such love and comfort tonight."

"I am filled with joy to have done so, my dear little one. And, before I stop speaking with you, please remember not to be so hard on yourself. You would not make the demands on others which you make on yourself. You are one of God's imperfect creatures. Please allow Him the joy of slowly bringing you to perfection. Don't rush Him."

I start to laugh, and he laughs with me. "Thank you."

"You are most welcome. Our Lord's love and peace are with you. I will see you again. Peace."

"Peace to you too, Angel of Comfort."

"My presence will remain with you as you rest tonight, and you will see the light of God which has been given to me, but I will not speak any more now. Rest now, little one. Rest in Our Lord's love."

And I did rest well, better than I have for a long time despite the shortness of the rest. I am amazed to feel such love and to realize that we are all loved like this. And if such tenderness can exist for us from the angels around us, what must Our Lord's love be! My heart and my soul sing praises to God. That He has shown me such love and mercy in granting me these conversations of love shows His mercy and kindness even more, because I am so very small and sinful.

# THE LIGHT OF LOVE

# Chapter 19
# PURGATORY:
# A JOURNEY TO SHEOL

That fall was, as usual, a hectic one. We arose at 5:00 every morning in order to pray before Eileen left for swimming practice. I usually worked until 9:30 or 10:00 at night in the clinic, seeing clients. I love this work. However, I had an uncomfortable feeling that I was running on empty. I suspected I had never really recovered sufficiently from the surgery. But I had enough energy to keep going, and that was enough for me at the time. Miriam and Eileen had begun their junior year in high school in September, and were already thinking of college. I spent odd moments wondering where my babies had gone.

Journal Excerpts:

Wednesday, December 13, 1989

The light is so beautiful and bright this morning. Sometimes I go for days without seeing it. Often I deeply pray to see it, yet do not. Then, often at such odd moments like this morning when I am so very tired and have been up all night with Gia and her bowel problems and my headache, I see it so gently and tenderly radiant. I think this is done in order that I will know more clearly, though so slowly, that I cannot make it happen. It is not something within my control, but is something given to me as a gift by my Lord.

Tomorrow is the one year anniversary of my tumor surgery. Glory be to God.

Tuesday, December 19, 1989

I have been very shaken today. My Guardian Angel took me on a journey to Purgatory. He tells me that the souls in Purgatory need our prayers so very much, and there is little talk of Purgatory in our Church these days. Some even doubt the real existence of Purgatory, saying that Purgatory, and even hell, are here on earth and are not real places. If only these doubters could live through what I have just experienced. God help me.

The light is so bright as I write this. Are the beautiful angels pleased that I am writing? One of them just said to me, "You were told you are to be a chronicler. What are you doing now?" Yes, I suppose I am, but me? Who am I to do this? But here it is.

My Guardian Angel took me to a gray and very cold sort of place. I believe that, though I was seeing metaphysically, the things of the spirit were shown to me in a physical way. I believe that what I was experiencing was being experienced by those in Purgatory in a physical way.

It was bleak. There were sharp boulders, rocks, small sharp stones, high mountains, deep and particularly dark valleys which seemed to go on forever. Each soul had its own way to find through this landscape, and each obstacle represented for that particular soul those things which kept him or her away from God — such things as pain caused to those still on earth and their own hardness of heart in caring about this or recognizing it. I was surprised to see that they also had to do atonement for the repercussions of their actions of cruelty or uncaring. The consequences of what they had done might go on here on earth for a very long time down the generations.

I saw quite a few of them lying face down in front of great boulders which they had to climb over. They also lay in front of deep gullies which they had to climb down into in order to face themselves. I thought at first they were lying there out of weariness, but was told it is not weariness but is a reluctance to understand and accept their part in sin.

Mike and Mary had told us that, as the souls grew closer to Heaven, they were in more pain then further away because they knew more and more clearly how they had offended God, and they cared more deeply about this the closer to Him they came. I saw this, too. For them, their little offenses loomed greater because they loved God more and yearned more strongly to be with Him in Heaven, the closer they came and the more their awareness of themselves, as His people, grew.

But some lay there not moving, suffering but refusing to go on, partly because of their increased pain further along but also because they did not want to acknowledge how they had hurt other people and themselves. It might take them a long time and a great deal of pain before they could face these things and go on. I was told that our prayers help them do this. Our prayers are very important to them, helping them realize God's mercy and love for them.

Some felt so worthless and hopeless. They had their hands raised in pleading and sorrow. I was not told this, but I had the impression they would have given anything to be back on earth to try to redress the wrongs they had done, to soothe the pain they had caused, to remedy what they had done in whatever way they could, no matter what that might entail. It was heartbreaking to me because they could see me and were begging my prayers for them. I did not see that they could talk to each other or in any other way give encouragement to each other. I hope that they can, but somehow I doubt it. This purification seems to be an individual struggle. An important part of the struggle seems to be seeing how everything fits together, and how our own lives and actions fit in to the whole pattern of life.

I was asked by my Guardian Angel to pray in particular for those who have committed suicide, those who have died in despair of God's love, and those who have died believing their cruelty to others is justified.

I saw a great wall with a door in it. The door would open periodically as I looked. Light streamed through the door, and a soul would enter through the door, greatly filled with joy. Many were on the other side to greet him or her with a joy beyond description. I don't know if those left behind to continue their purification could see the light or the door.

"It is so much easier for you to purify your hearts during your earthly lives," my Guardian Angel said. "One act of reconciliation, one word of kindness, one little courageous effort to reach out in love — these efforts and strivings to love during your earthly lives, if not made, bring countless eons of frustration and pain because you can do nothing in Purgatory about what you have done or not done in your lifetime. Please pray for all who are there, especially those who have taken their own lives or others' lives, both in physical fact and in the destruction of the spirit."

I will need a long time to ponder this and to pray. The angels have told me that we could not bear to be before the face of God as unpurified or tarnished souls. Our pain would be an agony beyond words. It would also, somehow, be impossible for us to be in the full presence of God as unpurified souls anyway.

I know that when suddenly I am brought face to face with my own sin, and, of course, just a small part of my sin, when I cannot pretend, justify or deny, when I come face to face with my deepest soul, when the pretensions and justifications are stripped away and I see clearly, even if only for a brief moment, what I have done and its consequences — then I feel as though my sorrow and self reproach may kill me. But it is also at times like this that my joy is deepest because it is in these moments of honest, painful clarity in which I realize more fully than ever I could in ordinary moments that I am totally and completely dependent on the mercy and love of my Lord and Love, Jesus Christ, the Redeemer.

I think of the souls for whom no one prays, either because they have been forgotten or unloved or because their relatives and friends do not know to pray for them. It is sad to me that so many Christians believe Jesus's sacrifice for our sins means that we do not have to face these sins or atone for them. Our Lord did not come in order to take away our responsibility for ourselves.

I have come to see Purgatory as part of the working out of Salvation which Our Blessed Lord made possible for us by His sacrifice and death on the Cross. But we are not babies, and Our Blessed Lord will not treat us as such. It is thanks to His mercy that this purification can take place at all. I see that now. "You will not get out," He says, "until you have paid the last penny."

But I will never again simply offer an empty intention for "the souls in Purgatory" because I can't think of anything else for which to pray. I still see them so clearly in my mind.

# Chapter 20
# AN ACCEPTED INVITATION

Friday, December 22, 1989

The changes in Eastern Europe are overwhelming. Who would have thought that the ignominious Berlin Wall would go down so quickly, would be sold for souvenirs? Now we hear of the horrible things taking place in Romania. At least now there appears to be a hope for elections. And all through this, the Russians do nothing. That is perhaps the greatest miracle of all. It seems sometimes that what happens in life is more unbelievable than anything anyone could ever invent, and that if one wrote factual events down and readers didn't know they were facts, the writer would be called a very good but fanciful storyteller. No writer of fiction ever conceptualized the events we are now witnessing.

It may be difficult for people of the future to understand the constant, quiet fear so many of us lived with because of the animosity of the two "super powers" and the apparent lineup of the world behind one or the other. Who would push the button first? And how, little nations asked themselves, could they best survive between these two giants?

So, now what? Are we going, so to speak, from the frying pan into the fire? In the exhilaration of these days I can hardly believe so, but the events in Romania seem to be a grim portent of what may be to come in eastern Europe.

Saturday, December 23, 1989

A little verse by Madeleine L'Engle goes through my mind today. It may not be exactly correct, but here it is as closely as I can remember it,

"This is the irrational season
When love blooms free and wild.
Had Mary been filled with reason
There'd have been no room for the Child."

When I think of our faith objectively, in a "scientific way", it seems almost ludicrous. To believe that a tiny baby born in a stable is the creator of the universe, that He lived and died among us and rose from the dead — I can hear myself and other arrogant professionals saying, "This must be scientifically tested. It must be a repeatable experiment. There are elements of this 'mythology' all over the world, so that proves it is all myth."

But it is the supreme arrogance to believe that people of other cultures and faiths could not have part of the truth, although distorted. Most of us have a hunger for God, for the One Who made us and loves us. These similarities show the truth of our faith rather than disprove it.

It is only because our Christian faith is familiar to us that we believe something so incredible as the Word Incarnate born to a virgin of body and spirit, and His resurrection as the key to our whole faith.

I want to look at my faith anew this Christmas and see it as I have never seen it before, as if I were a potential convert hearing of my Lord for the very first time. I think of what the blessed angels have told me, that Jesus Christ Our Lord would have suffered His Passion for each of us individually, had this been necessary for the opportunity of salvation for each soul. He would have suffered His Passion many times for each soul. They have told me that He would have, out of His endless love, suffered many times over for each soul, even the souls He knew would say no to Him and choose hell — just to give each of us the chance to say yes to Him, or say no. Love like this is too great for me to comprehend.

Monday, December 25, 1989

The light is so beautiful and bright. It seems to be everywhere on this Christmas morning. Happy, happy birthday, my dear Lord.

Friday, January 12, 1990

I am never sure whether I am a person of great faith or great doubt. I suppose it depends on what day it is, and what is going on in my life. This is a contradiction, of course. If I were a person of great faith, surely it would be a steady and an unwavering faith, not dependent on external or internal circumstances. I quail sometimes, thinking of what I have written in this journal, of what I know to be true. But how can I ever hope or begin to convince others of the veracity of what I have written? I have decided I will not try to convince anyone, that I will do my best to not let it matter to me whether I am believed or not. This has to be God's problem. It is too big for me. All I can do is record the truth, and thank and praise God for it.

A gentle angel came to me a few minutes ago. I tested the presence as I have been taught. This is not a verbatim conversation, but is the best I can do in reconstruction. The angel told me that the gift I have been promised can be taken away from me. He was referring to the special gift I was given on the Feast of the Assumption of 1988 to see the light of the angels and to hear them speaking when this is God's will. He told me that if this was all too difficult for me, it could be taken away. He said this with such kindness. I knew there would be no hard feelings if I refused to continue.

I pleaded that the gift not be taken, but I said, "I am concerned. I don't seem to be able to stop suffering and doubting myself. Wouldn't God's purposes be served better with someone who doubted less? My self–doubt and feelings of unworthiness get in the way so much of the time."

"No," he told me. He said that Our Lord has taken my doubting into consideration. He knew I would doubt before giving me this gift. He said that Our Lord knows me intimately and loves me, doubting spirit and all. He promised me that Our Lord will use my doubts for His purposes, and will bring about a greater love because of them.

Sunday, January 14, 1990

The light shines bright and gentle upon me. There are many angels around me this day. But "the light God has given them" is not just a light. It penetrates into my deepest heart. When I asked if I should speak with them, or if they wished to speak to me, one of them told me no. He said they are just there to give me Our Lord's love and peace. I blessed them with everything in me for their kindness, and I bless and thank my Lord for His generosity.

8:00 p.m. For the last few Sundays, two of Miriam and Eileen's friends have joined us for the rosary. Tonight the light from the angels was so beautiful and bright. It came from two different directions. I could not help exclaiming over it to the kids right before we started praying. I told them where it was and then said, "I can see this part of Gia's head," as she lay in front of me.

"Yes," Eileen said slowly, "that would be only about what you could see."

"How do you know?" Miriam demanded.

"Well," Eileen said without rancor, "from where she said she saw the light, that would be right about where it would be reflected off Gia's coat." She is very much fascinated right now with her physics class.

I was filled with such joy to be permitted to see this light and feel the peace and joy emanating from the angels that I cried out, "Please, if you wish to pray with us, all you blessed angels, do come, if God allows, and pray the rosary." I was amazed, for within a few moments of my saying this, there was so much light in the room that I could no longer distinguish direction or source. It was everywhere, even above me!

"Well," I thought, "should that surprise you? God, in His love and mercy, allowed them to accept your invitation. Don't give the invitation if you doubt that it might be accepted." Sometimes the only thing I can do with all these happenings is laugh in incredulity, with a thanksgiving in my heart that goes on and on and on.

# Chapter 21
# THE GUARDIAN ANGEL
# OF ANOTHER PERSON

Sunday, January 21, 1989

A few minutes ago two angels came to be with me. I could see their light, one on each side of me. The one on my left was my Guardian Angel. I had been reading an article for a class assignment. What a beautiful, and yet respectful interruption.

I grabbed scratch paper and began to write out our conversation. I asked the angel on the right, "May I know your name?"

He told me his name. I do not give it here because he is the guardian angel of someone who has hurt me very much.

"What do you want from me?"

"Your continued prayers."

I am dismayed at this. I really don't want to keep praying for this person. "How do you want me to pray?" I am hedging.

"With a forgiving and loving heart."

"How can I open my heart more to forgive?" Again, I suspect I am hedging.

"By understanding that you yourself also have sinned. There is no living soul on earth that has not hurt itself, others, and Our Lord."

"But what about the severity of the hurt? What if the person hurting me has purposefully lied? I don't think I have ever hurt anyone like this."

"The soul over which I have been given charge and whom I dearly love does not know how to be honest with himself or others, but he very much wants to be. He will not stop striving until he is. He is rigorous in his search for truth and honesty in himself and others..."

My Guardian Angel says gently to me, "You are so afraid of getting hurt that you can't see beyond your fears."

"But should I not be self-protective?"

"Yes, but know that it is God who is your true protection ... Know that you are loved by Him and by many others."

"I'm sorry, but in the case of this particular person who has hurt me, if this is being loved, I want nothing to do with it."

"He cries inside in a way you have never cried. Your grief is great and lasting, but his is a constant hurt because he accepts full responsibility and blames himself ceaselessly ... He does not know the mercy and love of God as you do. Even though your knowledge is small, it is greater than his ... He needs your faith and steadfastness, your gentleness of spirit, your kindness, to help him know of the gentleness and kindness and forgiving spirit of Our Lord. You are to be a mirror for him of the love of God."

I am shaken by this "Can I do it?"

"You can do it. You are so afraid of being hurt, of shortchanging yourself. You have wronged yourself before. You will do it again, but please trust ... Your gentleness and love, and your wish to please Our Lord are your great strengths. Always seek His guidance. He will not betray you.

... Pray for clarity and do not give up hope. This hope is not based in a certain outcome, but is based in faith — the faith that God, Our Lord and Creator, knows what He is doing and, despite interference, will finish His work in you and in all of His creation with the help of your prayers ... Please keep praying."

"I will try. I don't see the light from my Guardian Angel anymore."

"Your Guardian Angel never leaves you. He is able to do what you ask of him if it is allowed, and also still remain with you. He is not limited by space or time."

"Thank you for talking to me."

"You are dear to us, Bonita."

"Why do you call me that? It's very nice."

"You were so small when you came into this world. Your spirit has grown so, despite difficulties. But we will always think of you as the tiny little one Our Lord first created and blessed. A great tree will grow from a tiny, weak seedling, and those who have hearts to understand will give God praise for it."

"Is this tree me?!"

He says smilingly, "Yes. Are you so surprised?"

"Yes. I feel so small."

"You are not small when you are rooted in God and in His eternal love ... You are blessed because you are willing to wait for God's will to be manifested, and the little trust you have will be enough because of His mercy."

"Thank you. Thank you very much."

"Please try to wait. I know that it is the hardest thing in the world for you to do."

"Will I never not have trouble waiting?"

He says smilingly, "You will always have trouble waiting. You are one of those who, the more practice you get, the harder it is for you."

"Do angels know how to wait?"

"There are also some among us who have a hard time waiting, and we have had more practice at it than you! Offer your waiting as penance for your sins of omission."

"Why sins of omission?"

"Because the sins you commit by not doing or saying what Our Lord would wish for you to do and say are more numerous by far than your actively committed sins, and they are not thought of or repented of very often."

"I will offer this time of waiting for my sins of omission. Bless you. Is that all you wanted to say to me?"

"No ... thank you for your kindness towards my special charge. I know it is very difficult for you. I will not forget your kindness, nor will he when he knows of it."

"I just truly want to do whatever my Lord wishes. I despair of doing His will sometimes. ..."

"But you keep wanting to do His will. If everything were clear to you, there would not be the joy in Heaven that you give by struggling to do His will through your doubt, confusion and uncertainty ... Your desire to give Our Lord glory through all your difficulties and pain, especially (despite) your lack of clarity, give us and Him great joy. It will not be forgotten."

"That comforts me so much. Please thank Him for me and bless Him, that He has allowed you to speak to me."

"I will. But you can also thank Him."

"I do! I truly do! Thank You, Lord. Thank You."

This conversation is written out here only partially in order to protect the privacy of the person whose guardian angel spoke with me. The guardian angels of other people have come to me asking for prayers. I will not record these conversations here unless I can preserve the anonymity of the people involved and the conversations themselves have a broader interest and scope other than personal requests.

I would like to make it clear that when personal requests are involved or personal information is given, I very rarely remember what is said afterwards. This was at first frightening to me as I have a fairly sharp memory and can usually remember things in detail. I feel more relaxed about it now because I realize I am given the gift of forgetfulness because whatever is forgotten is

none of my business.

# Chapter 22
# THE NEED TO CHOOSE

Saturday, February 3, 1990

I have hardly been home in the last eight days. After returning last Sunday from a conference in San Antonio, I left on Wednesday to go to Austin to the Cris Cole Center there, run by the Commission for the Blind. I had a wonderful time on Thursday as I was shown computer equipment and access devices. They are great machines, but more importantly to me they can be of such help — if the agency will purchase them for me. I have been frustrated for the last year and a half trying to get computer equipment.

I was alone practicing with one of the pieces of equipment. It was late Thursday night. The light was particularly bright. I had noticed that it was very bright and beautiful all day. I go through my days sometimes so much enjoying what I am doing (and sometimes being frustrated and overwhelmed). The light from the angels is a steady reminder to me that this world is not at all the real place I belong, my true home. I receive such steady, gentle love and understanding from the angels around me. I feel it, even when they do not speak. I never could have dreamed of a gift like this from my Lord. It is so perfect. A great deal of quiet healing goes on in my spirit because of it.

After I had been working for about three hours, my Guardian Angel began speaking to me. He said affectionately that he had been waiting all day for me to pay attention. I told him I was sorry.

"It is hard for you to live in this world and have a share in the other," he said. He said it is hard for everyone who wants to be close to God to live in both worlds. He asked me to put a fresh piece of paper in my brailler. I did. I always wonder what on earth I am to write when I do this, and then realize I don't have to worry about it. He dictated what follows to me, "This is a time of deep concern in Heaven because it is now that the final choices must be made. Which master will you serve is the question you must ask and answer for yourself. There is no more room for waiting, for more proofs, for more signs. After this time, grace will be given to only a few to make this choice. Most of you, Our Lord's children, know in your deepest hearts whom it is you wish to serve. You waver because of the pressures and pains of this world. Do not waver any longer. No pain of this world is greater than the eternal pain of forever being cut off from God — the source of your life, the Creator of all that you are.

"Please ask your guardian angels for their love and protection as you make this choice. They will be doing everything they can to help you during this time. Your prayers will allow them to help you even more. Even those who have made the choice for Our Lord's Kingdom must pray, because Lucifer is on the prowl even more now. He is like a ravenous jackal waiting to tear out your soul and devour it.

"Please do not be afraid of what I am saying. Remember that you are loved by all those in Heaven, and that you cannot be separated from us and from Our Lord except by your own choosing.

"Please choose now to be with us and do not waver from that choice, whatever is to come. Though you may weaken and suffer later, your spirit will bear the mark of God if you choose now.

"A great battle rages and will continue to rage for your souls. Everything that can be done by those who wish to drag you into fear, darkness and hatred will be done to entice you thither. Please, please choose the light. Let the mercy and the love of God flow through you like clear water over a stream bed. Let nothing separate you from His love. Let nothing prevent you from expressing this love to those around you and to all those who cry out for it. It is in this way that Our Lord's Kingdom grows. Please choose to be a part of His Kingdom forever. Please."

My Guardian Angel made an exception to my silence with the dictation above. He said that it was so important for those open to this dictation to receive it, that I was to distribute it to several people. I asked permission from my confessor to do this. My Dear Angel had made it clear that no matter what the angels said to me, my confessor always is to have the last word. I am to be completely obedient to him and share everything with him, withholding nothing. He gave his permission for the limited distribution of my Angel's dictation.

My Angel tells me that this dictation grows in importance as time goes on, and the urgency of what he told me and all of us increases.

# Chapter 23
# OF THE HEART AND SPIRIT

Monday, February 12, 1990

Yesterday the girls, a friend of Eileen's, and I were praying the rosary. We were surrounded by the light from the angels as we did so. I hesitate to write this, but perhaps it is no more amazing than anything else I have written in this journal. The beautiful, bright angel next to me told me, as we paused in prayer, that he had been the angel permitted to announce Our Dear Lord's resurrection to the women at the tomb. I was so excited that I did not ask his name. I have always loved these passages in Scripture because the angel rolled away the stone from the tomb "and sat on it." That stone is the symbol of death, the symbol of finality, the symbol of no more hope, no way out, nowhere else to go, nothing more to happen, the symbol of the victory of heartache and endless tears—and the angel "sat on it."

I told the kids, and we were all amazed. The angel seemed amused at our amazement. He said, paraphrasing, "You are surrounded by angels who bear witness to the truth of these events."

Eileen's friend, always full of delightful questions, asked if there had been a lot of angels with Jesus during His Passion. The angel told us that all the angels of Heaven witnessed the crucifixion and death of the Lord — the redemption of the human race. How it must have broken their angelic hearts to see Him suffering and not be allowed to do anything.

Eileen's friend asked if all the angels were present at Our Blessed Lord's birth. "No," said the angel. They were celebrating everywhere, in Heaven and on earth. What about at the time of the resurrection, the angel was asked. "No. Many were attempting to give comfort to those in agony over Our Lord's death." The only time, the angel said, that the angels have been on earth in one place is during Our Lord's Passion and Crucifixion. He said this is the case so far. He implied that there will be another time in the future when all the angels of Heaven will be here on earth again.

All of these events make me more conscious of the real world, the Kingdom of my Lord. Our family and our close friends are drawn more and more closely into the love of the Kingdom of God. How can I explain this in words when the things that are happening to us are events of the heart and spirit?

Monday, February 19, 1990

Eileen has surgery tomorrow. She is more anxious about it than I think she would like to admit, though she feels better about it now since going to Doctor C. Doctor C. told her that in place of the surgery he could do "a long drawn out procedure that will probably cause you more pain and not be as effective as the surgery her doctor will do." This has boosted her confidence that the surgery is necessary.

Eileen was a member of the swimming team at Coronado High School. This was so important to her that she swam for three months with a dislocated shoulder, "not wanting to let the team down." Her coach had bullied her, calling her a wimp. It was only at the urging of a trainer that she finally went to the doctor and had the surgery which reconstructed her shoulder and has since caused her pain. She had not wanted me to know the extent of her pain for fear I might take her off the swim team, which, of course, I did do when I knew how serious her injuries were.

But Our Lord blessed her and us through this experience. Before this time, Eileen had not emphasized her school work very much. She is extremely bright, but swimming had been everything to her. Her energy and love is now going into majoring in theology at Christendom College in Virginia.

Monday, March 12, 1990

Today is my 37th birthday. I had a long day at school with a moment to drink something around dinner time. My last session tonight in our family clinic finished at 9:30.

As I came in our front door totally exhausted and rather downhearted because I had not been able to celebrate my birthday with anyone, Miriam rushed from her room. "I'm sorry, Mom, that I can't talk to you. I have a big test tomorrow," she said. She heated a bowl of stew for me in the microwave as I divested myself of my things. God bless her.

I was greatly hungry, and said grace quickly. I felt dreary and down hearted. Suddenly, the light grew amazingly bright. There were angels everywhere. I tested the presence. Then I heard them singing. To my shock, they sang the first bars of, "Happy Birthday to You." I couldn't believe my ears. Then they broke off and began singing a hauntingly beautiful song I can never describe. It was filled with joy and tenderness.

"This song," my Guardian Angel told me, "is a song of praise to our Almighty Lord. We are praising Him and blessing Him in thanksgiving for creating you." Of all birthdays, this one will stay with me forever. I am too moved to write more.

Tuesday, March 13, 1990

I returned from Austin a few days ago after more computer training. I do not feel comfortable with my trainer because of difficult circumstances which are not of my doing. I am also not learning what I need to know, but I don't know enough to ask the right questions. Our Lord will work it out.

While in Austin, I returned to the church I had visited there before. I am very shy about going to church in a strange place, especially in a strange city. The effort to get there and not get lost almost seems too great. So I had definite reservations about trying to find a church. But in this case, two parishion-ers greeted me as I went into the church, and they sat with me. One of them assisted me in going to Communion.

And suddenly the greatest miracle of my life happened again. The beautiful disk of light came toward me, was placed in my hand, and laid there glowing. When I moved to the side to receive Our Lord's Precious Blood, the liquid gold of the light from the chalice was there also. I became weak in the knees, and had a hard time standing. It was as though He said to me, "No matter where you are, in a strange city, in a strange church, remember: I am here." How could I think of myself as a stranger in this church when my Lord is there?

The parish had formed a Girl Scout troop, and members were being honored. It was a fun Mass. Afterwards, I had the strong wish to go to confession, though I usually do not confess to anyone but my confessor. I hesitantly asked the priest to hear my confession as I greeted him at the church door. He was very warm. He said if I could wait for him, he would be glad to do it.

After my confession, I was still so filled with amazement and joy over what I had experienced during Communion that I burst out with it. He listened quietly and then said, "Ordinary people tell us things like this sometimes. Some of my parishioners have said they see me and the Host surrounded by light during the Consecration. They, like you, are afraid I might not believe them. I hear other things too. Of course, some of it is probably fanciful. But not all. I think any priest who doesn't listen to his people about these things and give them at least some credence is passing by the living Body of Christ."

Sunday, March 18, 1990

I was in a great deal of pain yesterday afternoon, and am again this morning after a long night. Apparently not only are my neck muscles not healed properly (possibly a life long situation), but the implant in my right eye is pushing outward and must be removed.

That means surgery again. Perhaps I can hold out till the summer. It will be local anesthesia and then a few days of minor discomfort. In the meantime, I will offer the pain and hope I can make it till the end of the semester. I feel frustrated because of needing to rest today, but there is nothing else to do.

Saturday, March 24, 1990

There are little things the angels have told me which I must remember to record here. I asked one of the angels about the Immaculate Conception of the Blessed Mother. The Catholic Church teaches that Our Lady was conceived without sin, the only fully human being ever to be so. I have been puzzled by this. It has saddened me that this teaching has caused dissension among Christians, but the truth should never be compromised.

"Yes," the angel told me. "It is so. It would not have been possible for Our Lady to be that close to God, to bear Our Lord in her womb for nine months, unless she herself were without blemish. She could not have lived if it were not so." This is in accord with what I have seen of Purgatory, that nothing impure can bear to be in the full presence of God and survive. So she, the most perfect Tabernacle of all, could not have borne Our Lord otherwise. So, to assume that any sinful woman could have borne Jesus Christ is to deny His divinity, to assert that He is just an ordinary, fully human person like us. He is fully human, but He is fully God also. I understand this now.

I would be told later by my guardian angel that each of our souls is created by God for a specific and beautiful purpose. Of course, we have many reasons for being but there is a very special one for each of us. True loyalty, then, is doing everything possible to help another soul towards God and towards its reason and purpose for being; towards its unique and very specified work in serving God. Loyalty may not be at all to do what another wishes of one. As I would learn later, it is being falsely loyal to stand by or even assist another person to go against God for "reasons that are good for me."

My Guardian Angel said that the Mother of Jesus Christ was created by God to be the Mother of His Son. She was given special graces to do this because it would have been impossible otherwise for a mere human being to bring God to birth. The biggest reason for her great beauty, both outward and inward, was of course because of Jesus's love for His Mother. But he told me Our Lady could have decided, as we all can, not to follow God's way. She could have used the personal strength and charisma given to her by Our Lord for His good purposes for her own ends, as we all can.

He told me that she had such charisma and personal strength and beauty given to her which God wished to be used for Jesus's sake, and out of love for her, that she could have used to gain personal power. He said she could have drawn people to her and made them do what she wanted them to do because of their great wish to please her. She could have used her beauty and personal power to become empress of the world.

But she wanted to do Our Lord's will completely. She was always quietly in the background. He said that this choice of hers to use the gifts given to her by God for God alone and His purposes is one of the many reasons why she is so beloved by God and His angels and saints. We too, he told me, will be beloved for the same reason.

Sunday, April 1, 1990

This is the Sunday our family rosary was torn to pieces and never prayed because one of my daughters started fussing and complaining, telling me that "kneeling down is bad for your knees, Mom." All the blessings we have been given seemed to have affected us so little sometimes—and that includes me too. How can we begrudge so little when we have been given so much? Why do I have such a hard time sometimes praying a mere five minutes? All I can do at times like this is to hope that my Lord knows my heart will never be the same because of His patience and His blessings to me. I am despairing today, feeling so small.

# Chapter 24
# TENDER SORROW OF GOD

Friday, April 20, 1990

The light is beautiful and bright on days which are surprisingly or dinary. It usually happens that I see it when I least expect it. Even as I pray, I do not expect it. Sometimes I see it when I am not in a prayerful frame of heart or mind at all, sometimes too weary hardly to notice.

A beautiful, gentle, and a seemingly sorrowful angel spoke to me a few minutes ago. I wrote our conversation down as I was asked to do. He began, "You and all people are loved by Our Lord, Jesus Christ. His greatest desire is that you should share in the life He has given you. You want this too, but you believe this precious life can be grabbed and plundered from material things and from one another."

"I want to ask you more ... May I know your name?"

"TENDER SORROW OF GOD."

"Is God sorrowful?"

"Not in the same way you are sorrowful. His sorrow reaches into your hearts. It is your sorrow and all sorrow."

"What does it come from?"

"When you grasp and grab at what you think will make you happy, you hurt yourself and others. Many are effected, and what you do has repercussions which go on and on."

"This seems so hopeless."

"It can seem so, yes. But remember that what you do in love also bears fruit that goes on and on."

"Is this grasping and grabbing the source of all sorrow?"

"Most sorrow. Most sorrow could be avoided if it were not done."

"How can I avoid doing it?"

"By serving."

"Serving?"

"Yes. You have the strong desire to serve Our Lord, and that is your blessing. But you will start those little actions that bear continual fruits of love, and you will break the pain of sorrows caused by grasping when you serve."

"What about the concern in our time for people who have served so much that they have lost themselves?"*

"The root of their service is not love, but need. All people need. It is natural and right that you need each other. But when you do not know who you are, that you are a child of the Eternal God who loves and creates all things, then your needs become so great that you grasp at your own happiness in ways which are not clear and honest and which hurt yourself and others."

"Should we not want happiness?"

"Of course! But the root of your desire must be love, and the true fruit of that desire is and must be service, service from a full heart that gives without fear or resentment."

"How can I not be resentful and not be afraid of being taken advantage of?"

"By knowing that you are a child of the Lord of Life and Love. You may not be recognized as His precious child by those around you, but HE always recognizes you."

"What about those of us who reject God?"

"Because of their rejection, Our Lord and we in His Kingdom can give them only our tears, and even these they do not want."

"Please help me to serve Our Lord."

"You will receive graces to do this as long as you wish for them."

"I wish for them always."

"And you are given them always. Please trust that you are given them, even when you do not realize it."

"I will try. Bless you, and thank you, gentle angel."

"Our Lord's peace is with you little one."

As always, I have copied this conversation from the scratch paper on which I wrote as the conversation was occurring. May glory be given by my heart and spirit to my dear Lord of Life and Love forever and ever. Amen.

---

[NOTE: Many people who serve selflessly and lovingly in our time risk being labeled co-dependent. Perhaps this label is warranted in some cases. But as a counselor, I was thinking of our preoccupation and concern with co-dependency and the emphasis in working with people on becoming stronger through self-assertion.]

# Chapter 25
# GIFTS OF LOVE

Thursday, May 10, 1990

Friends of mine from Louisiana who have a special love for the angels came to visit me. They asked if we might pray. As we prayed, angels spoke to us twice. One beautiful angel said his name is SEARCHING THE HEART OF GOD. The questions were asked of him, "Why is Our Blessed Mother appearing all over the world, and why does it seem that the Holy Spirit is working so strongly in our own lives? Why now? Why in these times?" The answer was so simple and beautiful. It was, "That at least some of you may once again turn your faces unto the Lord."

Another question concerned receiving the Holy Eucharist in our hands. Though it is now allowed by the Church many seem to believe it is sacrilegious to receive the Host in our hands. I was curious about this question too. It is easier for me as a blind person to receive the Host in my hand, but this ease should not be a factor if there is anything sacrilegious about this. The angel said that there are many people who receive the Host in their mouths, but desecrate Our Lord's Body and Blood because of the uncleanliness of their hearts. He said that there are those who receive it in their hands who are like "little children with their hands out, reaching for the love Our Lord wishes to give them." He gently scolded us, saying we thought too much about form. "It is what is in your hearts that is important," he told us. If I paraphrase correctly, he said that what is in our hearts determines sacrilegiousness or determines holiness. We are much concerned with mundane matters. The love of God is everything. The love of God is the reason these wonderful things have been allowed.

Several weeks ago, I was praying using the little rosary I had been using the night over a year ago on which the little figure of Our Lord moved on the cross and was seen by my family and our guests. The little figure of the Blessed Mother was on the medal of the rosary and the other side of the medal was blank. As I have said, the little figure of Our Blessed Mother also moved.

I sat praying, holding the rosary. I begged Our Blessed Mother to please pray for me to her Son. "I'm just an ordinary woman," I told her. "You are my Mother in Heaven, and you've loved me from the very beginning. Won't you please give me some of the beautiful grace of Our Lord with which you are filled? On my own, I can't do what Our Lord wishes and what I want to do."

As I held the rosary, I suddenly realized that the other side of the medal was no longer smooth. There was something there that I could not identify. It felt clean and sharp, though delicate. I rushed out to my girls who also knew the back of the medal had been blank. The crucifix and the medal on a rosary that have moved are things that even sighted people take close looks at. My girls described the little emblem now on the back of the medal: A cross with an M at the bottom and on each side of the M, a heart—all surrounded by a circle of twelve stars. I discovered later that this is the Miraculous Medal whose image was given by the Blessed Mother to Saint Catherine Laboure in France around 1830. There is no way I could ever prove to anyone not taking my word for this, that the beautiful little Miraculous Medal which is truly miraculous has not always been on this rosary. But I know. I know with all my heart without any doubt, and I will give my word before God in thanksgiving for the kindness He and His dear Mother have shown me by letting me know through these signs of their great love.

I know my rosaries and crucifixes as, I suspect, a sighted person would not bother to know them. This is not a criticism, though it may seem so. I am sure there is just so much going on visually that many sighted people don't pay attention to what is going on tactually, to what seems to them to be minor details. But it is through my fingers that my heart is touched and my Lord in His love and wisdom knows this.

# Chapter 26
# JOY IN THE LOVE OF GOD

Saturday, May 12, 1990

A fter returning from dinner last night with a friend, I was washing up before going to rest when the light became beautifully bright. It was so luminous that I could see it reflected off the bar of soap I was holding.

I tested the presence. The angel asked me to get paper and write down our conversation. Here it is now, copied from my scratch paper. The angel began, "You hesitate to accept and be joyful in receiving the gift of the love of God from us, the angels, and from the people God has given to you to love you."

"Yes, I have sensed that too. Why am I so afraid?"

"You know it is because you are afraid of being hurt. But what is hurt if, even if only a few times out of many, love and joy might be exchanged between two hearts that love God?"

"I've never thought of it that way. Why is this so important?"

"Because the love of God, the heart of God, the Kingdom of God, can only grow through risking."

"Risking what?"

"Risking yourself. Even a miser will risk his gold before risking himself. It is the greatest chance you can take: to risk your heart in loving."

"Ah, yes, I know. What if I risk, and it is all for nothing?"

"It is never all for nothing if it is done for love of God."

"But how can I know if God wants me to risk everything as Jesus Christ did, to become totally vulnerable? Aren't there times when it would be only foolishness?"

"Yes. That is why Our Lord's guidance in everything you do must be sought always. But what is important is that you are willing, even anxious, to risk for His sake."

"You mean, take the chance I could lose everything materially, emotionally, and spiritually?!"

"You will never lose everything spiritually. Those who lose everything spiritually are those who will not risk. But yes, not just risking the chance of losing everything, but be guaranteed that you will lose everything that is important to you except the love and honor of the One Who loves and created you. And because you will always have these most precious of all gifts, you will have everything else."

"This reminds me of the verse from Scripture, "Seek ye first the Kingdom of God ... and all these things shall be added unto you.""

The lovely angel is warmly amused. "Everything you have written and will write in conversations with us is based in Scripture, and is there in some form. But Our Lord has a strong wish that it be said in many different ways, that clarity be given, that hearts might be touched. His love for His children is so great that He will never cease in trying to express that love for you in as many ways as you can receive it. He never wearies of trying to let you know of His love, because His love for you never wearies."

"This touches me so ... I should think Our Lord would grow weary of it all sometimes."

"He does grow weary of what you do to each other and that you have turned your faces, so many of your faces, away from Him. But He never wearies of you. You are His beloved children, whatever you do."

"You and the other angels have spoken to me in our conversations again and again of the love of God for us, and you keep putting it in yet different ways that touch me in new ways."

"Our Lord wishes that your heart should answer His love in as many ways as it can. The way that pleases Him most is your expressions of love for one another. This opening, forming, turning, changing of your hearts happens through your everyday lives, in grief of the deepest kind and sorrow of the deepest kind, and joy of the deepest kind, in ordinary moments and in memorable moments. This preparation of your spirit to give and receive love in many and beautiful ways is the reason for your sometimes very difficult and painful, but very short, lives here. To the degree that your hearts open will be the degree that you will be open to the love and the gifts of Our Lord, now and for all eternity to come."

"This is an incredible task we have, and a responsibility too."

"It is. But all the angels of Heaven will help you open your hearts at a word of request from you to Our Lord, and all the saints pray for you that you may open your hearts to the fullest to love — especially in painful and impossible seeming circumstances."

"How do the angels help us and how do the prayers of the saints help us?"

"Our dedication to serving God flows out to you because of the graciousness of God. Through your desire for it, it becomes more and more your own until it is inseparable from you and us and from our Lord Himself. This is how prayers, the grace of God, your own will and desire, and the actions that are the fruits of your love and of all love come together to give God glory."

"This is incredible."

"It may seem complicated. It is only necessary that you love, only that you love."

"I have been talking to you for so long, and I have not asked your name. May I know it?"

"JOY IN THE LOVE OF GOD."

"What a beautiful name! Every time one of you tells me your name, I think there must be a limit to how many names Our Lord could come up with, but your names are all so beautiful."

"It is because we are all named for Our Lord and for His love that our names are beautiful. It is He who is the source of all true beauty."

"Yes. I can feel that more and more as you and the others speak to me."

"You are blessed, little one. Do not forget that as long as you have the desire to serve Our Lord, you will. You will never be perfect in this life, but it is not perfection that He asks of you.

It is a willing heart. If you have a willing heart, He can accomplish all things in you that will bring you and many others to rejoice in His Kingdom for all eternity — and this is truly all that matters.

I will leave you now, little One. I petitioned before Our Lord to be allowed to speak with you, and now I will give thanks that I was allowed to do so."

"I am amazed that you should think of this as a favor."

"One of the joys Our Lord has prepared for you and all His children in Heaven is a greater understanding of just how precious each of you is to Him. All of you are loved by Our Lord and the angels and saints in ways that you cannot understand yet. It is our great delight to see your joy as Our Lord reveals this to you, both here and in Heaven. Peace now, little one. Rest well in Our Lord's love."

"May Our Lord bless you, kind angel. I feel your love surrounding me like a pair of loving arms."

"Peace, little one. Peace."

# Chapter 27
# PATIENT WORK OF GOD

Sunday, May 13, 1990

I am near the end of a second day of pain. Glory be to God that it is lessening. It is strange to thank God with one breath that I am better, and thank Him with the next that I have been given the pain to offer for the souls. One night as my head and eyes were particularly hurting, I felt sure I could not go on. What possible good could come of my strange, unsought offering?

I lay there feeling physically torn and mentally in anguish over my inactivity and feelings of vulnerability and helplessness. My Guardian Angel gently told me, "Look for a moment to see the souls your pain is offered for as prayers." I saw both darkness and light and, slowly out of the darkness about every ten seconds, hesitantly stumbled a form. Often its hands were reaching out as if to feel its way. "This is what your pain, offered as prayers, is doing," I was told. "The pain may stop if you truly wish." I continued to offer. Perhaps someone is praying for me too. It is a comfort to know that Our Lord God values our whole lives as treasured gifts when we give them to Him; especially does He value our pain.

Thursday, July 12

Last night I was very happy because I got home about 7:30 in the evening rather than at 9:00 or 10:00. It is out early and home very late these days. I was so exhausted I could hardly move or think. When the light became bright and I had tested the presence, I was rather dismayed. I wondered if I would be asked to write our conversation. It is not that I did not want to write, but that I felt so exhausted and drained I wondered if I could. I also knew I was too tired to think straight, and I thought I might be too tired even to talk or ask questions.

The angel asked me to get ready to write. I did this. I think I was asked by the angel if I wanted these conversations to continue because

I lead such a draining life with my work and my counseling, as well as my family responsibilities. But, oh yes, I do want the conversations to continue if this is what Our Lord wishes. I am amazed by it all—and most amazed by the kindness and love of God. The angel began, "Your heart cries out for love, but you have so little trust that Our Lord God knows your needs and is filling them in the ways that are best and most loving for you."

"I know this is true. I feel ashamed that I don't trust God completely, especially with the pains and desires of my heart in wanting to give and to receive love."

"You are not alone in distrusting. Very few of Our Lord's children have trusted so completely."

"I've asked one of you angels before about trust and how to have more of it. I still seem to have so much trouble. Before I ask you about this, may I please know your name?"

"PATIENT WORK OF GOD."

"Another beautiful name! Are you an angel of patient work, then?"

"All of our names reflect what we do in service to God and for you, to bring you closer to Our Lord."

"Why is it that you speak to me of trusting God with the things that I seem to have the hardest time over?"

"Because it is not even your heart, with its fears and wishes for love and to give love, that is the deepest thing you will learn to trust God with."

"Please. What is it then?"

"It is the trust that allows you to wait in quiet patience, knowing that your imperfections also give Our Lord glory, and therefore your willingness to bear with them with joy and without blame for yourself while, at the same time, striving to overcome them. To do this, you must know whom it is that created you. You must let time and love bind your heart to Our Lord's eternal Heart. Your great joy is not only that this will come to pass, but it is also in giving the Lord of all things praise as it slowly but perceptibly does happen, though hardly ever at the rate you would prefer."

"Yes. You and the other angels have spoken to me about impatience. Is impatience a sin?"

"Impatience itself is not a sin if it is impatience to serve Our Lord's children, and therefore to serve Our Lord. But it is a sin when distrust and fear are at its root. But there is no blame for you from Our Lord for your impatience unless it harms you and others—and then it is not blame that you bear, but the pain of consequences.

"But the Lord Who loves you and Who truly knows you has a kindness and a tolerance you could not believe if you even knew the tiniest part of it — a gentleness and kindness for His children who must struggle towards this patience of heart which has nothing of the burden of a beast's submission and lack of choice in it. It has in it only joy that what the Lord of all things, the One Who suffers for His people as they suffer, that what He is bringing to fruit in you will be good fruit because of the loving Hand of the Tiller and the willingness in joy of the tree, yourself, to bring about His glory."

I was interrupted by a phone call at this point, answered, and asked the caller to call back in a few minutes. The angel continued, "You are more patient and loyal than you know. You think of yourself as being such an impatient person, but you are slowly coming to know of God's trustworthiness, that He is truly faithful to His little ones, and that He hears all prayers. You have been shown by His acts of kindness to you that are tuned directly to your heart, and your heart alone, that the love of the God of the universe is a personal love for each of His children. It is only because of this personal love that it was possible for the whole universe to come into being. Without His love for the smallest and weakest of His children, how could care have been taken in the creation of anything? That is something many of your theologians and great thinkers do not understand."

"I had not understood it either, and I will have to think about it and ponder it. I still marvel that I, of all people, should have been blessed like this."

"All people are blessed. It is in their refusal to open their hearts to their bountiful blessings that causes a limit on what they can and do receive.

"You in your time believe that circumstances of birth and family and situation determine happiness. But you will find loving and happy hearts even in the worst situations. Happiness is not ignoring pain or in being oblivious to one's own suffering or the suffering of others. Happiness is giving thanks for what is loving and good and in trying as best you can, to resist evil and slights, and those things which will tear your heart out and devour it, which are the servants of the Evil One. It is a refusal to let these things conquer your soul in order that you may bring it safely, and with joy, to the One Who created you."

"Thank you for telling me these things. Will I ever share them with others?"

(Smiling), "They are the simplest things, the things which have been told to Our Lord's children down through the ages. But they are the things which must be repeated over and over again in new ways in order that hearts may open. And yes, you will share them. But it will be in Our Lord's time and with those He wishes. Stony hearts know only how to ridicule. Hearts which have been wounded and broken and yet are still open to faith and love will bleed tears of joy at these words. They will know and be reassured once more that there is a Lord of Life and Joy Who has not forgotten them and Who will always welcome them if they acknowledge themselves as His people.

When you acknowledge yourself as one of His people, this is not done for His sake but for yours; though it is Our Lord's joy that you should do this. It is only by doing this that your heart opens to love and happiness, regardless of what the world does or does not give you."

"I am so awed and joyful that my Lord allows these conversations. They amaze me so, and that He should allow this amazes me."

"He has allowed many things in your time which have not been allowed before—and all because of His love for you. You are blessed, little one, because you are slowly learning to accept with joy the gifts God wishes to give you. It is because of the prayers of the Queen of Heaven, the Blessed Lady who is fully human and who pleases God in all things, that much grace has been given to you and to all people. Glory, glory to God, and honor and joy be to the Queen of Our Lord's Mercy that all this should be.

"You do not understand how much your love could accomplish if your heart were open. Please open your heart, and know that the Lord of Love will not deny your request that your love not be poured out in vain. Your love will bear good and bountiful fruit if you allow the Lord of all Love to be the tiller of the field of your heart."

"Thank you. I sing glory to God too, blessed angel. Thank you."

"Are you willing that these conversations with us should continue, little one?"

"Yes. Oh yes, if Our Lord wishes it."

"Our Lord wishes it. Be patient. His timing is not yours. His ways are not yours. But His heart is yours. Our Lord's peace is with you, little one, and His grace flows out to you abundantly, and will sustain you in all that is important that you should accomplish. Trust Him in this also, and your heart will know the peace it craves. Peace, little one, peace.

"The light you see is the light Our Lord has given me, the light of love which is carried by all those who serve God or wish to serve Him and therefore serve Him by their desire.

"Please open your heart to the love I have been granted to give you tonight, little one. It is a singular honor for me to give you this gift. Peace now, little one. Peace."

Though I had been completely exhausted and drained before this conversation, afterwards I felt an exultation and quiet joy that made me want to sit and praise God all night, to smile at HIM and open myself to His smile. I felt so full of quiet, deep joy, and so at peace.

The light has been bright as I have copied this conversation from the scratch paper into my journal, sitting here at my desk at Texas Tech University. I live in the outward appearance of life as if everything were unchanged. But inwardly, in my heart, everything is changing, and so all outward things of my life are changing also.

# THE LIGHT OF LOVE

# Chapter 28
# CLEAR JUDGMENT OF GOD

The summer of 1990 was an eventful one for our family. For people living on a budget in which all the money coming in usually went out by the end of the month, we did a great deal of travelling. Though Eileen and Miriam would not be graduating from High School for another year, my parents gave them an advance graduation present. They gave them the price of tickets to Europe and Eurorail passes. They travelled around Europe with three other teenagers. They had little money for extras. They told me later that to eat fruit became a treat, and they mainly lived on peanut butter sandwiches. But they saw the great sights of Europe, and had the adventure of a lifetime. They spent their seventeenth birthday in London.

I had the unexpected opportunity to go to upstate New York to meet Father George L., a friend and translator of Mr. Josyp Terelya. Mr. Terelya is a leader in the Ukrainian Catholic Church. The Church has its own rites, but is under the Holy Father. It has a special love and loyalty to the Holy Father.

Mr. Terelya had spent a great deal of his life in communist camps for the sake of the faith. He was finally expelled from the Soviet Union. Before this event however, he had the privilege of being one of the over three hundred thousand people who witnessed Our Lady's apparitions in Hrushiv, Ukraine.

The figure of a woman began to appear over a ruined chapel in the little village of Hrushiv a year from the very moment of the disaster at Chernobyl. For several weeks, hundreds of thousands of people traveled from all over the Soviet Union to see her. What is unique about this apparition is that there are no visionaries. All of the people saw her, and most of them heard her, including KGB agents.

She pleaded with them for the conversion of the Soviet Union. She said that if Russia does not acknowledge her Son Jesus Christ as King, there will be a third world war. While in upstate New York, I talked not only to Mr. Terelya, who now lives with his family in Toronto, Canada, but also to other Ukrainians who saw and heard Our Lady at Hrushiv, and have since come to the United States.

Many conversions have taken place in the Soviet Union because of these apparitions. People have traveled in groups throughout Ukraine, spreading the word of the apparitions and exhorting their fellow citizens to a true conversion of heart, an unwavering dedication to Our Lord, and a devotion to the rosary as the most powerful prayer against Satan.

When I returned from Elmira, my work was waiting for me. I lived at Tech. Often I thought of the radio piece which had been broadcast quite widely a few years before, "Do you know where your children are at midnight?" I very often not only did not know where my children were, but did not even know what country they were in. There were some very anxious times for me.

Journal Excerpt:

Sunday, July 22, 1990

My dear sweethearts called from Venice this morning. They are growing up so fast on this trip. I have resolved to sit down and write in this journal tomorrow despite the work I have. The blessings and the love God is giving me and my family must be recorded.

But for now, I have another conversation to copy down. Yesterday I was busy washing the piles of laundry Miriam and Eileen had left scattered around the study room. Two friends came over and worked hard clearing the weeds in my backyard which had reached waist high proportions. They were more like trees than weeds.

Today has been quiet. I knew that if I did not rest, I would not be able physically to face the week. I am glad for this quiet time.

The light became beautiful and bright this morning, I tested the presence, and was asked to get ready to write. This is a different kind of conversation from any I have had so far. I wonder what Our Lord has in mind, but I wonder less than I have done before now. I am much less anxious about everything, not so much afraid of my unworthiness. So I am unworthy. There is more glory to God in this than there would be if I were a saint. I am, as the angel PATIENT WORK OF GOD said, slowly learning to accept the gifts God wishes to give me and, as he said so beautifully, learning that God is trustworthy. I hope I can be trustworthy too, with all my heart I hope this. Let me not write or do or say anything contrary to what my Lord wishes. May I understand clearly what is being said to me by the angels, and write it accurately.

Occasionally I have a difficult time with some of the things that are said, especially in the last conversation. I work with people who have been so damaged by their family and/or societal backgrounds, and the pain that has marked them for life seems to be very much beyond their control. And yet, there is hope in our choices, hope if there is no blame. I pray that the statement by the angel that happiness is not dependent on situation or family may never be used to blame or abuse. It was not meant that way at all.

This is the conversation today. The angel began, "You are known fully to God even in your daily lives. There is nothing that you do, feel or think that Our Lord does not know. This could be frightening to you, but it need not be so. Along with sorrow and sometimes anger at your actions which hurt you and others, there is also a tenderness and compassion for you and an understanding of you and your limitations from Our Lord that is beyond your comprehension for now. But you must know that you will be held to account."

"What is it that we will be held to account for?"

"You are held to account especially for cruelty. When you intentionally disregard another of God's children, when you do not at least ask yourself, "How would I feel if such and such were said to me or done to me?"; then you decrease your awareness of God. The love and tenderness you ask Our Lord to show to you is decreased in your own heart because of your refusal to show love and mercy yourself. When your own heart is closed to showing love and mercy, how can it be open to receive it?"

"Yes, I think I understand that ... May I please know your name?"

"CLEAR JUDGMENT OF GOD."

"This is a different kind of conversation than I have had with any of you angels so far. You are not just speaking now of the love of God for us, but of judgment too. I'm confused about judgment. Are we condemned by God, then? Have I misunderstood? I understood from the other angels that we condemn ourselves."

"You *do* condemn yourselves. You want freedom to decide for your-selves what you will do and how you will be, but you are not willing to take the responsibility that goes along with this freedom. Many of you, Our Lord's children, want freedom only so that you can pursue the lives you have decided will make you the most happy, and often these lives you have chosen seek only material gains and pleasures — all of which you justify. You ask for tolerance and understanding from others in the pursuit of these pleasures. This understanding is a false open-mindedness wrongly equated with love. Then you cry and complain because of the consequences of what you have done.

"God's judgment is a judgment of freedom. It is a judgment which respects your choices. It also grants you the ability to change your mind and choose Our Lord's way."

"I am confused about the teachings of some Christian sects nowa-days that only people who "accept Christ as their personal Savior" will go to Heaven or "be saved.""

"Only those who accept the Way of Christ and follow the teach-ings of the Lord of the Universe, whether early or late, will be able to stand before Our Lord in Heaven. You talk so much in your time.

"You talk, talk, talk about the teachings of Christ. When will you concentrate on yourself and live them? This is the Way Our Lord Jesus Christ was speaking of. Think also of what has been told you by Our Lord that you must take the boulder* out of your own eye before you can see clearly to remove the mote in your neighbor's.

"Why do you spend so much time pointing fingers at others? When will the weight of your own actions and inactions press on your heart so heavily that you will want a change in your own heart, and plead for it before the Father? It is only because of this constant desire that there have been some among you who have become one with Our Lord Jesus Christ, and therefore followed His Way. This desire to be one with God

---

[*NOTE: CLEAR JUDGMENT OF GOD used the word "boulder" rather than the word "log" which is used in the New Testament transla-tion I have. When he said "mote", I wrote it as "moat", thinking there was a meaning to moat which I did not know. I searched my cassette tape dictionary, and found that "mote" is an old word meaning "speck." Why these words were used, I do not know.]

is His Way, and takes all that you are, all that you are to become.

"How can you say you wish to be one with God while you condemn His children, of whatever race or religion they may be? Hypocrisy is rampant among those calling themselves followers of the Christ. They use religion only for their own ends, to feel secure, to feel superior.

"Woe to them when Our Lord God asks, 'And when I was hungry, did you give Me to eat? And when I was thirsty, did you give Me to drink?' He does not just speak here of physical food. All around you there are people crying out for nourishment of the spirit, for words of encouragement, for a pair of arms to hold them.

"Do not, please do not waste anymore time in your hypocrisies of superiority. Remember that you gain superiority only by humility and through love and service. If you are truly serving and are truly humble, you no longer desire superiority. The labor of love is all consuming. You have no more time or energy or desire to point fingers at others when you are laboring in love. The needs of others cry out to you. Your own need, the cry of your own heart to be one with God and to serve Him in any small way you can, fills your being. All else falls away and is irrelevant. You are then in the Kingdom of Our Lord Jesus Christ, and the Kingdom is within you.

"I and all the angels and saints of Heaven and the Queen of Heaven, The Lady of True Love, beg you to try to understand this and stop wasting time pointing fingers. There is so little time left for each of you."

"I am amazed by all this. I don't know what to say except thank you."

"It is Our Lord's wish that you, His beloved children, get your priorities in order. If the message of the Gospels were truly followed by those who most strongly profess them, Our Lord's Kingdom would be with you here on earth, and His will would be done here, as it is in Heaven. Stop pointing fingers. Stop judging each other. Stop deciding who will or will not stand before Our Lord. Those who truly love now and who have dedicated their lives to serving in quiet simplicity are already in His Kingdom. Most of you would not recognize them even if you were told who they are.

"Concentrate on yourself. Ask for grace that you may live the kind of life Our Lord calls you to live. The grace to do this is available for each of you in quantities which are immeasurable.

"You are growing tired, little one. This dictation has been hard for you. You are blessed. Please trust that you will be guided and protected as you write. Your consecration and dedication to all the angels has consequences you do not understand yet. Remember that with each willing heart, a new door opens through which many come rejoicing."

"I want very much to have a willing heart. I feel so closed to love sometimes and, I am sad to admit it, closed to you angels sometimes too."

"Peace, little one. You fret too much. Trust that Our Lord knows what He is doing with you and with all His children. You do not have to understand everything. Understand only that your love is necessary. The love of each one of you, Our Lord's children, is very necessary for full redemption."

"What about those who do not give their love?"

"More love is then needed from others. Peace, little one, peace. You are too weary to continue. Rest now."

# Chapter 29
# TEACHINGS ON THE FIFTH JOYFUL MYSTERY: THE FINDING OF JESUS IN THE TEMPLE

The Feast of Our Lady's Assumption was special, with thousands of people coming again to Saint John Neumann from all over the country. I had the joy of putting together a Scriptural Rosary book to be used on the Feast. I had to go into the Scriptures to find the appropriate texts (see appendix A). I have always been slightly impatient while praying and meditating upon the fifth joyful mystery: Our Lord Jesus is found in the Temple teaching the doctors and scribes. When I came to this mystery, I sat down in some frustration and prayed, "Please teach me about this mystery. I have always felt awkward meditating about it. I don't understand why it is included as a mystery along with such amazing happenings as the Annunciation of the Angel Gabriel to the Blessed Mother, or Our Dear Lord's Passion and Resurrection. Why is it here?"

My Dear Angel began quietly to ask me questions, "When Our Lord was twelve years old, what did the Holy Family go to Jerusalem to do?"

"They went for the Feast of the Passover."

"What happened?"

"They sacrificed a lamb as a recompense for sin, as was the custom."

"So that lamb was a symbol of the true Lamb of God. And immediately after that, Our Lord disappeared. His Mother thought He was with His earthly Father when they left early the next morning. His earthly Father thought He was with His Mother. They traveled for a day. This was the first day. When they discovered He was not with either of them, they returned to Jerusalem to seek Him. This journey back to Jerusalem was the second day. On the third day, they found Him in the Temple, teaching the learned of Israel.

"So for three long days of pain, He was being sought. How long was He in the tomb, counting days in the manner of the Israelites?"

"Three days also." The parallels between this pre–enactment of the Sacrifice of Our Lord, His absence for three days while in the tomb from those He loves and who love Him, are unmistakable. But I have never seen these parallels before, nor have I ever heard of them spoken of in a sermon or homily.

I thought of the verses in the Book of Revelations: 5:5-6 in which Saint John bewails the apparent lack of anyone worthy to "open the scroll and break its seven seals." Then he looks up and, as the New English Bible has it, sees a "Lamb with the marks of slaughter upon Him." The Lamb is surrounded by the elders and the four creatures. The wording seems to be an echo of the Blessed Mother and Saint Joseph finding Jesus sitting among the doctors of the Law.

I thought for a long time. This pre–enactment of a prophecy of Jesus's Sacrifice on Golgotha, His absence from those He loves for three days, and His return to them would have been obvious to Jewish Christians.

"Then," I thought, "Our Lord says to the Blessed Mother, "did you not know I would be about My Father's business?" I have heard this verse misused against Our Lady, but how wrongly! It must have been she herself who told Saint Luke about this one incident from Jesus's childhood. I was beginning to understand its importance.

Then the Scriptures say, "But they did not understand what He meant." What was it they did not understand? I had thought they did not understand that He was to be teaching and healing, going among His people. But surely they would know this was coming. Of course, they both knew of His divinity, His miraculous conception and birth. Perhaps they guessed at His Passion, but would not have known the details. This quiet pre–enactment of the Passion would be something they would not fully understand until later. And Jesus's continually giving Himself to His people in the Holy Eucharist: that is His Father's business, that He be the high Priest according to the order of Melchizedek.

He died once and for ALL as Saint Paul says. I thought with a new understanding and joy that He had died once on Golgotha for all of us, who would accept His gift and He is now going about His Father's business in the presentation of His Sacrifice to the Father in the Holy Mass. And every time I attend Mass, I participate and am present at His eternal, once and for all, Sacrifice.

I felt humble, realizing what a joyous mystery is the fifth joyful mystery of the rosary.

# THE LIGHT OF LOVE

# Chapter 30
# "WHO IS LIKE UNTO GOD?"

It was as I began compiling this chapter that MY SPIRITUAL DI
RECTOR, Father John Walch, told me the meaning of "Michael."
This question of awe and reverence, a query of love that is also a name,
rings out like a rallying cry. Perhaps it was a rallying cry for the angels
who remained loyal to their Creator.

"Who is like unto God?" This question is the essence of Saint
Michael's challenge to Lucifer's arrogance. As recorded below, I was
privileged to hear of this confrontation between Saint Michael and
Lucifer from Saint Michael himself. His ongoing battle with Lucifer in
which we are now defended is a battle for souls. To put Saint Michael's
question to Lucifer another way, what soul has made itself? And if we
are created by a being transcending our human limitations, who are we
to think we can make Lucifer's fatal mistake to believe we are "Like
unto God?" And yet, how many share in Lucifer's ultimate arrogance
and say, "I am God."

"Who is like unto God?" This query which is also the name of the
Prince of the Heavenly Host, cannot be asked in awe, love and respect
by anyone who has succumbed to the ultimate temptation of Lucifer:
to worship oneself. Self-preoccupation is the disease of our time. I pray
that the conversation I was privileged to have with Saint Michael —
this whole book in fact — may be an antidote for this fatal malady, this
cancer of the soul.

Journal excerpt:

Monday, August 27, 1990

Last night rather late as I was waiting up for Eileen, I turned around and
the light was so bright I could hardly believe it. I tested the presence.
All was well. The presence was so majestic and strong, but also very
protective and loving. Despite this, I was frightened because of the great
power and immensity I felt. It was Saint Michael the Archangel. I grabbed

my little Braille 'n Speak, a little mini computer on which I have been working, mostly trying to figure out how to use it. I didn't have my Braille writer or paper near. How amusing that such a conversation should be written on a little Braille computer, or on a computer at all, for that matter. But, of course, Our Lord is so kind.

After I knew it was Saint Michael I sat almost frozen, not knowing what to say or do. Then I began to shake. I could feel his quiet kindness, but I was still frightened. I think he purposefully waited for me to collect myself. I think that he waited for me to start speaking out of kindness for me. I said, "I should be on my knees to you, that Our Lord would allow this."

"Not to me, never to me. My Lord has raised me from the lowest of His servants, so it is He Who is great. That is something you do not realize, you and all Our Lord's children, that if you have any honor or greatness at all it comes from the Lord Who created honor and greatness in the first place."

"I am having so much trouble with this little computer. Would you like me to get a brailler?" (I was having trouble writing the text of the con-versation.)

Saint Michael is amused. "No. You must avoid the danger as much as possible, though. This is the danger of depending on things for what you want, and what you are trying to do."

"Why is this dangerous?"

"Because you begin to believe it is you who is doing what needs to be done, not realizing you are given the gift of things by God — even such things as computers — to help you accomplish great things.

But who is it that gave you hands? Who is it that gave you a mind? Who is it that gave you, most important of all, a heart capable of loving? No devices you have made make any difference except in how you use them."

"Saint Michael, why is it that you are telling me this? You are the Prince of the Heavenly Host."

"Because your distance as a people from the ways of God has become so great that all of us, the angels and saints of Heaven must, in whatever way is allowed by Our Lord, tell you, pray for you, in any way possible, plead with you to come to your beginnings; to the things that are now laughed at by many but which, if lost, will cause the death of your race in a physical sense, but more importantly will destroy your souls."

"This is very serious, but I am still amazed that you who are the Warrior Prince of the Heavenly Host fighting against Satan would come to me."

"When you were consecrated, you called upon me to be your sponsor, your protector, your guide. I have been deeply interested in everything you are doing since then, Pat. I am interested in you as a person. This is not separate from you as a warrior who has been called by the Almighty Lord to help us fight the great battles which are to come."

"I don't think like this, Saint Michael. I have always sort of prided myself on being a modern woman. This is all so amazing. People who know me will know I couldn't just sit here and write this. How will they believe, the ones who don't know me, that this is not at all my style?"

"Many will not believe. But, remember, it is because of the consequences for them if they were to believe."

"The consequences for them?"

"You yourself have had a hard time believing. You laughed, saying it would be easier to be crazy than to have these things happening to you. But you wanted to serve Our Lord. Also, your amazement and joy were great when you began to believe.

"But others have too much at stake, are too much invested in this world. What would they have to give up? How would they have to change if they were to believe that this world is temporary, is only like a tiny flicker of life before true life begins? How would this then change their lives? Many are not willing to understand this and feel it with their hearts."

"What will happen to them?"

"Some will come to know that what they have claimed as reality is not reality. When this happens, many will be frightened. Some know it already in their deepest hearts, that this is not what truly matters: this life that is so precious to them. It is only insofar as it matters in eternity that everything matters at all."

"Saint Michael, why does God allow Satan so much power over us?"

"Our Lord abides by His own rules of freedom and love. If He were to break them even once, they would be meaningless."

"I don't understand."

"Lucifer was given great power and honor at the beginning of the creation of all things. Great good and great love could have come out of this gift of Our Lord's. But Lucifer chose otherwise. Our Lord now must abide by the decision that was made at the beginning to give Lucifer this great power, though it could be taken from him. It will eventually be taken from him, but that must be in Our Lord's time and through love only. This, for Our Lord, takes time and heartache."

"Why was power given at the beginning to Lucifer if Our Lord God knew what he would do with it?"

"Why is power given to you, Pat? Why is power given to each of you, Our Lord's children? Why are you given freedom so that whatever you do, however you use it, you will be responsible for the fruits. They will be your fruits. If they are fruits of pain and sorrow, fruits of evil, you are held accountable because of the power you were given to bear good fruit, and you did not. If they are good fruits of kindness and love, you are drawn closer and closer into the heart of God."

"But Lucifer has so much more power than we, and can do so much more damage."

"His continued power is permitted that your love might be greater."

"This is hard for me, Saint Michael, because I see so much pain and evil in my work. I've seen it in my own life with betrayals and unhappiness. I've hurt over it in myself and in others. Can it ever be justified?"

He says tenderly to me with great gentleness, "No, dearest little one, it can never be justified. But it is the only condition under which freedom to grow toward God, or choose not to (grow towards Him), could exist. There was truly no other way. If there had been another way, Our Lord would have taken it. It is the hard way, the way of sorrow, that must be followed; the way of painful struggling toward the light."

"Have you angels ever had to do that?"

"Not in the same way you do, dearest one. But the temptation to follow Lucifer that we all faced was so great. He could and did make it seem so logical that God's way was crazy, that His plan for creation made no sense. 'How,' he asked us, 'could we think for a moment that suffering and sorrow could bring any good? Let it be everyone, each looking out for (as you say in your time), looking out for number one.'

"Even with the love Our Lord had poured out upon us, this made sense to many of us. Lucifer showed us a vision of Christ crucified and jeered, 'See! This is the King you would follow, a King who has no followers, who does not raise a finger to protect Himself against those who will torture Him to death. What kind of God is this?'

"He asked us, 'If you open yourself to love, what will happen to you but that you will be hurt? Look at this: The God of the Universe will come to earth to dwell among the lowest of the creatures who could knowingly praise Him, and what will they do but kill Him? And He knows beforehand that they will do this!'

"He jeered, calling Our Lord Christ many abominable names which I will not repeat to you, but which you will hear someday from his followers.

"He cried to us to be sensible, to think for ourselves, not to be blinded (excuse me, little one, I mean no offense to you), stupid followers who serve without question, who love with open hearts to the point of seeming destruction. He asked us how we could trust a God who could ask us to do such a thing. Was that God concerned for us at all, that He would ask it?

"Was He, for that matter, thinking of His own safety in what you would call in your time 'a healthy way?' No. What fools we would be to throw in our lot, our existence, our lives for all eternity with such a One."

"Did anyone answer Lucifer?"

Saint Michael is embarrassed. "I did. I asked Lucifer if he was capable of creating himself, if he was capable of creating the angels to whom he was speaking. I said that the wisdom of Our Lord could at times seem puzzling, but that was only because we are not God. I said that the Divine Love which had created us would not destroy us. Our Lord had made it clear to us that He is not a God of whim. He does not play with the creation He loves.

"I called on all the angels to stand firm. I said if God chose to be a man on earth, this would show His greatness and glory more than anything else. How could anyone, Lucifer included, say He is not one with you and with all that He loves? How, I asked the others, could we not trust a Lord Who loves even the lowest of those creatures which could knowingly praise Him that much — we who had been so gifted to be in His presence continually?"

"How is it possible that all this could take place in God's presence?"

"It was by Our Lord's wish that it should take place in His presence. Lucifer is now an enemy of the light for which he was named. This began when he thought he could hide from God, could speak with us secretly. Our Lord knew what was in Lucifer's mind and gave permission for him to appeal to all the angels publicly. This, my dearest little one, is the extent of Our Lord's love — that all who serve Him should do so of their own free will."

"May I know what happened then?"

"You have been told that one third of the angels of Heaven then sided with Lucifer, and the great battle began. But before it began, as one of my Angels has already told you, we who remained faithful were told that it was now that we must make an unbreakable commitment to Our Lord to serve Him. If we could not do this, we must go.*1 This service was not given for His sake, but for yours."

"For ours?"

"Yes. We are the servants of your souls, the servants of Our Lord who try in every way we can that Our Lord permits to guide your souls without interfering with your freedom. It is our desire beyond all things to guide your souls into the Kingdom of Our Lord.

"When we gave up our freedom to rebel, we were told this was asked of us because of Our Lord's love for you, His children, who would need true and faithful guardians."

"What about the angels who are not guardian angels?"

"They serve in other ways. All of us serve. It is our joy."

"Why has Our Lord allowed this conversation, Saint Michael? I am just me. I am so ordinary."

"Because you and all people are faced with the same choice we had to make, but for you it goes on through your whole life here. This may seem like a long time to you, but we smile at how short it is — though we feel compassion for you when you suffer because of what seems to you to be a long time."

"But, please, why now — this conversation, I mean?"

"Because the intensity grows, the battle is joined. Lucifer will not rest until he has proved himself right, so he will not rest.

"So many things in your time confuse you. Let nothing confuse you any longer. Make your choice again and again and again for Our Lord. Lucifer cares for no one but Lucifer."

"I don't know what to say. There are so many questions I have wanted to ask, but I can't think of any now."

"You will ask in the future, dearest one, and Our Lord will allow the answers He will allow.

Peace now."

"May I ask you another question?"

"Yes, little one."

"Why have you called me Pat? None of the others have called me by (my given) name."*2

"Because if I or any of the other angels were to call you by your true name, you or any other of Our Lord's children, you could not believe what you would then know about yourself. You would see the love of God for you at the time of your creation. You would see it now as you grow towards Our Lord. Those of you who love Our Lord would be filled with such joy that you could not remain a soul in a body, but would come immediately back to where you belong, back to Our Lord's heart."

"Oh, that is so beautiful. That is so beautiful. But, I mean, why did you call me by the name given me here?"

"You are maturing more and more. I and the other angels of Heaven will call you to serve. You are one of God's little ones, as we have said, but you are also stronger than you or anyone else knows.

"That is why Our Lord has called you to serve with us to bring souls to Him; to take them from Lucifer. This calling is not just a call to bring souls to Him, but to take them out of Lucifer's grasp before they are lost forever."

"What does this mean, please?"

"It is too soon for you to know this fully yet, little one. You are not ready."

"Will you stay with me a little longer?"

"I will stay. I and all my Angels will be coming and going here on earth now in these times. We will be protecting and shielding loving hearts, and praying for hardened hearts. This is a work that may sound simple to you: unimportant. It is what will make all the difference as to whether your souls will stand before Our Lord, or will not. Please join us in prayer. All people of all faiths must be united in these prayers."

"May I ask about what is going on now? How can we unite to pray for this when there is so much hatred between religions?"

"All who love will be spoken to as they can understand."

"That is comforting. May I ask about what is happening in the Middle East now?"

Saint Michael is in deep sorrow. He is grieving. He does not answer me. Then he says, "Pray for all who have anything to do with it.

Pray for all the leaders, even those you consider your enemies. Pray for those who kill innocent people. Only love can ever make a difference."*3

"I will try."

"Your trying is all Our Lord asks. Bless you, dearest little one. I will be close to you all of your earthly life. Let your heart not fear to serve your family, your brothers and sisters who are all Our Lord's children (all people.) Remember, Our Lord never requests anything of you without good reason."

"How can I know if it is our Lord's request?"

"You may test the fruits. You will never be chastised for testing the fruits."

"Thank you, Saint Michael. Bless you. Thank You, Lord, for allowing this conversation. I have a lot to think over, and a great deal to pray about."

Saint Michael laughs. It is a beautiful sound. "You do, dearest one, you do. But all you, and all others have to remember is the love and respect of Our Lord. Peace now, dearest one. I will stop now. Our Lord's peace is with you."

---

[NOTES:

*1 In a previous conversation, my guardian angel had told me when I asked him if the angels could rebel again that they had made an unbreakable commitment not to do so. He did not elaborate on this any further. He told me during this conversation that there is a favorite "Heavenly joke" which he wanted to share with me. He said that it caused great amusement in Our Lord's Kingdom to realize that no matter how much pain and sin Satan causes, there is one thing he cannot change. They are further amused at Satan's anger and frustration because he knows he cannot change it either, no matter how much he deludes himself or others. The thorn in Satan's side is this: God made him, he did not make God. There is nothing he can do to deny his creation.

*2 I did not remember at the time of this conversation that other angels had called me by my given name.

*3 As the Gulf War intensified, I asked my Guardian Angel about it. The only thing he said was, "It is the beginning of the beginning."]

# Chapter 31
# EARTHLY MATTERS AND
# ANGELIC LOVE

I thought after the conversation with Saint Michael that there would be a quick succession of other conversations, but there was not. My Guardian Angel spoke to me quite regularly during this time, but it was about little, personal things. A this happened, I felt myself growing closer and closer to him as a real friend. I began to know his character traits more intimately as one would gradually learn more about a friend as time goes on. This in itself was a gift to me, but I also believe it was done because I still suffered so from doubts. I did not doubt any longer that this was happening to me, but I could not get past the hurdle of, "Why me, of all people? Why not someone much more saintly, much more kind?"

My own shortcomings became sharper and more painful to me. I felt sometimes as if I were already in Purgatory. By His grace and His grace alone, I had grown closer to God. But now, as with those in Purgatory, things I would not have even thought twice about or simply pushed back with a guilty twinge bothered me. I did not think of Heaven or Hell. I felt badly in the immediate context of my relationship with my Lord right here on earth, right now, and I wanted as little as possible to separate us. I had had a small glimpse of the greatness and goodness of God, and I wanted to imitate that love and greatness of heart as much as possible. Things of the world such as recognition, notoriety, regard of others — I still prized them, but less and less so.

During this time, I began to see everything more and more in the light of an imitation of my Lord, Jesus Christ. In the back of my mind was the quiet question, "What would Jesus do?" or "What would Blessed Mary, the Mother of God, advise me to say?"

I was still not allowed to read anything which might have been helpful in the search to grow closer to my beloved Lord, aside from Holy Scripture, and this was at times frustrating. I was hungry to read theology books. I wanted to read what could teach me about God, everything written by saints while they were here on earth which might help me be closer to the One I was coming to love more and more with each passing day. The purpose of this command not to read was so that I might be able to state clearly that I had not read anything which might be the unwitting source for the conversations.

I did not feel "holy", but I felt rather as one does when one is coming closer in heart to the dearest friend imaginable. I began to see God's love as a gift to me expressed through the friendship and love of those closest to me.

In late September, my dear friend D. moved to Lubbock from Hawaii. She hoped her husband and children would follow within the year. Economic conditions in Hawaii for non-millionaire families are difficult. She lived with us for nine enjoyable months.

The summer had been unusually painful. As well as hard work and worry over where my girls might be, four people I knew had died. These were all separate incidents. Two of them were acquaintances, two of them were friends. I became afraid to answer the phone after hearing about the fourth death. One Saturday night had been particularly agonizing since I had heard of two of the deaths within an hour of each other. My awareness that eternity is much closer than we usually allow ourselves to know was painfully and yet also joyfully acute.

But as I grieved, I remembered one of the things my Dear Angel had shared with me. He had told me that the guardian angels of those who had been close to the souls were permitted a special honor at the time those souls entered Heaven. He said that he had been one of the angels escorting the people I loved to Heaven. He said this is the case when any soul going to Heaven is loved. The guardian angels of the people closest to that soul and those who have loved that soul the most who have already passed on are part of that soul's escort. He explained to me that there is a special bond between the guardian angels of people who love each other here on earth. Somehow, I am not sure how (he did not explain fully), because of the love between the people, a small reflection of Our Lord's Kingdom happens here on earth. This sharing in the Kingdom created by deep human love is what the angels participate in with us. This bond is not severed by distance or death.

I asked him what happens when love between people dies, and disruption or misunderstanding destroy human relationships. "Then," he said sadly, "there is grief among their angels."

A black and white, gray and brown cat I dearly love was lost shortly after our move to our new home. He never would have wandered off on his own. He was an unusual cat in his affection. He would follow me around, ask to be picked up, and put his paws around my neck and purr. He would usually come when I called him, and he would carry on detailed conversations with me in cat language — quite unintelligible to me, but that didn't stop him. He had been declawed, and I thought of him wandering and starving, looking for me. I did everything I could to find him with no results.

It broke my heart thinking I heard him meowing outside.

One night after I had come in from calling him and crying, my Guardian Angel said gently to me, "Everything which is good is preserved by Our Blessed Lord in some way. Nothing and no one that is good is ever entirely lost forever." I have taken comfort in this. I know of course that animals don't have immortal souls, but I thank my Lord for loving my kitty in some way.

My Angel spoke to me many times of offering pain — the pain of losing my kitty, Moses, and offering it; the pain of a headache, a cold, any discomfort at all. He said that pain can be offered in retrospect. For example, a grief experienced years ago can be offered for the salvation of souls now. The offerings of pure hearts and of children are particularly precious.

When he told me this, I thought of the caesarean I had undergone in giving birth to my twins. I had struggled for three days trying to give birth to them naturally. Finally, an emergency caesarean was performed. The spinal block did not take, and I was cut open still feeling. Because of fear that my little twins would be too anesthetized after birth and become critically ill, I was not made unconscious. I remembered this and other agonizing physical and emotional experiences. I offered them all as prayers for souls of God's choosing who were in imminent danger of going to hell now or in the near future. When I did this, I heard a diabolical scream of rage. I was frightened beyond words.

"You hear this," my Guardian Angel said, "so that you can testify to the truth of what I say through your own experience. If others could only know the good they could do in offering their pain: past, present and future, many more souls would be brought to Our Lord God, and those offering for them would be blessed in their offering, both here and in Heaven."

He also told me that the age of reason, as it is called, is much earlier than seven years old. He said that children of a young age, usually about two or three years old, begin to make little decisions which form their ways of looking at the world and responding to other people. These patterns may be changed, but they are important because very often they become the foundation from which other decisions and ways of being grow. He said that the most important thing parents can do for their children is to set an example of kindness and love. This, more than anything else, he said would help the children to form these ways of being for themselves. "Harshness and cruelty only teach harshness and cruelty. Self-discipline teaches self-discipline. Fairness teaches fairness," he said. He said that we are afraid to be firm with our children in our time, that we get firmness confused with unkindness or harshness. He said many parents either do not know how to take responsibility for the gift of parenthood God has given them, or else are too lazy to do so. "They have decided other things are more important," he said.

During this time of pain, there was one private sorrow which made the others even harder to bear. I do not normally ask my Dear Angel idle questions. I try just to let be, and open my heart and soul to whatever Our Lord wishes to be said through my Guardian Angel and any other angels Our Lord permits to speak with me. It seems to me that idle curiosity is not respectful, and I also know Our Lord has His own good reasons for allowing this precious gift to me.

But in a moment of particular pain I cried out to my Angel, "Why didn't you tell me about — (the painful situation in which I found myself.)? This could have been avoided if only you had told me."

In tender kindness he answered me, "You would not have done the will of God if you had known." I wonder how many times in life that answer is the reason we are kept in ignorance of what we think in our arrogance we have a right to know.

I have always wanted to be on the best terms possible with the people around me, and when this does not happen I feel badly. One day while on the campus of the University of Hawaii when I was about nineteen years of age, I was bemoaning the fact that no matter how considerate or kind I tried to be, one particular person seemed to shut me out without any regard for my efforts. I was complaining to a good friend. Finally, he said in complete exasperation, "Pat, they crucified Christ. What makes you think you're any better?"

I was reminded of this incident one day when my guardian angel spoke to me about sadness I felt over a disrupted relationship with someone I had thought was a sincere friend. "You are accountable only to One," he told me. "If you stand before Him with humility and a sincere heart and all is right between you, that is all that need concern you. Everything else will be as it should be with others. You cannot stand before Our Lord for them. They must do it for themselves."

One evening I was praying and thinking of the great Intelligence of God, the brilliance of the Mind of God which held the idea of everything before it was created, the power of God which had created EVERYTHING out of nothing, and the Compassion and Patience of God which kept me and everything else in existence. I pondered something a wonderful priest liked to say, "God made everything out of nothing, out of nothing!" How could anyone conceive of this even dimly and question Him?

I am so small and insignificant. It is only because He cares for me and bears me in mind that I exist. If He made everything out of nothing, it is only by His grace that anything exists at all. Even if He is all-knowing and all-powerful and infinite, how could I matter to Him?

As I thought this, my Dear Angel said to me, "You still do not know what 'infinite' is. You, and each one of Our Lord's dearly loved ones, are loved by Him as if you were His one and only love, His one and only creation and heart's desire. Do not doubt this."

One morning when the light was particularly bright, I wondered why there were some times when I could see the light so clearly but other times when it was not there at all and I was as I had been before the Feast of the Assumption of 1988. "Our Lord's light of love is always there," my Guardian Angel told me. "You don't always see it. But it is there."

One day as I was working, my Dear Angel interrupted me long enough to tell me something which I thought about for days afterwards. He said that Our Blessed Mother had seen me crying at the fountain on the Feast of the Assumption of 1988. "She saw your tears, she felt your pain," he told me. "She prayed to her Son Our Lord for you. She asked Him for a special gift for you, since you did not wish to receive your physical sight. "This gift," he said, "is the gift of the love of the angels and the ability within God's will to speak to us and hear us. The light of the angels will be your sight," he told me.

One Monday night, my family and I were at Mass at Saint John Neumann, with the rosary to be prayed afterwards. For some reason, I was particularly aware of just how blessed I am in my daughters, my two very different and special twins. I began to thank and praise my Lord for them.

"There is another angel here with me," my Guardian Angel told me. "This angel is special in your life, and in the lives of your daughters. He was given to you during the time you carried your daughters. Our Lord knew what a painful period of your life this was. He knew you would have a hard time giving birth to your children. He gave you a strong and beautiful angel to help you and them. This angel has a special love for you and your daughters."

He told me that we are given angels by Our Lord at different times in our lives, especially during times of pain and temptation. He said we can also ask that we be given angels during different times of need, and Our Lord always hears this prayer and grants it.

Then the angel accompanying my Guardian Angel began to speak to me. He said that this was the first time he had been permitted to come to our family since I had given birth to my girls. To my sadness, he reminded me of an incident in which I had not been as protective and loving toward my two unborn children as would have been right. I had not been as responsible and aware of my unborn children as I should have been. I had not thought of this incident for years. As he spoke to me, it was as someone who loves me very much speaking to me of an incident of wrongdoing which lay between us which had to be discussed in order to make things right.

He said he had been given a special charge by Our Lord to help me and my children in this grave time, and my negligence had interfered with this responsibility of his to us. I knew I must and would confess the incident. He left us with great love. We are his earthly family. As he departed, he told me he would be continuously praying for us before Our Lord.

I thought then of that difficult time. So my Guardian Angel, my children's guardian angels, and this beautiful, powerful angel had been with us. I marveled. My dear Guardian Angel reminded me that Our Lord is continuously giving gifts like this, and wishes to give them especially to those who think to ask.

On another evening, my Guardian Angel began speaking to me about the names of the angels. "We are all named for Our Lord," he said. "Whatever our particular name is, that aspect of Our Lord is what we most try to express and glorify." He told me that when a new and infinitely beloved soul is created, it is immediately assigned a guardian angel. "But," he said, "it isn't just any angel. "Each soul is created to serve its Creator in a special and unique way. So the soul is given a guardian angel who will be a perfect teammate for it, who will work with that soul most beautifully of all the angels to bring about the purpose for which the soul was created — always without interfering with free will."

The Heavenly match making that takes place between each soul and its guardian angel is very special. When I was asked later why people should become closer to their guardian angels, the analogy was given to me that the match making between a soul and its angel takes place in Heaven. But as the relationship deepens between you and your angel and your wish to be open to his love and guidance grows, then you become the team Our Lord had in mind, and you say, "I do." You are saying yes to the gift God has given you in your angel.

My Guardian Angel also told me that because of the great spiritual need in our country, the devotion to the angels would (because of the compassion of God) become a great devotion in the United States. "You will need to know for certain that your guardian angels are with you and will never leave you unless you choose damnation," he said. "We are always with you, loving you. You will need to be more aware of us and our love in order to be strengthened for the difficult times to come." He would tell me more about this later.

Near the beginning of November, he told me my time of silence was over. "You will speak now and write for others, but always under the guidance of your confessor," he said. "You are to obey completely those in authority over you."

# THE LIGHT OF LOVE

# Chapter 32
# GENTLE WISDOM OF GOD

On the night of Tuesday, November 6th, the light became bright as I sat studying. I tested the presence. All was well. The angel speaking to me asked me to get ready to write. He began,      "You and all people are dearly beloved by Our Lord, Jesus Christ. There is not one soul that has ever lived or ever will live that He would not have suffered and died for, again and again, if that had been necessary.*1 His suffering of spirit is great now because of His love for each of you. Once a soul is lost, it causes a wound to His Sacred Heart that cannot be healed in the way in which you think of healing.

"You in your human relationships go on with your lives after suffering the loss of someone you love. Please try to imagine the eternal loss of someone who is more loved than you could ever comprehend, with a pain that is eternal — what that continual and deep pain forever in the heart of God might be. It is a pain thousands of times greater than the deepest pain you have ever known. And this is the pain of the Lord of all things, felt over the loss of one soul — one infinitely treasured and dearly beloved soul.

"The price paid for each soul was an agony of body and spirit you can only be dimly conscious of, and even with this price, there were no guarantees. Each soul is free, always free to choose."

"Thank you for talking to me like this. It seems like a very long time, though, I have felt your love and the love of the other angels and I have seen the light. Please go on with whatever Our Lord wishes you to tell me."

"You are beloved, little one. I know you have many questions and fears in your heart. If you knew even the tiniest part of the love of God for you, even the worst circumstances and pains of life would seem minor. You would be aware of and praise and thank Our Lord always, but especially in painful and difficult situations. You would do this at these times most especially because it is during these times that the love and kindness of Our Lord can be most manifested.

"Even the distraction you have right now of your cat about ready to have a cat fight would not ruffle you from writing what I am saying to you. Minor things and big things you would see as opportunities for love. ALL LIFE IS AN OPPORTUNITY FOR LOVE. That is why it is so very precious. That is why those who are in Heaven in Our Lord's Kingdom are so filled with joy — because it is there that they can most freely and joyously give and receive love.

"But the difficulties you face here strengthen you if you will allow them to do so. They will permit you to love and be loved abundantly here and in Heaven."

"Your words are so simple but beautiful. Thank you so much, and THANK YOU, Lord. May I please know your name?"

"GENTLE WISDOM OF GOD."

"That does fit you so perfectly!"

"Remember, it is my Lord I am named for."

"Yes. I'm sorry."

"You are not to be."

"Thank you. May I ask, should I start working on the manuscript now?*2 My Guardian Angel told me I was not to read anything about angels or theology until after the manuscript is written. I don't know anything now, and that seems to be best."

---

[NOTES:

*1 Later my Guardian Angel clarified what GENTLE WISDOM OF GOD was saying. Our Lord would have died for each individual soul not just once, but again and again, if this had been what was required for that soul's salvation. He would have suffered and died for every soul which has damned itself to Hell, of course, knowing it would do so, just to give every person the right to choose, whether we choose Him or not.

*2 My Guardian Angel had told me to begin writing down the conversations in print, as well as the notes I had taken on the other incidents and smaller exchanges between me and the angels recorded here.

I feel slightly apologetic about my own denseness in this conversation. I was very tired, and I realize in rereading this conversation that I hardly responded to what the beautiful angel GENTLE WISDOM OF GOD was saying to me. But somehow I know this will be all right too.]

"Start working on it slowly and with patience for yourself. Pray continually for guidance from the Holy Spirit in your writing. Ask others to pray with you. You will be shown whom it is you are to ask. You were guided to your first special petitioner the other night."

"Yes. Thank you, GENTLE WISDOM OF GOD."

"I will speak with you again, little one. I will remain with you tonight. Our Almighty Lord has granted me this."

"May I ask for wisdom too?"

"The greatest wisdom is patience without drudgery, love without bitterness, kindness without demands. Ask for these things first, little one. Our Lord's peace is ever with you."

# THE LIGHT OF LOVE

# Chapter 33
# THE PLEA TO
# REORGANIZE PRIORITIES

I had become close friends with Jeff and Celeste Benoist. They had first come to Lubbock in 1988 for the Feast of the Assumption at Saint John Neumann Church. Their little boy, Vincent, had severe cerebral palsy because of complications at his birth. Within days of returning from Lubbock, he had shown remarkable and medically unexplainable improvement. We had become friends when they returned to Saint John Neumann in 1989 to give thanks for the Feast of the Assumption of 1988, and the blessings which they had received from Our Lord through the Blessed Mother's intercessory prayers.

In 1990, Celeste and Vincent came again for the Feast, and with them came one of the most down-to-earth and kindly people I know, Rita Roach. We spent a wonderful time together.

With their priest's support, they invited me to speak about the angels in their parish Church of Saint Andrew's in Moore, Oklahoma.

I went to my confessor. I told him my Guardian Angel had said my silence was over, but I did not know if I should accept the invitation. I asked him what I should do. He told me I might speak, but he was concerned about several things. He wanted me to be sure to speak with Father George Pupius, the pastor, before talking. He wanted to be sure that Father would be there, and that the talk would in no way bring about the possibility of sensationalism, that it would be a quiet and spiritual experience for the people. He was worried for me. These conditions were met.

I am not a public speaker. Even after the years of education I have had and practice in speaking after countless presentations, I can't speak in front of people with ease at all. I shake too much.

But this talk and others at Saint Andrew's began a series of publicly given talks in various places. I never speak without my current spiritual director, Father John Walch, whom I met on the second trip to Oklahoma City. Inevitably before I speak, I am nervous beyond words, convinced I will not be able to do it. Father is calm and reassuring, knowing that the gifts of joy and peace will be given to me by Our Lord as I speak and, if I am in pain, somehow that pain will be suspended and I will carry on as if it were not even there. There have been times I was to speak and almost had to be carried to the podium, I was in so much pain. This is not noticeable once the talk begins. I write about this because it is a continuing miracle to me that it should be so, that Our Lord would use me despite all the difficulties. It is certainly His work, not mine.

On this first trip, I came to love Father George Pupius, the pastor of Saint Andrew's in Moore, Oklahoma, and later would come to know other people of the parish as personal friends.

After my return, it seemed no time at all before we were preparing for finals — and Christmas. How unfortunate that the two are insepa-rable for students.

D.'s children were to arrive in Lubbock to spend Christmas with us on Sunday, December 23rd. Her husband was not able to get off work, but would arrive a few days after Christmas. That Sunday morning we were busy getting ready for the kids to arrive.

I took out my crucifix, the one I wear on a chain around my neck, the crucifix which turned from tarnished silver to gold on the Feast of the Assumption of 1988, and which has changed so much tactually since. As I held it, I realized that the little figure on the cross was mov-ing quickly.

I rushed out to the den where D. was, and showed her the cross. D. saw the figure moving. She said later that seeing the little figure move was so traumatic for her that, though she knows with all her heart that she saw it, it is too painful to talk about or remember in any detail.

We walked back to the bedrooms and called Miriam and Eileen. As the figure continued to move, we prayed. My Guardian Angel be-gan to speak to us.

"If Our Lord Himself were here asking you please to pray five mysteries of the rosary each day as a household, would you do it?" he asked.

"Yes," I said shaking.

"If He wished you to also read a chapter from Scriptures and offer personal intentions during this time, would you do it?"

"Yes!"

"If you have a test to study for or an event to go to, you have no trouble getting up an hour earlier to do this. Our Lord is here, and He is asking you to do these things. He asks you to spend this hour each day with Him as a household, plus your personal prayer time. He also asks that you return to the Monday night Mass and rosary at Saint John Neumann."

"Is this all He wants us to do?" It seemed to me that this was very little to ask of us, considering the graphic understanding right in front of us which we were being given of what He had done for us.

"This is all He asks," my Dear Angel said. He seemed almost amused. I think he knew that, despite my awe and good intentions, this would be enough to ask for now. "Our Lord asks that you make sure to pray in the morning," he said. I believe Our Lord was clear about the time because He knows that our family would spend more time arguing about when to pray than actually praying.

I suddenly realized that there was a figure standing quietly behind my Angel. "I give my peace to your home," He said gently. And then He said to me personally, "I will walk beside you." Since this very time I have felt His presence as if a physical person did walk beside me.

We collected ourselves with difficulty. I felt rather sick to my stomach. As a blind person, I think I tend to imagine situations in their immediateness. So when I think of the crucifixion, I imagine as fully as I can how I might feel suspended with huge nails through my wrists and feet, sick with agony, throat parched, and no help. I have found that sighted people often believe that lack of sight protects one from the pains of the world, i.e. we as blind people don't see distressing situations so are shielded from them. This sometimes may be true, but I find that more often pain is closer because as a blind person I experience life in a closer way, through my immediate senses. I feel other people's pain.

D. left to pick up her children, Scott and Kelly, at the airport. I went into my room and was very quiet for a long time. I found it difficult to pray, my feelings were so deep. I hoped that my Lord would accept this deep love and pain in my heart as a prayer.

At difficult times in life when I have known I had little or nothing to offer my Lord, I have offered my nothingness to Him. This is a poem expressing this:

GIFTS

Please accept my hopelessness
When I can no longer pray.
Please receive my emptiness
When all that I can say
Is God, O God, O God,
And wander through the day.
Please welcome what I have to give
When nothing else remains
But numbness of heart and lack of faith
And a belief my life's in vain.
Sometimes these gifts are all I have,
So proffered without shame.

Did Our Lord empty Himself willingly so that He had only these gifts also? Mine was an emptying through painful circumstances. His was a willing surrender.

We did not tell Scott and Kelly right away what had happened. But on Monday morning, Christmas Eve, Kelly asked about the events I had written of in my letter. I began to tell her more about them, and the changed crucifixes. As I showed her the crucifix on my rosary made of Job's tears from Hawaii, the figure began to move without altering its dislocated shoulder position. It moved up and down, arms straightening and bending. Kelly saw it. She was gripped with the same combination of amazement, horror and wonder we have all felt.

Her mother D. also saw, and left us abruptly. She told us later she had not been able to look any more, she had felt nauseated. The cruel reality of what Our Lord has done for us is a wondrous but difficult gift to experience directly.

"Auntie,"* Kelly whispered, "what color is your crucifix?"

"Silver," I told her.

---

[*NOTE: It is the custom in Hawaii for adults close to young people to be called "auntie" or "uncle" as a mark of respect and affection.]

She did not say anything more. Later she hesitantly told me, afraid I would not believe her, that the crucifix, especially the figure, had looked gold to her. She said there was a golden light around my hands as I held the crucifix.

Why are we given so much? I think of the Scriptural verse which says to those who have been given much, much will be expected. I am afraid of this expectation, but surely if Our Lord is asking something special of us, He will grant us the grace to give. I have heard it said that signs and wonders are for those who have little faith, that those with a great faith do not need them. Are we being given these gifts in order to have the opportunity to bolster our faith?

# THE LIGHT OF LOVE

# Chapter 34
# A CHRISTMAS STORY

It was a joy to have Scott and Kelly with us over Christmas. We had decided that since neither of our families had much money, in fact we were both near broke, we would not try to buy elaborate gifts for each other. We would buy a few necessities and a few things that we knew would be loved and appreciated. After that, we had decided, we would pool all our finances. We would then go shopping together to get Christmas gifts for a family in more need than ourselves. There was a real joy for us in doing this, because we would notice the sacrifice and therefore be reminded of the joy of giving.

D. had rented a car for the time Scott and Kelly were in Lubbock. We went to a warehouse and began loading shopping carts. We picked up a twenty-five pound bag of rice, canned goods, potatoes, flour, and some fresh vegetables. We also found a wonderful buy on frozen chicken and other meats.

Then we started having fun. We knew the ages of the children. We began to buy specific Christmas gifts for the family members, though we did not know their names.

"Auntie Patti," Scott said to me, "please take this. I'm just a kid. I don't need it." He handed me at least thirty dollars. A few minutes later, Kelly came up too. She had been busy gathering things in another aisle and had not witnessed Scott's generosity.

"Auntie Patti," she said to me, "I really want to buy these things (referring to her cart load.)" She handed me her spending money too.

So I walked up and down the aisles crying. Eileen passed me. "Mom," she said, choking up too, "I haven't felt as if it was really Christmas all this time. But it's Christmas now isn't it?" My girls too had contributed their Christmas money.

I had a careful tally of the money we had, plus the money I had been given by the kids. As we paid for our cart loads, my figuring came within two dollars of the amount owed. I was relieved. We had about two dollars left. We had been able to give Our Blessed Lord a gift of our love.

As I walked outside, the weather had grown colder. I didn't have any mittens, so I put my hands in my coat pockets. "What's this!" I cried. Out of one pocket I took five bills.

"It's five twenties," Kelly told me. None of us would have had that much money left over. Where had it come from? I knew I was much more careful with my figures than that!

As we sat in our living room, I felt very tired but more happy than I can say. Eileen and Miriam, Scott and Kelly and D. wrapped the personal gifts, putting little amusing notes on them. We all had such fun making up these amusing little notes to strangers who seemed so close. Suddenly my Guardian Angel spoke to me. "Our Lord is very pleased with what all of you have done this night," he said. "He will remember you in your time of want." The promise sent a quiver up my spine, partially of fear because of the certainty of a time of want to come, but also of excitement to know how intimately Our Blessed Lord is involved with us.

We loaded ourselves into D.'s rented car and began to search for the address of our family. We drove and drove and drove.

"We're going to Egypt," Miriam exclaimed.

Finally in a run-down area of Lubbock we found the apartment building. The four kids unloaded all of the goods. One of them went ahead to scout out the territory to be sure the Christmas gifts would be left with the correct people. They then loaded their arms with as much as they could carry, calling a warning to us to be ready to speed away the moment they came back and jumped
into the car.

"Hurry up!" they yelled as the last one got back and the doors slammed. They were giggling.

"The little kids saw us," they said. "They started to squeal. There was a big black guy watching us drop the gifts off. He was laughing at us. 'You got busted early!' he said to us." They were so joyful and excited. I have to say that it was rather like a get-away, screeching brakes and all.

Midnight Mass was beautiful. Christmas Day started off quietly. My friends, the Valerio family from Midland, had called to ask if they could stop by.

The four of them arrived late in the morning. Eileen and Miriam were gone, and D. was resting. Kelly and Scott and I sat talking to the four Valerios.

Valerie Valerio had seen one of my crucifixes, and she asked me if I would show it to her family. I did so. They held it for a long time. Then I realized from their quiet exclamations that they were seeing the figure move. Scott and Kelly saw this also.

It was, as always, traumatic. This gift of love wrapped in pain is never totally joyous. It affects us individually each time, and in different ways each time. Why it was given to us on this celebration of Our Lord's birth, I do not know. It meant everything to those who were seeing it for the first time.

# THE LIGHT OF LOVE

# PART IV:
## "TAKE UP YOUR CROSS EVERY DAY AND FOLLOW ME"

# THE LIGHT OF LOVE

# Chapter 35
# HIERARCHY

On Friday, January 4th, 1991, my Guardian Angel told me that the conver-sations, for this time and in their present form, were over. He asked me to begin writing them down in print. I asked if the angels would still be speaking with me. He said, "Yes. That is a gift which has been given to you." I asked if I would have a chance to ask questions. Again, he said, "yes." It had been a great delight to me to converse with the beautiful angels.

On Monday, he told me again what he had said on Friday. He added that I was to continue writing, continue taking notes. Then he said, "You have other work to do for now."

Within a few weeks time I began to learn more about what at least part of this work would entail. I was asked several times to suffer for a particular soul. When I consented, a pain that is both physical and spiritual would descend on me. It was intense. But when it was gone, it was entirely gone with no repercussions except tiredness. I will write more about this later.

It was made very clear to me that in no way was I ever to wish this pain on myself or try to bring it about, no matter how desperate or worthy the cause seemed to me. The Lord always must be the One to control this.

Journal Excerpt:

Wednesday, March 20, 1991

Our household was all together praying the rosary on this evening. As we prayed, my Guardian Angel asked if Saint Michael and many other angels might come to be with us to pray. Of course we said yes. Soon the room was filled with a beautiful, gentle light. I had expected the light would be much brighter with so many angels in the room, but it was gentle. This gentleness seemed to be there in order to protect us. I believe if we had seen the full radiance of God from the angels, we would not have been able to bear it. The light was everywhere with no distinctions. Usually I can see distinct lights in different places, but now there was only the beautiful, warm light everywhere, with no breaks in it.

After praying the rosary and asking Our Lord's blessing, we prayed a Litany to our guardian angels. After this, Eileen asked why our guardian angel is said to be "a ruler" over us. This is part of the Litany. Saint Michael answered strongly and amazingly forcefully. I did not copy word for word what he said, but we took notes afterwards, and we all did our best to reconstruct as accurately as possible what he said. It amazed me that we were able to do this quite clearly, sometimes remembering word for word. It was clear we had been given a gift by Our Lord to recall what had been said to us.

My daughter Eileen was particularly good at doing this. It was almost as if she were given a photographic memory for the moment. Here is what Saint Michael said as closely as we could reconstruct it.

"You are like little children who say, 'I will only listen to God' and then are disrespectful to those authorities given charge over you by God. You use God as an excuse to do your own will. This has caused an abomination of insubordination: Heresies against the Church with many going their own way in the past, and with deeper and more serious heresies to come because of this prideful attitude. There is rebellion against parents. There is disrespect to the Mother of God who was chosen by God from all women to bring The Word to physical birth among you. You ignore or are disrespectful to your guardian angels who have been given charge over you to guide your souls to Heaven, into the arms of God Who created you and loves you beyond telling.

You are being disrespectful when you claim God as your authority in order to do your own will. Does not God have the authority to order His creation as He sees fit? You are all given dominion. You are all responsible to God, just as all the angels and saints of Heaven are responsible to God for what He has placed in our keeping, to be cared for and loved. The Blessed Mother of God, the angels and all the saints, have been given a great trust. We are responsible for what God has given into our keeping: to pray for you and to guide you into Heaven.

You are responsible for the lives God has given into your care, for your care of the earth and its beauteous bounty so thoughtlessly despoiled, for its creatures. You are responsible for yourselves. You are responsible for your relationship to God. You are responsible to God, just as the angels and the Mother of Our Lord are responsible.

You must understand that the Church is given authority over you. Those in authority are given authority over you so that God will be glorified. You think this diminishes God's glory but, in fact it enhances it. You are all part of Our Lord's plan. If there is an abuse of this authority, especially in the Church because here the entrustment is greatest, then those who abuse are held accountable to God — and seriously so."

Saint Michael was angry. It was not an anger directed toward us personally, but was present because of the disrespect shown to Our Lord, and the use of God for our own selfish gains and purposes. It was made clear to us that obedience in unjust cases and obedience to superiors who were in disobedience to their superiors were not included in the command to obey and respect those in authority over us. We were strongly enjoined to understand and ponder what had been said to us. Saint Michael said to us, "Now you know this. Share it with others. You have no further excuse for usurpation."

Saint Michael and many of the other angels then departed from us, leaving a "lesser angel" behind to instruct us. My daughter Eileen asked about the term "lesser angel." Democracy is a strong value of hers, and mine too — within reason.

The "lesser angel" was amused by the question. "Please do not quibble over 'lesser' or 'greater.' Lesser and greater have no meaning in Heaven because we all serve God, each in our place. All are important. But all must obey in order to serve. How can those who are not subject to Our Lord's will serve Him?"

My personal views have been quite liberal both in politics and in Church matters. This strong request of Saint Michael's for obedience is not something I would have subjected myself to in the past. I am undergoing a definite change of heart in understanding and accepting what Saint Michael and the other angels have told me — solely because of their influence and persuasion. I am beginning to feel a great joy in obedience. Immaturity is believing that freedom lies in doing what one wishes. The paradox is that limitations wisely used can build character and strength, and ultimately free the spirit.

The blessed angels would later explain to me that an understanding of hierarchy is crucial to being in union with God's creation and with oneself. The concept of hierarchy is woven into our whole universe, both our physical world and our spiritual plane. The blessed angels would later emphasize again to me that dominion means responsibility. We do not have a right to destroy the gifts we have been given, from the material world around us to our own lives.

We are all important in this hierarchical structure no matter our place in it, and our question should always be, "How can I best serve God where I am, being loyal to those in authority over me and responsible for those for whom I am accountable?" Bearing this idea of hierarchy in mind in our families, our work, our whole lives, and understanding that EVERYTHING is a gift from God and praising Him for it; we begin to rejoice in His perfect Kingdom.

Thursday, March 21, 1991

The "lesser angel" was with us this morning as we prayed the rosary again. We were told that our relationships, especially with our fami-

---

[Note: I was reminded later by my Guardian Angel that we have the flame of God's Spirit in us and the mark of His love on our souls. He said we are to respect our bodies as treasured vessels. They are not to be abused or used by us or anyone else for purposes of impurity: sex without marriage, use of drugs and alcohol, etc. He said our souls are not to be sullied with impure thoughts and fantasies, or our minds put to the use of extending evil. This is a stricter code than I had adhered to. Like many in our society, I had believed that "If it doesn't hurt anyone else, whose business is it? I am an adult." But through my Guardian Angel's teaching I have come to realize that no act, no thought, is totally separate from others. I do not have the right to do with myself as I wish because I belong to God. True maturity is not license to do as one wishes, but is a trust of God's love given to one with its main element being responsibility. These conversations and teachings have caused me to begin the process of reorganizing myself. We are not given our bodies, our lives, our families, or our world to dispose of as we wish but in trust from God. We are held accountable to Him for them and their use or misuse. This causes me to see the need for a whole reorganizing of the way I view myself and this world.]

lies, are entrusted to us by God and we are accountable to Him for their care. We are accountable to God for everything that we have been given, including the care and use of our bodies. We are ultimately accountable to Him for the state of our souls.

"Remember that dominion means stewardship. Anyone who abuses what has been given into his keeping is held accountable. You think being given charge over and being given power over means to exploit or to hurt or to enjoy as you see fit. Even Our Lord, as a human being, was under the authority of Saint Joseph and the Blessed Mother of God the Father had appointed. This was because He was under Divine authority, which had put them in charge of Him. Until He was released from His Mother's authority, He did not begin His public work among His people."

The angel blessed us and told us that the Scriptures would be used to instruct us.

# THE LIGHT OF LOVE

# Chapter 36
# SYMPATHY FOR SAINT PETER

March 29, 1991

This is Good Friday. I am in Oklahoma City with Celeste and Jeff Benoist and their little boy Vincent. On Wednesday I spoke to Father George's parish about the blessed angels. I was comforted to know that there were two priests and several nuns present. They are firmly rooted in our faith and its teachings, and in Scripture. There are so many influences now which are not of the Scriptures or of the teachings of the Church, and God only knows where most of them come from. I felt relaxed and secure knowing they would interrupt me at any time if I made a statement contrary to the Church's teachings, or even just slightly questionable. To me, being obedient to the Church is a safety net. Our Blessed Lord has promised to be with the Church till the end of time and "the gates of hell shall not prevail against it." That comforts me.

On Holy Thursday, Celeste and I kept Our Lord's vigil in Gethsemane with Him. We asked that, since God is not limited by time or space, we be allowed to be with Our Lord, that somehow He would know we were there in spirit.

It was not until near the end of the vigil that I knew without any doubts that our prayer to be with Our Lord as much as that is possible had been granted. Suddenly, I was in the Garden with Jesus and the disciples. I was not afraid because I felt the presence of my Guardian Angel beside me. I could feel the wind on my face. I could not physically see. I was standing near a tree and could hear the branches of the tree rustling overhead. I was standing about four feet away from Jesus.

Then I heard them coming. I was surprised, because they were not trying to be quiet. I would have thought they would try to take Him by surprise. Some of them sounded drunk to me — loud and vulgar. I said, "Oh God, I can hear them coming!"

Celeste said later it felt to her as if she could not move, as if everything including time had stopped. "It's 12:07," I heard her say.

Then I heard Judas's voice, sneering and triumphant as if to say, "You thought you were hot stuff, didn't you? But see what I have done?" Then he said, "Rabbi!" He said it with such mockery and slimy triumph that I felt sick to my stomach.

It was horrible to me how fast it all happened. I heard cries of fright coming from those who had come; then a moment later the sound of pounding feet running away. Then the Garden was silent. All I could hear was the wind in the tree and little night noises, crickets or cicadas; empty, nothing but empty. The desolation of the garden was nothing to the desolation in my heart.

I knew my Guardian Angel would have taken me further, would have gone with me to follow them. But I did not have the courage to follow them. I have always rather smiled condescendingly at poor Peter. I have thought that if I had the chance, I would have stood by Jesus. But I couldn't even follow Him as a blind person, and only in spirit. I was thinking too much of myself and what it would be like for me to stand by and hear His pain. I was not thinking of the comfort one friend might have been to Him.

But Peter did follow them, even if he denied Christ. But I, God help me, did not even have the courage to follow along behind them though I knew my Guardian Angel would be right there with me and that it would be only in spirit that I went. God, help me. I am so sorry, Jesus.

The memory of my failure to follow my Lord is now one of the most painful I will bear. Perhaps I have a small taste of the pain Saint Peter carried till his dying day. I frequently ask Saint Peter to pray for me now.

Later. I was asked this morning to suffer for a soul. It was a very serious matter. The pain went on only for a few minutes, and then suddenly my Guardian Angel told me that was enough. I would not be permitted to continue. I was disappointed because I truly wanted to do more. I knew the job had only just been started. But my Guardian Angel told me that my strength would be needed later, and I would not be allowed to become too drained. He told me I would have more pain later on this Good Friday.

11:00 p.m. Tonight at Saint Andrew's Church, the Stations were so beautiful. They were the old Stations of Our Lady's pain. I have been told by a friend who is a convert to the faith and knows more about it than most cradle Catholics that the Stations of the Cross were begun by Our Lady herself. During her life, she visited in progression the spots of her Son's deepest sufferings. She prayed at each spot. The practice was continued by the Church itself. The Stations of the Cross commemorate Christ's Passion, suffering and death. They end as His body is taken down from the cross and placed in His Mother's arms. They are particularly meaningful because one journeys with Christ, and His suffering becomes very personal.

I am shy to write about this next event because if there is any pride or haughtiness at all in me, the best I could do would be not to record it at all but keep it in my heart and pray for forgiveness for my grandiose arrogance at the thought of recording it. But I have searched my heart, and what is there is not pride but sorrow because I am now more deeply aware of my Lord's sufferings. I am sad because I moan and groan over such little things, and I now have a better idea of my Lord's pain.

While we were at church, my left wrist began to hurt terribly. It felt as though a rod of fire ran through it. It would not stop. Later, a group of people including Father George went to Celeste and Jeff's house to visit. I did my best to carry on as usual, not wanting to draw any attention to what was happening to me. I was given grace to do this. Under normal circumstances, it would not have been possible because of the excruciating pain. At one point, poor Father George exuberantly grabbed my left wrist to show me something. I scared him by yelling in pain as my face twisted. To minimize it and calm the poor man down, I jokingly said, "Here, try this one," and offered him my right hand.

To think one wrist could hurt so much, and this only a small example of Our Lord's agony. I am sure I was not given even near the pain in that wrist of mine that He felt in His left wrist. Whether it was a gift from God in a supernatural sense or a gift from God in a purely physical sense does not matter to me. What matters is that I had a small chance to share in a small way in my Lord's Passion. I am grateful that God does not consider worth in these things.

I come to understand more clearly all the time that all pain is a share in the Passion of my Lord, or at least it can be if it is offered in union with Christ's sufferings, if the desire that it should be united to Christ's sufferings is present. What an unexpected road I am traveling,

I who have been so intellectual and proud of it, wanting proof for almost everything, but yet having a spirit which knew there was more to everything than could ever be proven or should ever be proven. Without faith, we will become robots. Without accountability to God, anything becomes justified, morality is situational and negotiable, and no one is safe.

We are going to protest abortion tomorrow. Celeste asks me to promise to go, but I do not know what sort of night I will have. I want to be available for anything required.

Saturday March 30

This morning I awoke feeling fresh and strong. I flexed my wrist. There was no soreness in it at all as there would have been naturally had my wrist been hurt in a normal way, considering the amount of pain I had yesterday. It was as if nothing had happened.

So we leave now to pray for an end to the destruction of the people we would have called our descendants. Why is this, and so much else, allowed to happen — and, I am sure, done by people who sincerely mean well, as long as they do not delve too deeply into their own souls?

# Chapter 37
# OFFERING EXPLAINED

Friday, April 26, 1991

Today I was asked to suffer for the soul of a heroine addict dying from her addiction. When my Guardian Angel asks me to suffer for a soul and I have consented, very often I am shown the soul and some aspects of his or her life. This woman had led many others to addiction for her monetary profit and to support her own addiction. Our Lord wished to save her soul and was able to do so because she had loved her baby sister who had died many years ago. Even this small openness in her heart many years ago gave Our Lord His needed opening to give her His grace through my offering. If she had been totally closed to love, He would have had no way to give her His grace without violating her free will, which He would not do.

He needed our prayers and pain offered as prayers for her, and that is why the request was made of me. I wish to state again here that Our Lord is no blood-thirsty God wanting pain before He will forgive. He Himself is limited by the gift He has given us of our free will. My offering and the offerings of other souls asked to do this work frees Him to pour out His grace to a given soul without violating its free will.

I have been told by my Guardian Angel that because the custom of offering pain as prayers has almost died out, Our Lord is now asking certain souls all over the world to suffer, as I call it, to provide a "margin of grace" for souls in desperate need.

There have been times when I have known that other people were helping as I suffered for a particular soul. This assistance from others occurs when I am weak and feel unable to hold the soul for whom I am suffering back from damnation. I cry out for help to the angels as I have been instructed to do, and their love and the love and offerings of other people in this work combine with my physical and spiritual strength.

Trying to explain what this suffering is like and how it happens is difficult because there is very little in my previous experience to which it can be compared. I feel as though my whole being becomes a rope or an anchor holding a soul back from the abyss of damnation. The struggle for a soul is truly a tug of war. I mean this literally. The pain is physical, emotional, and spiritual. For a time, I become one with the soul for whom I am offering. For the time of the offering, this oneness is complete. I cry out in my pain for forgiveness for my sin, because for that time of suffering that person's sin is my sin. I have willingly taken it on at Christ's request through my Guardian Angel, following His example.

The pain is physical and spiritual as I have said, but it is a torture of heart which can be best described as the deepest regret imaginable. It is as though for this time of suffering I become completely one with the soul I have been asked to offer for, and I feel and experience the deep sorrow of repentance necessary to redress the imbalance of wrong done by that soul, enough to hold that soul back from damnation. But no substitution can be made if the soul being prayed for in this way is completely hardened against God and refuses to regret serious wrongdoing if given the opportunity and understanding necessary to do so.

My Guardian Angel has made it clear to me several times that in no way am I ever to bring on or seek this pain. It will either be given to me through natural causes or by request from Our Lord or the Blessed Mother through the angels. Others who are not called to this work are also asked to offer their emotional, spiritual, and physical pain brought about through ordinary living. Even such things as a bad cold, a headache, a personal slight, the rejection of a friend — all these can be offered by anyone who is willing. As I have said, I have even been told that past pain may be offered. For example, the pain suffered years ago can be offered now. But we are all strictly ordered never to induce pain, as was done during zealous times, through such things as flagellation and self-torture. We must be requested to offer extraordinarily induced pain, and we must be under close guidance by one in authority as we do so.

The pain of ordinary living may be offered by an act of your will to do so. It is a wish on your part that your pain should be transformed into a prayer of love. Then the pain itself, which seemed to be your greatest enemy and stumbling block to prayer, BECOMES your prayer. It is offered for an intention of your choosing, or something for which you believe Our Lord wishes you to pray. This prayer of pain is one which unites you with Our Blessed Lord, Jesus Christ, through His love and your desire. I try to concentrate on His agonizing Passion as I suffer the pain. Then the unification of your heart with His through your faith that it is taking place DOES take place. In this way, all human suffering can be united with that of Our Blessed Lord's, and therefore is transformed because of His Passion into a prayer of love.

Around April 20th, I was asked to suffer for a woman dying of her fifth abortion. She was a whore, and had chosen to be one. She had a little son, about six or seven years old, who ran the streets uncared for. He was already choosing evil at his young age. My Guardian Angel said to me again that children of quite a young age can and do make choices for good and evil. I was not shown why Our Lord had particular mercy on this soul, or why I was asked to suffer for her. I was glad to do this because of His request alone. Quite a few of the souls I have been asked to pray for in this special way are those of women who have had abortions.

As I witness the mercy of God shown to souls in different ways according to their circumstances, I wonder, "Am I witnessing part of the first judgment, the individual judgment, for these souls? Is this the individual judgment each of us will face before the last and final judgment of the whole world?"

Another soul I was asked to suffer for was a man who was so totally evil that he was repulsive to me. As I gave consent to the pain and began to suffer it for him, I heard Satan's voice screaming at me, asking me why I was doing this for such a disgusting bit of refuse as this soul. I answered that I did it because my Lord asked me to do it. That is enough for me. Then I would no longer answer him. The sense of deep sin was all about me, but the love of God for this soul was much stronger than any evil could ever be.

This man was so evil that no one knew there was a little bit of goodness in him. No other human being knew. The man himself did not know. His guardian angel did not know, and was in deep sorrow for him. Only Our Blessed Lord knew that this man did have this little goodness in him, and that knowledge He guarded for the man's protection.

As we prayed, this little bit of goodness was taken by Our Lord, and the soul was placed in the bottom of Purgatory. It was like watching someone gently put a tiny, delicate bird's egg with a thin, breakable shell into a safe nest. Thinking of Purgatory as a "safe nest" was a great surprise to me. That Purgatory, a place of painful purification and long suffering, should be a haven amazed me. But when I thought of the alternative, damnation forever, I understood.

The soul was surrounded by all the evil and spiritual filth he had accumulated during his lifetime. It was horrible. The little good of the soul would have to grow just as an embryo grows, becoming stronger, and then finally begin to do what most other souls can immediately begin to do — start the long process of sorting through the enormous pile up of evil in their lives.

This would all have to occur over countless ages before this soul could finally stand purified in the full presence of Our Almighty Lord. My Guardian Angel showed me this in pictures and through explanations. What struck me most as my Guardian Angel showed me this was the incredible mercy of God. I see this mercy in different ways with each soul for whom I am privileged to suffer.

I was too weak to hold on to this soul. I cried out for help to the angels. I felt their strength and love joining me, especially the total love of the man's guardian angel. I felt other souls of living people coming to help us. I do not mean that their souls came literally, but that the strength of the love of their souls expressed through their pain offered as prayers was joined to our spiritual strength.

Then, as I have said, I saw the little goodness of the man's soul placed in the bottom of Purgatory by Our Lord. What a relief and joy.

Another soul for whom I offered was that of a woman. At first I thought she was a man because she was very masculine seeming. She had been very hard and manipulative during her life, using other people to get what she wanted. She was cruel, and no one chose to be around her unless out of fear or because they thought they might get something out of the fact that she was powerful in a worldly sense.

When I met her, she was living that "timeless" moment before death, the moment of grace given to her by Jesus Christ in hopes of repentance.*

---

[Note: As I was privileged to offer for other souls, it was made clear to me that there is a timeless moment before death offered to some souls for whom there may be mitigating circumstances in life which Our Blessed Lord in His mercy considers. In this timeless moment of grace, He attempts to reach the soul in some special way, giving the soul an opportunity to accept His grace.]

My Guardian Angel, Our Blessed Lord Jesus and I were with her. We were on the brink of hell. She could see hell below us, and she was terrified. She was so terrified and desperate with fear that she would have thrown her own Mother or Grandmother into the flames, if she thought she could avoid going there for even a moment. My Guardian Angel wordlessly told me this, how ruthless her desperation had made her.

Because of the stark reality of hell before her and her fear, she was like a person drowning. She was so frightened that she could not stop to receive the grace Our Blessed Lord was trying to give her. My dear friend D., who was praying for this soul as I offered for her, pleaded the Passion of Our Blessed Lord, all His terrible sufferings, for this soul. Suddenly, Our Blessed Lord showed the woman a vision of His crucified agony.

The woman froze. She stared. "You did that," I said to her.

"I didn't mean to," she said.

"If you had your whole life to live over again," Our Blessed Lord said to her, "would you live it as you have lived it?"

"No," she said, "I would not."

"That is all I need," Jesus said to me and my Angel. He told us she would be placed in the bottom of Purgatory to begin her purification. He blessed us, including D., and thanked us. His blessing and His thanks are such balm to my spirit.

This gift of being able to imitate Christ and give, through our suffering as if the person we are suffering for had repented of sin, is our special grace from God. In my case, it certainly has nothing to do with my own merits but is truly a gift. The joining of my soul to another is strictly a temporary union and is not burdensome later. In fact, I am protected from remembering too vividly. At the end of my suffering, I am no more united with that soul than before the suffering began, though I believe I am given the gift of a greater compassion by God every time I offer. I remember what has happened as I would remember an incident repeated to me by someone else.

The total involvement and union with the soul ceases. I believe this is a spiritual protection for me, given by my Lord. I think of it as being rather like the way the people who watch the sun dance were protected from sun blindness.

It has taken me a long time to understand these things as I have gone through these different experiences and heard the quiet explanations of my Guardian Angel. The suffering began within a few weeks after I was told the conversations were over, at least for the present. What is most amazing to me is the kindness of God to permit this, especially at the very last moment, for these souls so dearly beloved.

As I experience this pain, of course the pain is great. But the joy I feel is deep. It is hard to explain this. It is not masochism, the enjoyment of pain, nor is it an oblivion to pain. The pain is agony. The joy does not come from the pain itself, but from the knowledge that I am helping just a little to bring a soul to Our Lord, and that I am being allowed to help even a little. By my Lord's kindness, I am being given the opportunity to "take up my cross and follow Him." And I am being allowed to take a little of the crosses of others as well. Our Lord could ask anyone to do this. I believe if people knew how important this is, almost everyone would be willing to do it. The awareness of how important it is grows for me each time I am asked.

Another soul for whom I was asked to suffer when this began in January was a woman who had not done anything truly evil. She had gone through her life rather automatically. She did what she had to do in order to live marginally, just to exist. She had no warmth or love for others in any way. There was no kindness in her. She had no friends.

Our Lord's mercy was not able to touch her because of her quiet hardness and indifference. I had not thought of indifference as a sin before, but it became clear to me in this offering that it definitely is a sin because it shuts out not only those God loves, His precious people, but it shuts out God Himself.

As with most of the souls for whom I have been asked to suffer so far, this woman was near to or on the point of death. My family and I were praying the rosary when I was asked to suffer for her. The pain began, and they joined their prayers with my prayers of pain for her. I don't know whether it was right before she died or right afterwards, but for a brief moment her soul was present in the room with us. She knew we were praying for her and offering for her, and she was greatly surprised. She had lived her life in such chosen and hardened isolation that she had never felt so strongly before, not even the emotion of surprise. It was as though she was taken unaware by our prayers. There was no other emotion for her but surprise: No gratitude, no anger, just surprise.

My Guardian Angel explained to me later that this reaction of surprise, this one show of spiritual openness (her surprise), combined with our prayers and offerings was Our Lord's "in" to her soul. Without this reaction, He could not have reached her.

A few minutes later, her guardian angel was with us. He kept saying over and over, "Thank you for praying for my lady. Thank you for praying for my lady." He told me he would be with her in Purgatory until the judgment. But he was so filled with joy and gratitude because he had thought she would be damned by her own indifference. He sang a song of praise to God for His mercy, and told me he would pray for me and all of us present "until you are all before Our God's throne in Heaven."

# THE LIGHT OF LOVE

# Chapter 38
# MY LORD AND MY GOD

About two months ago, the little inscription above my crucifix which turned from silver to gold on the Feast of the Assumption of 1988 was lost. I was surprised this should have happened since so many extraordinary things have occurred where this inscription is concerned. The inscription had been a simple lettering at the top of the crucifix before the Feast of the Assumption at Saint John Neumann Church in 1988. When the crucifix began changing physically, the inscription moved from the very top of the cross down to right above the head of the figure of Our Blessed Lord. It became larger and changed into a squarish scroll in appearance and feel.

In November of last year, I took it out to make a point about faith to D. as we sat talking. It had changed shape from a squarish scroll to an oblong inscription with pointed ends. D. could clearly see the difference in shape. My children could also see the difference. They said it was one of the clearest changes in the crucifix they had seen and could attest to. They told me it looked like a banner.

So when the inscription fell off, I wondered why this had happened. I felt sure there was a good reason for it. I prayed about it and asked my Guardian Angel. He said to me, "That sign was put above Our Lord Christ in ridicule, but it is the truth. But when you suffer, there is no sign above your cross, at least not yet. Our Lord wants you to know that He is completely with you in your suffering. The inscription's absence on your crucifix is to remind you of this."

Monday, April 29, 1991

Yesterday I asked my Guardian Angel if he knew beforehand that we would be talking to each other. Did he know before the Feast of the Assumption of 1988? I had asked this question before but he had not answered. Yesterday he did answer.

He told me that he had not known until the grace was granted me on the Feast of the Assumption of 1988 at Saint John Neumann Church.

It was a gift of love to him from Our Lord, just as it was a gift to me. As I write this he says lovingly to me, "Our beautiful Lady, Queen of Compassion for the children God has given her to love, saw your tears. Her motherly heart asked for a special blessing for you in this, since you did not wish to see in a physical sense."

Saturday, May 11, 1991

May 9th, two days ago, was Ascension Thursday. I knew so little about our feast days in the Church before the Feast of the Assumption here in 1988. In so many ways, I am a convert to the faith. Perhaps if we don't stagnate in our faith, all of us must be converts.

I love the image of Jesus on the Feast of the Ascension. As He speaks to His people who are now the Church, He raises His hands in blessing. And as He does so, He begins to rise, "and a cloud took Him from their sight," as recorded in Acts.

I laugh at the description of them all standing there looking up into the sky. Then suddenly, two men dressed in white stand beside them. "Men of Galilee, what are you doing looking up into the sky?" they ask them. They tell them Jesus will return just as they saw Him go.

After the events of the Feast of the Assumption and my own incredible experiences, I know it will truly be just as they have said. With what amazement faces will be turned up toward Heaven as Our Lord descends, escorted by angels!

Yesterday as we prayed the Sorrowful Mysteries of the rosary my Guardian Angel took me, just for a moment, to Our Lord's scourging.

I stood several feet away from Him as the Roman whip opened His back. The blood splattered on my face. I could feel its warmth as it sprayed. God help me. This, along with the Blessed Mother's showing me the blood of the innocence, is something I hesitate to write down. It may seem macabre to some. Though I have experienced deep personal pain and felt the pain of others, I have not watched films of great suffering. The most direct way I can experience this realization of my Lord's suffering is in the way I experience everything else, through touch, hearing, smell, feel, taste. I felt as if my soul were being ripped in sorrow for His suffering. I was in anguish knowing that I have had a share in causing this suffering — no matter that all of us human beings have contributed to it.

But I also felt a great joy that He would do this for me, for me!

Today as we prayed the last Glorious Mystery of Our Lady's Coronation as Queen of Heaven and Earth, my Guardian Angel told me that it would be well if we remembered to call Our Lord's Mother "the Mother of God" in referring to her. He said that by not honoring her as "the Mother of God", not seeing her as the Mother of God, we deny the divinity of Christ. I have never looked at it this way before.

He said that Our Lord Jesus Christ's divinity would be questioned more and more in our very own Church! He did not say this directly, but I had the impression that the honoring of the Mother of God affirmed Our Lord's divinity in a bigger sense than I can understand. How could this be that we would cut out our own hearts by denying Christ's divinity — and all probably in the name of intellectualism, worldly sophistication and good old common sense? I am in shock over this.

# THE LIGHT OF LOVE

# Chapter 39
# JUST LEARNING TO WALK

Tuesday May 21, 1991

I have such differing days. Some days, like yesterday, I could hardly move for weariness and pain, though I felt peaceful in spirit as I almost always do. Today, I was filled with energy. I would have died of boredom if I had been made to stay at home or inactive. I was up and doing and filled with the joy of it. I worked for hours and got a great deal accomplished. I love days like this so very much. I would enjoy a life that could be full of them. But then perhaps they would become the norm, and I would not recognize them as the gifts to me that they are. My heart is singing praise to God on days like this, when I can work in the way in which most people do ordinarily. So perhaps it is a blessing that days like this are not the norm for me, because I get so much enjoyment out of them when they do come. I enjoy them too much to ever wish them to become routine and ordinary.

As we prayed tonight, I smelled roses so beautifully. It has been a long time since I have known it was Our Lady's special roses I smelled. The last time was unusual, to say the least. D., Miriam and I smelled them in a restaurant as we sat talking about Our Lady. We thought the scent might come from potted plants nearby. But when we went into the undecorated, dusty entrance of the restaurant to leave, we were hit so strongly with the scent of roses that it was as if Our Lady were joking in loving kindness with us. It was as if she said to us, "You're not going to say this is potted plants now, are you?"

Tonight no one else smelled the roses, but they sensed a peacefulness and a presence of gentleness. All the animals were quiet — something unusual. Gia and our three cats were looking in one direction — towards our front door.

I did not hear her voice as before, but she seemed to be comforting us. My heart has been so sore over my children. Will they forget what we have been given and live as if ... nothing had happened or been given?

Last Sunday was Pentecost. Nothing was mentioned about Our Lady at Mass, but I thought quite a lot about how she is the Bride of the Holy Spirit. Of all of us human beings, she has been most filled with the Holy Spirit. She was so filled with the Holy Spirit that she conceived in her womb, physically and spiritually—she conceived God. That is true grace. To be that filled with grace, to be that filled with God that God would become flesh of your flesh and bone of your bone! Glory to God that it should be.

Who could ever have invented this? Stories of Virgin births in mythology are common, but it is through lust of a god or through gold coins or a bull or something else that they occur, by water itself in one myth that I remember. But never like this, in humility and purity, in quiet submission as a channel of grace for all of the human race.

I thought about these things and began to pray, asking God that whoever gave us a ride home from the church (we still did not know whom it would be) would not mind stopping to get some flowers for the Mother of God and the Bride of the Holy Spirit.

As well as a Pentecost Mass, it was a recognition Mass for the seniors graduating from high school, and an honoring of their parents. Since both my girls are graduating from high school shortly, one of their friends had come to see me, asking for pictures of them for a slide show. I only have baby pictures since Eileen and Miriam are not happy with their later pictures and are embarrassed to give them to me. I wish they knew how much I would value those pictures of my dear girls.

After the slide show, the parents of the seniors were called up to the altar. Unbeknownst to me beforehand, we were presented with red roses. I received two roses — one of the benefits of having twins that come along every now and then and are so special when they do.

So within a few minutes of my prayer, there I stood holding two red roses. I always think I have to assist God with granting my request. It was so perfectly right that the roses should be given to Our Lady, who has prayed with me for my girls and loves us so very much.

As she sat praying tonight after everyone had gone to bed, D. saw the roses in the vase on our little home altar next to the statue of Our Lord's Mother. She came into my room a few minutes ago to tell me that perhaps I had smelled the roses as a little "thank you" from Our Lady. Our Lady and Our Lord are always so appreciative of the smallest things we do.

We think now more and more as children without much sophistication—foolishly, the wise ones of the world would say. We see God and the angels not just in situations in which we would never have thought of them as being involved before, but we noticed situations we would never have recognized before and see God there.

D. was telling me tonight about the great joy she feels in watching the sky, the birds flying, and so much else. One day during the winter she felt as if she had stepped into fairyland because of the glittering ice over everything. It seemed to her that no one else really shared her joy, perhaps because they were used to the scenery and had seen it many times before — so really did not see it now.

The verse, "Unless you become as little children you will not enter the Kingdom of Heaven" has new meaning for me tonight. Might it be possible as C.S. Lewis wrote in THE LAST BATTLE, one of the Narnia chronicles, that some of us could be in the midst of joy and beauty—Heaven itself—and not know because of our arrogance of spirit, pride in our own accomplishments and knowledge, and hardness of heart? Does God prepare us, little by little, step by step, and then stop when we stop? I cannot believe that this preparation starts only in Heaven. As the angels have said to me, what else could life here be but a preparation?

The Blessed Mother said right before the Feast of the Assumption at Saint John Neumann Church in 1988 that she was not preparing us for the Feast of the Assumption. Father James exclaimed at this. "No," she said, "I am preparing you for eternity." This also seems to be what the angels are trying to explain to me. Is part of that preparation an opening of our hearts, if we say yes, to a little bit of Heaven here in a beautiful sky, a kind word, a fairyland of glittering ice, a lovely song, and a unlooked-for act of consideration? The angels have told me that our lives here determine how much of God's love we can give and receive in Heaven. Perhaps it is as though we build our vessels of love here. All vessels in Heaven are full, but some people have built vessels which can hold and therefore can give in great quantities of love, while others are like little cups—precious but small.

But I see more clearly now that this preparation is and must be both in the receiving and in the doing. As I write these thoughts down, I feel like a child in kindergarten who has been given a college text by the angels and by life itself. I write these thoughts down for myself because anyone reading the conversations or perhaps any other writings about God would know them already. But I must take the tottering steps of a child just learning to walk toward understanding, because I must keep learning these things again and again in new ways, as one of the angels said.

But perhaps learning these basics again and again in new ways also means learning them well and from different angles, never as something quickly learned which is superficially understood and probably quickly forgotten. I must know these things completely to be one in heart with my Lord. To be one in heart with my Lord is my ultimate prayer.

I must know these things so completely that I don't know I know them, that they become so much a part of my being that nothing in the whole universe could separate them from me because they ARE me.

This can only occur if I am so concentrated on my Lord that I do not wonder how this or that is affecting me, how I am growing or changing, what my reaction is. Then the main emphasis of my heart is not on myself, but on my Love. Then growth in loving, changing to a greater capacity to love, are by-products of this love between us. They are there, but totally unnoticed and indescribable.

Then it is no longer knowing, but being. Just being, with no awareness at all that I am, that I exist. This is not at all the same thing as oblivion in the void of nothingness and non-personhood. It is a full flowering of myself so centered outside myself that I become fully myself. What thoughts tonight!

Wednesday, May 22, 1991

My heart is so heavy this morning, and yet God's love and grace is all around me. I am thinking of an incident here in fundamentalist West Texas which brings it home to me how closed to the love of Jesus for His Mother and for us some Christians have become. I have been there too, but mine came out of a sense of unworthiness. Do I not trust my Lord to open their hearts to knowing Him and honoring and loving His Mother? But they have free will as we all do. How easy it is to buy Satan's line that a love for the Blessed Mother somehow diminishes

Christ or is disloyal to Jesus. This would only be true if Jesus and His Mother had been at odds and His family, at least His immediate family, had been disunited and had not followed the Law of God. Do those who dishonor Jesus's Mother believe He broke His own commandments?

This morning the light is so bright and the little figure on my cross moves so quickly. D. could see it this morning changing positions within seconds as I could feel it. If this could become a commonplace, what God could do—anything God can do for us—can be minimized and belittled as either ordinary, explainable or routine. And if we cannot give one of these three labels to a blessing, then we simply dismiss the wonder without a label. We just refuse it.

The only thing I can do is pray for others, and for myself as well that my own heart will stay as open as it possibly can. We have been given so much and yet ... and yet how closed we still are.

There are so many who have turned away despite the love they have been shown. If this great love is not what they want, what do they want? But in order to receive any love at all, human or divine, a relinquishing of self to some degree is necessary. A person capable of giving and receiving great love can do this relinquishing of self without a diminishment of self. But when these two—relinquishing versus diminishing—get confused for us, then we fight love. We are afraid that relinquishing ourselves means we lose ourselves and are lessened as people. Perhaps when one is trying so hard to hang on to oneself because one is not mature enough to know that one can let go from a position of love and strength, then one believes one has to resist the vulnerability of love because one may be swept away into oblivion.

But I have been reassured by Saint Michael that genuine Love never does that, no matter what it may seem, and that's where trust comes in. What more apparent proof of diminishment and oblivion could there have been than the mental and spiritual agony followed by a tortured death on a cross?

But yet how wrong it would be to say that Our Lord diminished Himself. No. He relinquished Himself, and His Resurrection made this clear. Perhaps our relinquishing of ourselves makes our own Resurrection, first spiritual and then physical, possible. We are clearly told to follow Our Lord's example in this, as in everything else.

Relinquishing is not at all the same thing as diminishing. I realize with surprise that a simple act of will, through love, can change a diminishing experience that appears to have no choice in it into a relinquishing one—and therefore turns it into a noble sacrifice. I can decide to make this transition because of the grace of Jesus.

What the angels have said to me stays in my mind quietly, and I am almost always thinking about them and Our Lord in some way, even as I do other things and think other thoughts. What an adventure to be on this road.

# Chapter 40
# CONFESSION

On the morning of Friday, May 24th, 1991 my household and I were pray-ing the Sorrowful Mysteries. I was asked by my Guardian Angel to suffer for a soul. He told me that this suffering might be particularly difficult. When I consented, the pain came quickly and hard.

During the time span of one mystery, it was excruciating. Then one of my family prayed for the soul, pleading the suffering and the Blood of Christ be given in retribution for the sins of the soul. The pain diminished quickly.

My Guardian Angel told me that it had been necessary for a human being among human beings to suffer for the sins of all who would accept His gift, and to do this the human being who was entirely a human being had to be also entirely God. He asked, "How is it possible for sin to be fought with sin? It is not possible." He said that Jesus had suffered and died so that sins could be forgiven at all. Before this, sins could not be truly atoned for or forgiven. He said we still had to atone for our sins, but Our Lord Jesus had made complete forgiveness possible. We had to ask for forgiveness, but now forgiveness is possible because He has paid the price.

He explained to me that before Christ's suffering and death, although many souls had atoned for their sins they were, so to speak, on hold. They were waiting for the complete grace of Jesus's sacrifice so they could be forgiven. Then their own suffering and atonement for their sins could be applied once the price of Jesus's suffering had been paid.

For a moment, my Guardian Angel took me to the site of Our Lord's Crucifixion. I heard Our Dear Lord speak the words, "It is completed."

Then I stood in a place that reminded me of Purgatory, though I do not know if this is actually where we were. My Guardian Angel's presence was close beside me. We stood in a very large crowd of people. The crowd seemed endless, but they were very quiet. There was hardly a murmur among them, though they could speak with each other. As I have said, I have doubts based on what I have experienced that souls in

Purgatory can communicate with each other, so this state or place seemed not quite the same since the souls could communicate with each other. I do know that these souls were not in pain, were not being purged of sin. They were simply waiting. I don't dare hazard a guess as to what all this means. I will only describe now what happened rather than try to interpret anything else.

The crowd faced all in one direction toward a great wall. Suddenly Our Lord stood facing us. My Guardian Angel showed me that He was freshly off the Cross. He was not there in the flesh, but His spirit bore the wounds of His body. How to describe the bloody and torn wreck of His poor body, as illustrated in His spiritual form, is beyond me. There was no part of Him that was not hurt and bleeding. I know very certainly that He showed the clear, horrible marks of His suffering.

He stood there for a moment in silence, and the crowd was totally quiet. He did not speak, but I had the sense that He said to each one of them personally, "I got here as soon as I could." It was almost an apology for keeping them waiting, and this amazed me. I would almost say I was stunned that He, being in His mortally wounded state, would think with such love for all those waiting for Him. Even in this state, He put them and their needs above His own.

He turned to the wall. His back was to us for a brief moment. What He did I don't know, because there was no door in the wall before He turned His back to us. But suddenly there was a great door, and He had opened it. It was a wide door. He stood just inside the door's margin, with a side profile to us. Our Lord did not go any farther into Heaven at this time.

Then slowly, quietly, and in perfect order the souls began to come forward one by one. Each soul stopped in front of Our Lord facing Him. I believe He spoke a brief word to each soul. He raised His hands in blessing, but it seemed to me that He could not raise them entirely outward.

His hands were almost in front of His face about four inches away. His palms were turned outward toward the person in front of Him with His hands downward. It was obvious that He could not raise His arms and hands outward any farther than this. What most struck me was the blood dripping down from His wounds, dripping down His forearms, which were turned outward toward the person in front of Him. Each soul, in great joy and yet great sorrow at Our Lord's pain, then moved passed Our Lord through the door into a region of beautiful, warm light. Jesus did not move beyond the door, but stood immediately inside it.

"There have been many false speculations and errors construed concerning what Our Lord Jesus Christ was doing between the time of His death on the Cross and His Resurrection," my Angel told me. "This is what He was doing, freeing each soul from the chains of its sin." Jesus gave each one of them His blessing of forgiveness as they entered the door to Heaven which He alone could open. This forgiveness flowed out to them in His life's blood.

All of us there could see the signs of His past torture. This scene of Our Lord freshly off the cross blessing each of the people is one I can never forget. My Guardian Angel told me that this blessing of forgiveness, Our Lord's crucified arms dripping blood, is what happens every time we go to confession and receive absolution at the hands of a priest acting for Jesus.

Baptism cleanses us of original sin and whatever other sins we have committed. Confession is an extension of the grace of baptism. My Angel begged us to go to Confession much more often than is now customary. Our Lord forgives us all the time, but it is necessary for us to ask for this forgiveness so that we ourselves can be open to receive it in the sacrament of Confession. Without our openness, Our Lord's forgiveness is a gift waiting to be given. "Confess your sins," Saint Paul says. Part of my penance has always been to speak my sins aloud. Speaking them aloud forces me to claim them, to face them, to admit them as being my responsibility. No wonder we must be urged.

"His hands are always raised in blessing for you," my Angel said. "But you must see that and accept it."

"You cannot just confess your sin and then go on as if nothing had happened," he said. "You must show by a change in your own heart, your life, your relationships, that you have repented.

You must atone to God's children for the hurt done to God. The hurt done to God's children is done to God Himself." He said that a misunderstanding of this is one of the biggest errors and problems in the Church today. He said that when we go to Confession, this is a grace given to us by Our Lord. It is as if Our Lord says lovingly to us,

"These are your trouble spots. Go out and work on them in your daily life, and know that I am with you. I only want you to be close to Me."

He said that these troubled spots are not eliminated by Confession. They are forgiven by Confession, but we must eliminate them ourselves in our daily lives with others. The sin itself is removed, but without our efforts the repercussions of that sin will remain and we will probably commit the sin again. Our own efforts are crucial in this process of growing closer to Our Lord. This does not negate the grace or the gift given to us by His sacrifice. It makes us partners in our own salvation.

My Dear Angel explained to me that God could not get close enough to our sin to forgive it because of His own perfection. Though Christ never sinned, He was and is fully human as well as fully God and therefore could be the mediator, the bridge of forgiveness and reconciliation between humanity and God. Our Lord God wished above all things for this bridge between Himself and humanity regardless of our sinful state. Drastic measures were needed, and they were taken.

My Angel told me that the crowd in which we stood was composed of souls from every past nation, every past religion, who had lived as just and kind a life as was possible for them on the earth, or regretted not doing so. Their righteousness and desire had taken them as close to God as they could come without the redeeming sacrifice of Our Lord. That sacrifice now opened the door of Heaven to them all.

I was quite overwhelmed and awed by all this, having never thought much about the sentence in the Apostles' Creed, "He descended to the dead." My Guardian Angel smiled at me and said, "That is enough."

# Chapter 41
# THE CHURCH UNDER PERSECUTION

Eileen graduated from high school on May 31st and Miriam graduated on June 1st. I left for an internship in Saint Louis on June 2nd. My parents had, to our great shock, left Hawaii after 40 years and retired in San Antonio. They arrived for the hectic but exciting weekend. We also attended the graduation of a friend of Eileen's which made three graduations in two days. I had dreams of hearing lists of interminable names all night.

Monday, June 24, 1991

The light grew bright but gentle as I sat working. I tested the presence as I have been taught. The voice was a human voice, the loving voice I have come to know as my Lord's. He asked me to write. This is what He said "Those who are power hungry will not stop until the Church has been destroyed in your country. It will lie in ruins. Those who are faithful will be silent and in despair. Those few to speak out will be silenced, not just by the "new" church but by all others in government and in other sects. They will whisper only to each other. They will meet in small groups and pray in despair.

"But out of their prayers shall rise a great spirit of love. It's greatness will lie in that it can even love those who have crushed it. Do you not know that I Am God, and that all apparent evil is turned to your good? All pain is permitted that renewal might come. You faithful ones are the people with whom I have chosen to work most, and who is to gainsay Me?

"Those who are arrogant in their ways have no voice. Their voices became a whimper when they tried to make Me into a concept, a doubtable idea. I then could be dismissed.

"But now that I have been dismissed from their minds and banished from their hearts, who are they? What are they? They are children wandering in a desert, too afraid even to know they are there. They need your prayers far more than it is possible for you ever to fear them. It is only My mercy that will save them from themselves. They are to be pitied far more than those who never found their way to Me at all. Forgive them, and give them into My hands, which is where all healing takes place.

"Be strong, my people. Be strong in love. You have no other weapon but love. But I have told you over and over again that, with love, all things are possible in love. Nothing apart from love endures, though it may last for a very long time. This is because nothing but love truly has being.

"Be at peace. Let your hearts be untroubled by appearances. I have promised to be ever with you. I do not forget."*

On June 29, 1991, Father Walch was wondering aloud what his guardian angel's name might be. When a priest becomes pastor, he receives an angel to assist him in his duties. Father wondered if this angel was still with him since he no longer has the responsibility of a parish.

---

[NOTE: I was later told by one of the angels that the hierarchy of the Church in this country would assume they could keep the "American Catholic Church" intact and under their control after "getting rid of Rome." However, it would not be very long before this "new church" splintered into many small groups with many people simply leaving for older Protestant groups. The "new church" would not be an entity for very long. I was also told by my Guardian Angel at this time that the Church, as the Body of Christ on earth, would undergo a series of events which would parallel the events of Our Blessed Lord's Passion: His Agony in the Garden of Gethsemane, a great betrayal of some sort, a horrible scourging, a crowning of mockery, a walk to death, and finally a cruel death. "But," my Dear Angel said, "when you see the Church established by Our Lord Jesus Christ while here on earth hanging dead on the cross, mutilated beyond recognition, please, please remember the Resurrection." We are also never to forget Our Blessed Lord's promise that He would be with His Church, and that "the gates of hell will not prevail against it."]

My Guardian Angel began to talk, but he had spoken only a few words when Our Lord's voice began speaking. His warm, rich voice full of melody, gentle and light but yet with a strength and power I cannot describe, is so beautiful. He said:

"You are still a pastor.
You meet your people everywhere.
The pain of My people cries out to Me,
And their agonizing cries echo day and night.
Their voices lament to Me:
'Where are You, Lord?
Do You remember me?
Have You forgotten Your promises?'

Tell them I have not forgotten.
Tell them in the congregations,
In the streets—
In byways—
On the mountains—
In the valleys—
In the slums—
And in the mansions
That I have not forgotten.

Show them by your actions,
By your words,
And through your love
That I have not forgotten them!"

# THE LIGHT OF LOVE

# Chapter 42
# YET CLOSER TO MY LORD

Christmas of 1991 was quiet for us, mainly because we were ill. Our big Christmas present that year was rest. But right before Christmas, my Blessed Angel asked us to place a crucifix on our door.

"When you place this crucifix on your door," he said, "you will be making it clear to whom your home belongs. You will be marking your door with the blood of the Lamb of the New Covenant." He said this was akin to the Children of Israel marking their door posts with the blood of the slain lambs for the first Passover in Egypt. "When your door is marked with the Blood of the Lamb," he said, "much evil will pass by you."

The crucifix we now have on our front door was Miriam's Christmas gift to me. The head of the corpus was slightly away from the cross and to the right. It now hangs completely forward as I have never felt it on any other crucifix. The corpus has fallen, Jesus's left shoulder is in a distorted and dislocated position, and the body truly hangs by the nails. Our door is certainly marked with the Blood of the dear Lamb of God.

On New Year's Day of 1992, my computer crashed. I was distraught and discouraged. Not only did I lose a great deal of work, but I lost six months of this journal. I will now try to reconstruct events with the blessed angels as best I can. It will probably be a haphazard reconstruction, but I tell myself (and believe) that what Our Blessed Lord wishes recorded will be recorded.

I was coordinator for the rosary group at Saint John Neumann Church. For the Feast of the celebration of Our Lady's Assumption into Heaven of 1991, many of the regular rosary group were involved in other things, so those few of us remaining were kept busy leading rosaries and were very sore throated by the end of the day.

There was a crowd of about four thousand people at Saint John Neumann that day. Many people, including my confessor of this time saw the outdoor statue of Our Lady weeping. Others saw the statue of Our Lady of Fatima in the church also weeping. She always warns us. Since the beginning of this century in particular she has warned us. She warned of World War II. Though we were saddened, there was a great joy in the crowd — joy over being there.

Bishop Michael Sheehan celebrated the evening Mass, and his respect for the faith of the many pilgrims was heartwarming. It is not necessary to believe in order to respect.

Because of the wide circulation of my lengthy letter concerning the events at Saint John Neumann Church in 1988, written originally to friends and family, many copies of which had been made by people and passed on to others, quite a number of people in the crowd recognized me. They were lining up to talk to me, wanting to ask questions about the angels and other things. I had not received permission to speak to them from my confessor, who almost certainly would have asked me to be discreet and quietly out of sight. I felt this way too, but did not know what to do. I also did not in any way wish to have anything sensationalized. But I didn't know what to do.

I have been hesitant to ask my Angel about things in everyday life, thinking it was better he speak to me as Our Lord wishes. But this time I did cry out to him for guidance as to what to do. He would later tell me I was to feel comfortable asking him for help and guidance at any time. He said it would be up to Our Lord to decide how and what he should answer, or whether he should answer at all. Now he said to me, "Please lead the people in praying the rosary all day as you had planned. I will not speak to you again today."

He not only did not speak to me for the remainder of the day, but did not speak again for a month. I saw the light fairly often and felt my Angel's kind and loving presence with no censure of me at all in it, but he did not speak. I felt more peaceful about the silence than I have ever felt about other silences before. More and more, I am peaceful and not concerned about the times my Guardian Angel does not speak to me. It is Our Lord's decision.

Around this time, an acolyte of our church asked me not to receive Our Lord as I had been doing: taking the Sacred Host in my hand and dipping it in the Precious Blood of Jesus. I did it this way because several years before I had knocked the cup out of the hand of the Eucharistic minister, spilling its contents. I felt terrible and, rather than trying to take the cup in my hands, I would dip the Host into it.

The acolyte asked me to take the cup in my hands, saying he had seen the Precious Blood fall on my coat one day as I dipped the Host in the cup. I felt very badly about this and went into the church to pray. Perhaps the fear of committing sacrilege, perhaps better put by saying the fear of offending someone you love so very dearly, cannot be understood by non-Catholics. But I was mortified.

I felt my Lord's quiet, real Presence beside me in the same way I sense the presence of everyone. As a blind person, there is no difference for me when Our Lord speaks to me and is with me. I do not mean in any way to minimize this wondrous gift given to me. It is only that He is so real, truly human, and truly God.

He said to me gently and even a little humorously, comforting me, "My Precious Blood has fallen on many places less hospitable than your coat." His tenderness and understanding are something I cannot express in mere words. I now receive Our Lord only in my mouth, and I hold the cup and pray there will be no more mishaps.

One evening at Mass, my Dear Angel asked me to pray in particular for the Holy Father, Pope John Paul II. He said, "He is dearly beloved by all in Heaven and has been especially chosen to guide the Church founded by Jesus Christ through this difficult time." He told me that the Holy Father's guardian angel's name is "Fortress of the Lord." As I have been told, the name of one's guardian angel directly bears on what one is to do on earth for God. Each of our beloved souls is matched by God to a special angel in Heaven, an angel perfectly suited to help each of us live the life we are called by God to live, fulfill our earthly purpose, and finally to be fully reunited with Our Lord. Our guardian angels' names are directly related to our purpose and mission here. When I heard the Holy Father's guardian angel's name, "Fortress of The Lord," I wondered. "How can it be that God needs a fortress?" I was perplexed.

"Wait just a moment and you will understand," my Angel said to me. In a moment, we sang the last song. I had had no idea what it would be. As we stood singing, I understood that the Holy Father and

---

[Note: In the spring of 1993, right before Easter, the Holy Father's guardian angel came to me pleading for prayers for him. The light from this angel was so bright and huge that I thought at first it was Saint Michael.]

his angel are to be God's fortress for the Church, for us. Here are the words we sang,

> Though the mountains may fall and the hills turn to dust
> Yet the love of the Lord will stand
> As a shelter for all who will call on His name
> Sing the praise and the glory of God.

This is also one of my favorite songs because of the verse,

> Could the Lord ever leave you?
> Could the Lord forget His love?
> Though a mother forsake her child
> He will not abandon you.

I can't remember at the moment which psalm the song is based upon, but it is special, considering that millions of mothers have forsaken their children in our time, offering them as human sacrifices to the gods of convenience and personal wishes.

"What is this?" I exclaimed.

"Test!" He said sternly to me.

After I had tested the presence, he asked me to pray and ask others to pray that "the channels of God's grace will be opened for the Holy Father by your prayers that he might have the time and the strength to protect the Church in the way God wishes him to do before he (the Holy Father) must leave." I don't dare think of what these words may imply.

I pray diligently now for the Holy Father, and beg you to do so as well. I pray he will have a trustworthy friend beside him always, that he will be given great strength and wisdom by God, and that he will know how loved he is both as a person and as the 264th Vicar of Christ on earth.

Around this time, I asked my Dear Angel why it is so important that we ask our guardian angels to pray for us and with us. Just as we ask friends to pray for us, we ask the angels and saints to pray for us. But why, I wanted to know, is it particularly important that we ask our guardian angels to pray for us.

My Angel told me that our guardian angels are our special gift from God, our personal messengers and petitioners who will, at our bidding, go directly into the full presence of God. These guardian angels are our personal messengers and petitioners, just waiting to be asked. He told me that when we ask them to pray for us, they go into the full Presence of God, right to the throne of the Lord of the universe, and give our petitions as we gave them to our angels. We can, of course, pray directly to God but He in His love for us has given us special messengers to formally petition Him as an earthly king would receive petitions, but so much more majestically.

My Dear Angel told me that our petitions, whether our guardian angels believe they should be granted as they are or not, are not changed in any way by the angels in their presentation of them to God. The petition of a child to his or her guardian angel, a narrow prayer, an unthinking prayer, a loving prayer: all are presented as they are given to God by the angels, and Our Lord does as He in His infinite wisdom sees best. My Angel said the angels, not just our guardian angels, love to petition God for us and they will join our guardian angels in doing this especially at our request.

I did not ask a question about this, but one morning my Dear Angel told me that Our Lord's creation of the universe began "with His wish for a family." It was this wish that began all of creation. He said that Our Lord God had created angels first. But, he said with wry humor, "we weren't enough." With great affection He said of God, "and He's still at it." He spoke with such love and affection for Our Lord, with friendly closeness and yet also with such deep awe and reverence, that it was for me yet another glimpse of the relationship I may have with my Lord some day. He told me once again of the great love Our Lord has for each of the souls He creates.

In the middle of October a woman of our parish who had been fighting cancer for three years, died. As we were praying the rosary at her memorial service, my Dear Angel spoke to me. He said that Our Lord had "allowed her presence" to remain with her husband and children to comfort them. "But now," he said, "because of her great suffering and sincere atonement her full spiritual being is being called home."

He told me that when a soul is called by God to Heaven, there is an ecstasy of joy for that soul which cannot be known here on earth. "I have been given permission by Our Lord to show you in a small way what this great ecstasy is like," he told me.

Then I felt a rush of joy which is indescribable. The best way I can describe it, though, is to say it was as though you were to throw your arms above your head in unabandoned exhilaration and your whole being were to rise up and up and up in a swoop of joy and freedom that might last forever or be only a second. True and beautiful purpose was at the heart of this exultation, the purpose for a soul now going to its Creator. How I wish I could give you in your own heart and feelings, as well as in the joy of your mind's understanding, what was given to me.

On the feast of Saints Peter and Paul, I had gone to Mass not knowing it was their feast day, or that it was any feast day at all. The light in the church, the light which I see, was very bright. It was bright even before the Consecration. Usually I see it, but it is gentle. Then, at the time of the Consecration, it often becomes so beautiful and bright it is a constant wonder to me. This does not always happen. It happens, perhaps about 60 per cent of the time. But on this day it was very bright and became brighter still at the time of the Consecration. I wondered if it were a special day.

Then, as naturally as if two warm and loving new friends had come up to me to introduce themselves, Saints Peter and Paul were standing beside me. They were very real and human. I do not mean by this that they had bodies. I sensed their presence in the same way I sense the presence of anyone, human or angel, as a blind person would sense it, of course. I know my blindness is used by my Lord in these experiences and it becomes an asset because I am not limited to visual perception.

Saint Peter was warm and friendly, not as I had imagined him. He was outgoing and very kindly. I could imagine him striding along the shore of the Sea of Galilee chatting with people and joking with and playing with children. He was not at all a leader, it seemed to me, at least I would not have thought of him as having leadership qualities. Perhaps the word I would use to describe him is lovable. I knew within a few moments why Our Blessed Lord loves him.

Saint Paul was more serious and intense, but even here there was a warmth I had expected even less than I did Saint Peter's warmth. I have had a difficult time with some of the things Saint Paul wrote about women in the scriptures. I also noted, however, the love and respect he had for people like Priscilla and Damaris. Saint Paul said to me with total sincerity and firmness, knowing my feelings about him, "You have absolutely no idea at all how hard it was for me to get those people just to listen to me, let alone live what I was trying to teach them." I feel differently about him now, though it would be hard to put the difference into words. I have also noted more clearly to myself while reading the Scriptures how lovingly he speaks of certain women by name, giving them great and automatic respect, apparently due to their merits as true Christians.

I have taken a warning from this experience: Be careful what you think and what you say concerning saints who are already in Heaven! You, after all, Patricia, are not there yet.

I learned that Saints Peter and Paul, according to Church tradition, were martyred together in Rome; that is why they share a feast day. Saint Paul was beheaded as a Roman citizen. Saint Peter, after telling his executioners he did not feel worthy to die in the same way as his Lord had, was crucified upside down. What struck me so about them is that they seemed to me to be such ordinary people. Can ordinary people be so brave? Could I be? By the grace of God we can be courageous way beyond ourselves for people we love. For the Lord we love how much more then, but only by His grace and with His aid because we are such ordinary people. We may have a chance to show our love in this way. If I am called to this, may I please not be a coward out of fear of pain.

# THE LIGHT OF LOVE

# Chapter 43
# THE TWO SOULS

On New Year's Day of 1992, my Blessed Angel began talking to me. Father Walch was visiting us. He had arrived in Lubbock from Oklahoma City four days before.

I ran back to my room to get the little computer, the braille 'n speak, I use most of the time now for writing. I began to write down what my Dear Angel was saying. That is when the computer crashed, losing everything with no backups. I lost not only the journal, but telephone numbers, calendar, etc., and two and a half months of school work. Father tells me he hopes never to see the expression on my face that he did that New Year's morning.

Here is what my Blessed Angel said, as closely as I remember it.

All of Heaven, he said, was rejoicing because Our Lord God had given the year of 1992 to Our Blessed Mother as a gift. She had been praying for this gift very deeply. She has been given this year of 1992 completely, and will have (by the love and grace of God) full power to do as she believes best for the sole purpose of bringing souls to her Son. My Angel told me that all of Heaven was mustering behind her, ready to do her bidding to help her bring as many souls to Our Lord as possible. All the Saints and Angels were in unfathomable joy over all this.

So, I asked him, is it sort of like a Marian Year in Heaven? He was amused and told me all eternity is "Marian." Since the Mother of God is Our Lord's masterpiece, His delight, then all of eternity is a celebration of His creation.

He then told me that our country has, for the most part, been spared the catastrophes hitting the rest of the world. He said that practically every place on earth in this century has suffered natural disaster or war or both, but that our country as a whole has not experienced this to the degree others have. Our civilian population has not suffered the direct horrors of war as so many have, and we have been spared major natural catastrophes. He said this would change now because our country as a whole does not wish to continue trying to live the values taught to us by Almighty God.

It is not, he said, that calamities will be sent but that a special protection we had as a country, gratuitously given to us by God, is now being removed by Our Lord to allow nature to take its natural course. This is, at any rate, my understanding of his words to me. He said there would be major disasters, particularly flooding. I saw whole cities inundated. He did not say when this would happen. He warned that each soul should live as close to God as possible, knowing its time here is short. I was reminded of the visions I saw at the fountain at Saint John Neumann Church of 1988. I experienced an earthquake on the west coast of the United States in which suddenly there was nothing beneath the buildings. There was destruction of crops and vegetation, death of livestock, contamination of water in the mid-west, and the rise of a lawfully elected government in this country which would turn so evil it would be more evil than anything humanity has ever known. I remembered seeing the horrible illnesses, especially two. One disease was lingering and wasting. The other affected its victims so quickly that those who contracted it through simple contact with others were dead within 36 hours.

Devastation was great in Europe. I could see nothing but blackness, and the red of fire. Conditions, relatively speaking, were fairly good in Central and South America, though there was political and economic chaos and disorder. I was not allowed to see my beautiful Hawaiian Islands, nor could I look into the Pacific Ocean area at all.

I asked about the horrible government in the United States, when it would come. I received no answer. Then I asked, "Who are these people?" – meaning the government in power. I saw a great fire with people dancing around it. I heard a cruel and evil thundering voice saying, "Go forth and do my work!" What people, united in kinship with Lucifer, will rule?

I have not dwelt on these horrors, suffice it to say that I believe I have been shielded from dwelling on them. I have understood that they will occur, but that I and others are to pray and to love. We are to hold fast to our faith and our love, even and perhaps especially to hold fast to our love for those hurting us. As beautiful Sophie Scholl said, "I will stand alone before God whether my soul goes alone or whether I perish with millions."

It is only important to live the best lives we can every moment of every day, praying that our lives will be completely pleasing to God. It is up to us to remain in the state of grace, and then trust everything to Him.

On the evening of January 2, 1992, after the celebration of the Holy Mass by Father John Walch, now my guide and confessor, we were gathered together in my home. Father Walch, Miriam, D., and Mike Slate were there. My Blessed Angel said he had come straight from the presence of God to deliver these words.

"Our Lord, the King of the universe, His Majesty, the Lord of all things, thanks His servant and friend, Father John Walch. He blesses him because of his efforts to protect His people. He promises these efforts will bear fruit, not just in this present time, but continuously into eternity. He gives His blessing to all who strive to give Him glory. Amen."

Father John was deeply touched by this, and believes the statement refers to his efforts to track down a bogus priest who had come to our vicinity and who is traveling around the United States masquerading as a Roman Catholic priest.

On February 3, my little God-daughter Claire Rene Benoist was safely born. Her mom, Celeste, is also all right. Glory be to God. We had been praying deeply that this would happen since Jeff and Celeste's first child, Vincent, had unexpected complications at birth which caused him to be handicapped. He is the little boy who received such beautiful healing blessings, though not a complete cure, at the fountain on the Feast of the Assumption of 1988 at Saint John Neumann Church here.

---

[Note: Sophie Scholl was a young lady who grew up during the Third Reich in Germany. She and her friends were members of the Hitler Youth, but during their university days in Munich, they formed a resistance group called the "White Rose". The Group secretly passed out leaflets denouncing Hitler, the invasion by Germany of other countries, the exportation and murder of Jews, Gypsies, and other minorities, and the suppression of freedom at home. The members of the White Rose were greatly influenced by reading the early Church Fathers, especially St. Augustine. When they were finally captured, they were allowed a short time together before being taken out to face individual firing squads. They hugged each other and said, "See you in a few minutes."]

This day was also special and unusual for another reason. I was asked to suffer twice on this day. The first time was in the morning for a soul near death who did accept the blessed mercy of Our Lord. The second time was in the evening.

My Dear Angel asked me to suffer for two souls at once. They were a man and a woman. They were fairly young. This offering for two souls at the same time has never happened before. My Angel told me the two people had been closely linked in life, had done much evil together, but had cared for each other. It was this goodness of caring Our Blessed Lord wished to use to try to offer them His grace.

I began praying the Sorrowful Mysteries for the souls, and near the beginning of the second Sorrowful Mystery, the Scourging of Our Lord at the Pillar, I began to suffer the pain I have described, the total pain of body, emotions and spirit.

My Dear Angel took me to the brink of hell. I have pleaded never to be shown hell. My prayer was answered and my wish respected in a surprising way. All of my strength, all of my energy, went into trying to hold onto the two souls for whom I was offering. As I have previously described, I became a rope (in a metaphysical sense) holding them back from the precipice of hell. My Angel showed me the dark abyss below the two souls. There was fire down there, but somehow it was not bright fire, but horrible and black. There was a sickening stench in the air which I could not identify.

But, as I have said, I was so concentrated on holding the souls back, focused on using my entire being to keep them from the brink in my offering that I really was not frightened. I would say that I was too busy to be frightened.

I don't know how long I offered the pain for the souls or held them back with my whole being in offering. There is a timelessness about these experiences. It could have been a few minutes, it could have been an hour. But at last my Guardian Angel, who had never left my side, said gently to me, "They do not wish in any way to receive the grace Our Lord wishes to give them through your offering. Please let go of them."

I felt as if my heart would break, but I did not hesitate to let go of them at my Angel's command. They fell. When they were not quite half way down, a horrible creature came up out of the abyss. It came very quickly, rising much faster than they were falling. He was like a huge long worm. I felt his presence, his personality I might almost say. What horrified me most about him was that he was so completely complacent and self-satisfied. Nothing for him existed outside himself.

He snapped up the two souls, which had been very obviously human souls as they fell. By this I mean that though they had done great evil, they still had Our Blessed Lord's life in them, or mark, or something of humanness and of God. I can't describe what I mean very well here. Though they had sinned greatly they were still people.

When the vile creature snapped them up, it began a horrible grinding and sucking. It was so delighted with itself, so completely self-satisfied and pleased. My Dear Angel showed me that it was sucking all the life of God out of them, all the things which are good that God gives us, His very stamp of His image on our souls; all of this was being sucked out of these two human souls.

When it had finished sucking, the creature spat them out. They were unrecognizable to me when he spat them out. They were two totally inhuman little black wisps, like horrible gnats flitting around. They were little disgusting demons with no resemblance to human souls any longer. They fell the rest of the way into the flames below.

My Guardian Angel immediately turned me away from the brink so I did not see what the monstrous being did after this. My Blessed Angel told me gently that Our Blessed Lord had wished me to experience this and to see and understand that, no matter what gifts of grace and love He wishes to give, there will be some who will not, even on the brink of hell, accept His love and mercy. The only way He could have given those two souls His mercy would have been to force it upon them, and this of course He will never do. My friend, my Dear Angel, told me that the pain I had offered as prayers for these two souls would be given to souls who would accept it.

It would become an offering, a redress of the balance for their sins. It would be the pain of their repentance in order that they could be open to the cleansing of Our Lord's love, the cleansing of His life's blood. My Blessed Angel said it was Our Lord's particular wish that I see this in order that I might clearly know that there are some who will not be salvaged no matter what is done to help them.

This experience haunted me. For weeks afterwards I could not pray the most commonly known Fatima prayer without crying.

Fatima Prayer, "O my sweet Jesus, forgive us our sins. Save us from the fires of hell. Lead all souls to Heaven, especially those in most need of Thy mercy. Amen."

By the grace of God, these experiences are used as a means of grace for others. They are also, however, always a means for Our Lord to help me to grow in love. As I have written before, I had for the most part a credo of "live and let live." I had moral standards and I very much wished to be a true follower of Jesus, but I was also anxious not to judge others. Judging others is God's right, never ours.

But as I have these experiences, I see that there is a divinely given code of right and wrong which is apart from us, which is non-negotiable. We may know clearly and without doubt that a sin committed is wrong. We may say so. What I must never judge is whether I or another person will be given or should be given the tender mercy of God. That mercy will be given if the individual's heart is even a little open, and I can never know whether another person will see the wrong done and regret it. That is what I must never judge. Judgment that an act puts a soul in jeopardy is an indication that prayers are truly necessary.

If I know that someone is doing wrong and I am cruel and destructive about my criticisms, or if I do nothing about it out of fear of appearing judgmental, I will be held accountable to God for that soul if I do not at least pray for him or her. How many souls are there now in hell who would not be there if someone had seen and acknowledged that they were breaking the laws of love, and had prayed for them? Will that be one of the reproofs with which Our Blessed Lord will face us?

# Chapter 44
# A PURE SOUL

One of the first souls I offered for was a young girl. By what I saw, I believe she came from a non-Christian, third world country. She was the youngest of a large family. Her parents were both severely handicapped, her father being totally bedridden. They lived in a one-room, little shack on stilts of some sort. She was the only one left at home to care for her parents. She was the only one of her brothers and sisters who did care for their parents, and she had resolved to do so until they did not need her any longer.

What little she brought home by working was not enough to feed them, and they were hungry and malnourished. They lived in a continuous state of starvation.

This dear young girl was raped, and found she was with child. My Guardian Angel told me that if she had been on her own, she would have carried her child to term. But because of her responsibility for her parents, she went to a woman of the community who did such things and was now dying of a botched abortion.

I could hear loud lamenting from the people of her village. She lay on a mat in a dingy hut. Though she had sought the abortion, she grieved over her little one.

In a timeless moment right before death, she met Jesus face to face. She recognized Him as One she dearly loved but had not known she loved. Jesus gently reproached her for the death of her baby, but it was clear He understood the circumstances in which she lived, and had the deepest compassion for her and her parents. She accepted His reproach with humility and sorrow. I will never forget how they looked at each other with such tenderness, and the compassion in His eyes.

She was able to separate the horrible event of the rape from the innocent existence of her child. As she passed from this world to the next, I caught a glimpse of Purgatory. Then, to my amazement, I saw the beautiful door in the wall of light open for her. I was not told this, but I conjecture from what I saw that if she was in Purgatory at all, it was not for long. She is in Heaven now with her child.

Such is God's love and mercy. Though he is a God of justice or perhaps BECAUSE he is a God of justice, he is truly the Lord of Mercy.

# Chapter 45
# TEACHINGS ON THE ROSARY

M y Guardian Angel, my friend, spoke to me about the rosary. He said that the rosary is the most potent weapon we have against Lucifer, the strongest weapon there is, because with each Hail Mary we remind Lucifer that he is only an angel, and a fallen one at that. He is reminded of this because, with each Hail Mary, he is brought face to face with the miracle of God using a mere human being, a woman!, to bring about His purposes. He said that Our Lady is a perfect mirror of God's grace. That a human being could be a perfect mirror of God's grace is like saying that the lowest of the low could be raised to perfection by the might and power of God, and so the greatness of God is clearly expressed in Our Lady. With each prayer of the rosary, Lucifer is reminded of this (see Appendix A).

The perfection of this miracle of love by Our Lord is contrasted in each one of our prayers with the imperfection, pain, and sinfulness of the situation in our lives for which we are praying. We ourselves, my Angel said, in our sinfulness are contrasted with this perfection which God has achieved through His grace in His creation of the Blessed Mother and, through her, God Himself becoming a human being among us. Through this continuous contrast as we pray the rosary, grace is poured out to us and deep and lasting change occurs. If we are praying from our hearts, the mysteries of Our Lord's and Our Lady's lives begin to actually come to life in us. We begin to live Our Lord's life in our own lives.

We do this, he said, by approaching the purity of the human being God created to be His Mother. As we become more and more like her, we can and do live Jesus's life and suffering in our own lives.

He said something else which I found very amazing. "As you pray this prayer of the rosary which encompasses deep contemplation on yourselves and your lives and situations joined in contemplation on Our Lord's life, the perfect grace given by God to Our Lord's Mother can and is poured out to you. You become living rosaries. You yourselves become a living prayer."

The image he showed me which most remained in my mind was the constant contrast, with each Hail Mary, of our pain and sinfulness, our impossible-seeming situation, with the perfection of God's miracle of a pure human being and bringing Him into the world. I interpreted what I saw, this continuous contrast between perfection and pain with each Hail Mary, as a quiet lessening of this great gap between the situation being prayed for and God's perfect love. A slow perfecting of those who pray with all their love also takes place.

I saw a clear and right mirror of God's love being held up, then a blackened and tarnished image which resembled the first only in that they were both mirrors. With each Hail Mary, the blackened image more closely resembled the bright and beautiful one. The blackened image was the situation needing prayer, as well as the heart and soul of the person praying. So both the situation we pray for and we ourselves are changed by the powerful prayer of the rosary, which is both the prayer of the entire life of Jesus Christ and His Mother and the great mysteries therein and an offering of our own hearts in prayer and union through Our Lady's graces.

# Chapter 46
# KINDLY SPIRIT OF GOD

March 20, 1992

T he light grew bright as I sat working at my desk about 5:30 this evening at Tech. The light was not as bright as it has been in the past, but it was gentle with a hue I can't describe. I tested the presence as I have been taught, and received gentle assurance. I was a little at a loss as to how to begin when I was asked to write, since I had not been asked to write for a very long time.

I finally began, "May I ask your name?"

"Kindly Spirit of God." (Meaning the warmth of fellowship and closeness among those loving God. I was puzzled by the name and the angel clarified it for me in a type of wordless but very clear communication something like the way I am shown pictures.)

"Is this a regular conversation?"

"No, I am here to give you comfort and reassurance."

"I haven't deserved it at all, but I am very grateful."

"You are a human being with many limits. Our Blessed Lord needs your limits as much as He requires your strength. If you had no limits, how could your frailty serve Him?"

"I feel as though I have a lot of frailties with which to serve Him."

"You have many, and you will be given more. But you will also be given the gift of joy in your frailties. The special people God has given you are there to help you and to love you, and all of you together will praise Our Lord by your lives dedicated to love. You will be given special graces for the times to come."

"There is so much talk of the times to come. May I know anything more about this?"

"There is emphasis about the physical difficulties you will face in the times to come, but the greatest pain and stress will come from your spiritual battles against those forces which are trying to rend and destroy your souls. Physical discomfort, great suffering and even death are temporary when seen through the glass of eternity. But what affects your souls: that is forever, that is for always. Each one of you have a priceless treasure to guard: your soul. Guard it well, and help others to guard theirs. This is the basis for all the commandments you have been given by Our Almighty Lord."

"That we should guard our souls?"

"Not simply to guard your souls but to cause them to grow in strength through great love and quiet sacrifice. As you give, you receive many times over; though the fruits of your patience may not be immediate."

"But it is so hard sometimes to swallow hurt. And what about abusive situations?"

"Think always in terms of eternity. Ask yourself how what is happening affects your soul and the souls of those who are joined with you. You have each been given a guide in your soul because your soul is made in God's image. This means that He has put His stamp upon you. You have, to the degree that you need it, an understanding of how you, each in your own way, can best reflect His image. Each of you does this differently because Our Lord is God, but each of you can be a pure image. You become purer as your love grows, and your love grows as you choose to love. You decide.

The other night you chose again. Each time you choose sincerely, you grow in strength and love. You have believed that weakness makes you less able to serve. But your honest understanding of your weakness, of your own deep inability, frees you to serve because you do not look to yourself quite so much. Do you understand, little one?"

"I think so. I have thought about some of these things too, but I have felt so guilty."

"It is right that you should feel guilt. Guilt is said to be very bad for the well being of a soul in your time. But unless there is true remorse for doing wrong, how can there be sorrow over sin followed by forgiveness from God and those whom you have hurt? Guilt is not good when you do not understand that you are God's beloved one, and that a repentant heart is never turned away. On the contrary, a repentant heart is the joy of Our Lord because a repentant heart is an open heart to be molded to greater love."

"That is so beautiful. But this is sort of a conversation again. One of you blessed angels is talking to me more than at any time since January of 1991."

"Did you think you would be left bereft? Our Lord will work through you always if you are open, and you will write much more than you have done so far. But the conversations you will have now are to be written carefully and shared with only those close to you and with those to whom you owe obedience until their word permits otherwise."

"Will there be more conversations then?"

"Patience, little one. Let it be in Our Lord's time and as He wishes. Your questions are a worry to you. Let them be."

"I'm sorry. I am really so very happy to be talking at length with one of you again. I have missed it so, and wondered if I would be blessed like this again."

"Blessings are never repeated exactly. (The blessed angel is smiling at me.) You will be blessed even more this time because your heart is more open to receive Our Lord's blessing."

"I praise You and I bless You, oh my beloved Lord."

"And I sing praise with you, little one. Our Lord gives you His peace and love. He asks that you remember your earthly Holy Father, the steward of His Church, in your Lenten offerings. He promises you again that your father, the one you love so very much, will receive His mercy with an open heart one day. Our Lord has seen his good works and His kindness, and much wealth in Heaven is his." (Here, the blessed angel was speaking of my father for whom I have been praying greatly.)

"Thank you so very much, blessed angel. Your words comfort me. I will offer for the Holy Father, Pope John-Paul II, and I thank you for telling me about my own dad."

"Please be careful with the gift Our Lord has given you, little one. Your soul is most precious to Him."

"Please help me to be careful."

"You have the love of all the angels of Heaven, and the prayers of all the saints in this. Our Lord's peace is with you, little one. Peace."

I was filled with a beautiful, peaceful joy as the light faded quietly, and then later that evening with an exuberant exultation. Our Lord is so very kind to me, such an ordinary and weak person. I marvel at all of this so very much.

The blessed angel asked me to be careful with the gift Our Lord has given me, and I knew it was a gentle but very serious warning. He gave it, I am quite sure, because several days ago I did something my Guardian Angel had clearly asked me not to do. I felt terribly about it and asked forgiveness, begging for help in being given the strength never to do such a thing again. I still feel very badly about it, but hope and know that Our Lord has taught me more about the necessity for obedience. I feel His beautiful love and compassion for me, and I know from repeated experiences that He doesn't ask me to obey in anything unless it is for my growth and my good. He is like that, bless Him.

And yet He is stern for our good too. When I had disobeyed, my Guardian Angel said to me, "On which side do you place your love and loyalty: on the side of the Lord of Love or on the side of the Lord of darkness?"

I said, "I thought I had decided that."

"Have you?"

"I thought I had."

"Have you?" He asked me again sharply.

This painful questioning made me aware that we are always to be diligent in obeying the commandments of God which we have been given, and continue as Saint Paul says, "to work out our salvation in fear and trembling." A diligent soul is a faithful one.

# Chapter 47
# THE HOLY EUCHARIST

About April 5, 1992, the question of why we as Catholics may not receive the bread of Protestant services was raised by a convert to Catholicism who had been mistakenly told at the time of his conversion by the priests teaching him that he might receive the bread of Protestant services "if he knew it was not the Lord." I was horrified by this, knowing that we are not as Catholics to do this since it would be a mockery for us to receive something that is not Our Lord (though of course it would not be at all a mockery for non-Catholics to receive the bread of their own services.)

I was disturbed by all this. My Dear Angel spoke to me about it after long prayer. He said, "No exclusion is meant, but a clear stream has been preserved and tended with graces poured out by Our Lord through His sacrifice and completed with those who choose. He did not offer His Body and His Blood to the crowds, but only to the Twelve with Him at the Last Supper. You know that Our Blessed Queen was there. But she did not eat supper with the Twelve, but received Our Lord separately from them.

"Because you live in a physical world, it is by physical means and through physical laws that the pure stream of grace given through the Holy Eucharist has been and must be preserved. This is a sacred trust – – not just for you, but also for those who will be one in Our Lord in the future.

"If these physical laws are muddied or distorted, the gift itself can no longer be given. Our Lord 's full Presence among you is too precious a gift to be handed over to whim, dispute, or controversy. It is a treasure of His Church, held in trust until He comes again.

"Do you feel better?" he asked me. I said yes.

Going to Fatima in Portugal was one of the greatest events of my life. I will not write much about it here except to say that the bonds of love and friendship with the people I know from that trip and the people I got to know will always be special to me. I received an answer on that trip about my future which was painful and joyful at the same time.

One of the places we visited was Santarem, where one of the Eucharistic miracles took place and where the actual Body and Blood of Our Lord Jesus Christ, visible in a supernaturally produced monstrance, was seen by our group. Though of course I did not see it, just to know it was there moved me to my depths. The people asked me later if I saw the light which I very often do see when Our Lord is present in the Holy Eucharist. I did not see it. I think Our Lord was letting me know that whether He is present under the appearance of bread and wine or in the miraculous way at Santarem, He is there. He is on the altars of the world everywhere whether I see the light or not.

We were troubled by some of the secrecy we found from Opus Angelorum, and within a few days of our return the controversy over Opus Sanctorum broke. I, however, have a great deal of personal faith in the people involved in Opus Angelorum. I pray they will be totally obedient to the Church, as it appears they will be, and use the corrections from Rome to make themselves stronger and in complete accord with the Church. I appreciated very much what my Angel said about corrections being necessary at times.

In the early spring I had been invited to speak at a conference held in Tulsa, Oklahoma, in June of 1992. Father and I felt it was too soon for me to speak about the angels, but we were invited nevertheless, and our fares and lodging paid for. This was a very special Marian conference. I had felt I should attend it, but because of responsibilities with my work and bad health, plus of course, not having money to go, I said, "Lord, if You want me to go then You know there are certain things I do really need. I need to fly there because of my headaches and neck pain. I would need a place to stay with no charge or paid accommodations, and conference fees — all to be paid without loss of money to me because I just don't have it. If going to this conference is just a whim of mine, let's forget it. If You want me to go, please provide these things I genuinely need in order to go." Our limitations are nothing to God.

The Holy Spirit is being poured out upon us in this time in a way we could not have imagined even ten years ago. We are living in times which, in my mind, are akin to those of the early Church at Pentecost. This is wonderful, but it is also a heavy responsibility. So many people talk to me about "receiving messages." But if they are, then what? Have they been guided as to what to do with them? Are they under obedience? Do they know what they must do to be in tune with what Our Lord has in mind as He gives this gift, assuming He has given it? To "receive a message" is not at all the same thing as being asked to deliver it.

It must always be the Church which has the final word on everything. We know how much discord, confusion and division has been caused by people doing their own thing, all in the name of doing God's will. But He is not a God of discord or division, and He has promised in the Scriptures that one day there will be one shepherd, and one fold.

On Friday night at the conference in Tulsa, Oklahoma, I was among the close to two thousand participants and was in the middle of the crowd. I was very startled when my Dear Angel asked me to suffer for a soul. "How," I wondered, "could I follow this request in this mob?"

"Please give me privacy if this offering is truly Your will, Lord," I prayed. Within a few minutes I was in an infirmary room off to the side with only Father John, a lovely young man who had come with him, and a nun who is now very dear to me, present. I think she left before I began to suffer. She told me later that when I had come in I looked very white. If Father Walch had not told her it was a spiritual offering, she would have wanted to call a doctor. No need.

We started praying the Sorrowful Mysteries, as I always do when beginning to offer. I got a glimpse of a man stealing a consecrated Host. I thought for a moment that it was someone at the conference. Then I realized it was not someone present at the conference.

I was in what seemed to be a large room with a great door. I could hear cries beyond the door, distant but sharp. The pungent smell I have come to associate with hell was faintly present in the room.

My dear Lord Jesus was there. He said to me, "If he does not repent of this sin, no matter how much I am willing to forgive him he cannot enter even the bottom of Purgatory. That is why I am here, to try to help him. That is why I have asked you to help too, little one."

He went out of the room. A moment later, the man who had stolen consecrated Hosts regularly during his life was there. My constantly faithful Angel stood quietly by my side. He showed me that this man had routinely stolen consecrated Hosts. He did it for fun, for kicks. He appeared to his friends and family to be a faithful Catholic. But he took secret delight in stealing the Hosts. It was almost as if he was saying, "I can get away with something you don't know about. Look how smart I am, and cunning." In short, he got his thrills by doing this. I was horrified, and amazed that Jesus would still love this foul soul so much after its desecration of His entirety: Body, Blood, Soul and Divinity.

Our Blessed Lord entered the room. He was not whole as He had been when He first spoke to me. He stood before the man terribly mutilated. All the wounds of His abuse and crucifixion were upon Him. One recoiled in horror, not from Him but because of His horrible wounds. I felt sick to my stomach because of them.

As I was experiencing these things, my body was in great pain. I was nauseous and retching. I think I was literally trying to spit out the man's sin which I had agreed temporarily to take on as if it were my own so that it could be repented in union with Christ's sufferings for this soul. I was in more physical pain than I have been for most other offerings. I felt as if my poor body might be torn apart from the pain and retching.

Under normal circumstances I would have been frightened for myself, especially for the harm which might be done to my neck and head. But I was too engrossed in offering for the soul my Lord wished to save from damnation to think of this, and I also had a sense that I would come to no personal lasting harm because of this offering, though under normal circumstances this surely would have happened. I felt sick with the evil of the sin, just as one would feel revulsion at a physically repugnant odor. Two people who have been present when I offered have said they felt revulsion during the offering too, but had not known what it was at the time.

So our Lord Jesus Christ stood before this man, His dear Body horribly lacerated. "Your desecration has done this to Me," He said quietly, looking deeply into the man's face.

Then suddenly He stood whole before the man. In His hand He held what seemed to me to be a whip with knives or spikes of some sort attached to it. He handed this evil looking thing to the man.

"Strike Me," He said. "You will not be hurting Me again. Your sin has already done that, though I experienced My Passion two thousand years ago. I bore Your sin then, before you had committed it. But now, you must clearly see and understand what you have done or you will not regret it and you will be lost forever, if you cannot regret it. Strike

Me so you may see what you have already done to Me through your sin of desecration."

The man held the whip, whimpering as he did so. "I can't hit You," he said over and over, "I can't hurt You with this."

"You have already done so," our dear Lord replied calmly. "now you must see. Begin."

His voice and His manner were so quietly filled with firm authority that the man raised the whip and struck Him. He then shrank back, saying again he could not go on.

"You must," Jesus told him. "You must see what you have done or you cannot repent of it. Go on."

After a few strikes like this, the man put his head down, closed his eyes and struck again and again. Then he collapsed sobbing, saying he could not go on. He looked up in horror at what he had done to Our Lord.

"You have not seen fully what you have done," our Blessed Lord told him. "go on."

"But I can't! I can't! How can I hurt You?"

"You have already done so. Go on."

This whole scene and exchange was agony for me. If I did not know how desperately my Lord wished to save this precious soul He loves from eternal agony in hell and how dearly He wished to eventually bring him to Heaven, I would have thought I had gone mad or Jesus had or somebody had. How could this be actually happening? Jesus had forgiven him His sins; He had said so; but perhaps the man had to be open to that forgiveness before he could receive it. Why did the man have to repent fully of this sin before even entering Purgatory?

Then I remembered one of the few things I can recall from my Catechism class and which I learned as a small child. It is not possible to go even to the bottom of Purgatory with a mortal sin on one's soul. "Is that why this man has to repent of his purposeful desecration of Our Lord in the Blessed Eucharist?" I asked myself. "I can offer for him, and the pain of my prayers can open the channels of my Blessed Lord's grace for him, but he has to repent fully of the mortal sin of desecration entirely by himself before the graces of Jesus are available to him, and before he can receive the graces my Blessed Lord wants to give him through my offering in union with Him."

I felt very inadequate, not having much knowledge at all about our faith except what I have learned through the Holy Scriptures, homilies, and what I have been told by the blessed angels. I was afraid I might come to the wrong interpretation of what I was witnessing. I knew that what I was witnessing was entirely correct, but I did not know if my interpretation was accurate.

As I thought this, my dear Lord turned to me and said gently, "You understand." Then he turned back to the man. The man continued to lacerate Him, and sobbed heartbrokenly as he did so. Finally Jesus said to him, "It is enough. You see fully now what you have done by your secret desecrations." The man sank to the floor, crying bitterly.

"Can you ever forgive me, Lord?"

"I have already done so." As Jesus spoke, drops of His blood from the scourging the man had given him fell on the man on the floor. He had completely forgiven the man before all this began, but the soul in immediate danger of eternal damnation could not take advantage of this forgiveness without realization of his wrongs and sorrow over them. When our Lord tells us to forgive, it seems to me it is more for our cleansing and healing than for the sake of the one doing the wrong. The wrongdoer's cleansing only comes with realization and repentance, on his or her part, and this realization and repentance must be a result of complete free will; not forced upon the soul by others. I thought about these things only later, after everything was long over.

My Beloved Lord turned to me and said with a gentle smile on His torn face, "See. The wrongs done to me by this soul and the Blood I shed because of them; these are the very things I use to bring about his salvation." This, more than anything else in this offering, amazed me.

He then gently raised the man up. "Go in peace now," He said, "you will be with Me eventually." The man walked through a door across from that which I knew lead to hell. It is my assumption, not shown to me, that it lead to Purgatory.

My Beautiful Lord then turned to me. He blessed me. "Thank you," He said simply. That was all, and my suffering was completely over.

As the pain faded, I was amazed. After all the pain and retching, I would have been totally weakened under normal circumstances. The pain could not have drained away so quickly, within seconds of my Lord's last words to me, if it had been natural pain. But I was completely free of it, and free of any after effects. I was tired, but nothing else. I was told later that my color also returned in those moments and became normal again. "You were as white as the sheet covering you during the time you were offering," Father told me afterwards.

I felt such an exultation of quiet thanksgiving that one more person would share in the love of God forever. It was chilling to me, however, to realize that, even with my Lord's best efforts and unconditional forgiveness and love, the man still had a choice and could have hardened his heart. Thank God he did not do so.

Sometimes, as I offer for these precious souls, the sense of their sin is so overpowering that I feel as if I am being asked to jump into a cesspool of slimy excrement. I apologize to anyone who finds this too graphic a description. It is not vivid enough to describe what is happening. A few others have also sensed this tangible presence of sin, and it has revolted them also. It is a token of Our Lord's love that He immerses Himself in our sin and degradation out of His great love and wish to salvage us. What a heartbreak when a soul refuses this great love.

For our Blessed Lord, each human soul is as important as the whole universe, so a battle for one soul is a battle for the universe to God.

I think of the seeming paradox one of the angels told me, "You are more precious to Our Almighty Lord than anything or anyone in the whole universe, and each soul is this precious to Him, and shares in this great love as if there were no other beloved one."

# THE LIGHT OF LOVE

# Chapter 48
# A PRAYER FOR PURIFICATION

April 30, 1992

The Monday following Easter, we went to Saint John Neumann for the Monday night rosary. The light was beautiful and bright, more especially so than is usual, though I hesitate to use the word "usual" because there are times I do not see it at all.

I wondered if the Monday after Easter has a special significance of which I am unaware. As we prayed, my Dear Angel told me that this day after Easter is held very dear in Heaven. "It is the day," he told me, "when all martyrs, all those who have died for Our Beloved Lord's sake, are honored. Especially honored are those who are not remembered or are unknown on the earth."

I thought of the thousands of Japanese martyrs who died under tortures which would have been unimaginable in many cultures which have been considered cruel in their methods of torture. For some reason, I have a special call to pray for the conversion of Japan. Being from Hawaii, I have had many friends of Japanese descent, as well as friends of mixed ancestry from China, Korea, the Philippines, and Polynesia. In some ways, my cultural background is closer to these cultures than to Western culture.

Now my spirit is called to join with those who were martyred in Japan, to pray for their country's conversion. Our Blessed Lord has not forgotten the blood of those martyrs.

As I looked at the beautiful, glowing, penetrating light I felt as if my spirit were being raised into a joy and peace beyond description. I was given a small taste of the joy of Heaven that night. I want to go there as soon as my Blessed Lord has no more use for me here. In His mercy, I know He will not wait a moment longer than necessary before He takes me.

The martyrs seem closer to my heart now, my brothers and sisters, because of Jesus Christ. Would I have the courage to suffer so terribly for my Lord, I, an ordinary very weak person? But they were "ordinary, weak people" too. It certainly must be love that makes the difference. But I think of the cruel intelligence of those who tortured in Japan during the persecutions of the later 16th century and onwards. They tortured the people and told the priests they would stop if they, the priests, recanted. That would seem quite effective. But could they not know that such a denial would be a false one? Perhaps they didn't care that it was a false denial. Perhaps all they were interested in was obtaining a denial to weaken the faith of the people. In such a case, would not a denial like that be an act of love, done for love of those being tortured? I don't know. I don't know.

June 6, 1992

Prayer dictated by my Guardian Angel for someone I know as well as all others wishing to be cleansed and brought closer to Our Blessed Lord, "I give my Lord full permission to show me in all ways, no matter the pain to myself, all things which prevent me from being loving, devoted, sincere AND honest. I ask my Lord to show me all those things outside MYSELF and inside MYSELF which cause me to be indifferent, disloyal, false, and without integrity.

"I give You this permission, Lord, so that by Your grace you may cleanse me and rend my heart for Your good purposes. Amen."

My Angel warned that any person praying this prayer regularly would be taken at his or her word. "You may suffer a great deal if you pray this prayer because Our Lord God will take you seriously, and begin your purification immediately. But it is much better for you to be purified here than to be cleansed in Purgatory, where you can do nothing about the wrongs you have done, and where the pain is much greater and of longer duration."

June 19, 1992

I was being given Our Blessed Lord in the Holy Eucharist here at home. I had not been feeling very well, and was particularly hurting over the betrayal of someone I had thought to be a loving friend. As I received the Host, I felt Our Blessed Lord beside me. His presence was as a normal human presence would be. I felt His loving hand over mine. He said, "I forgive sinners. I work through sinners. Through unclean hearts that wish to be pure, I pour out My graces. Through stained and tarnished vessels which allow Me to cleanse them I perform wonders. Through the filth of the world wishing to be made whole, a new heart is made. I need only your openness to do this. Come to Me. Let Me work through you, and all shall be well.

"All some souls need is to know that they can never be worthy of forgiveness, but that they are given forgiveness as a gift if their hearts are even a little open to receive it. Worth has nothing to do with it. A sorrowing heart has everything to do with forgiveness."

June 21, 1992

Again today, I was blessed to receive my Lord here at home. He spoke to me right after Communion once again, His loving presence and warm love quieting my troubled spirit. He said, "Remember that those whose hearts and spirits I allow you to know clearly, especially in their sinfulness, degradation and wrongdoing are those I call you to love because in them you see most clearly the reflection of your own sinfulness, degradation and wrongdoing.

"When you condemn them, remember you condemn yourself. You are to point out their errors to them, but remember always to see your own. You are not to submit to the wrong they do, but you are also not to submit to the tendency of your own heart to sin. The wrong you do damages yourself far more than the wrong done to you.

"The sin you commit separates you from God. The sin committed against you, if you so choose it, may be offered and may bring you to My Father's heart.

"My love is always with you, and My heart beats with you in all your joy, and aches with you in your sorrow.

"Peace be with you. My peace be with you."

# THE LIGHT OF LOVE

# Chapter 49
# DEVOTIONS

July 1, 1992

When the controversy over Opus Angelorum (The Work of the Angels) broke, I was concerned. I asked my Guardian Angel for guidance, and this is what he eventually said to me after deep prayer, "You are correct in believing that you have been protected from what is not of Our Lord. Remember, however, that it is not at all unusual that what is of God is persecuted. Pray deeply and obey completely what the Church of Our Lord dictates. The prayer for discernment of what is of God given to you by me, your Guardian Angel, is one to be found as approved by the Church.*

"The concentration upon us, the angels, is not what we wish. It is not what is best for you. The devotion to us is only useful to you when it leads you closer to Our Almighty Lord. So it is with all devotions: to us, to the holy ones in our Lord's Kingdom, to the Queen of Heaven. When you in your humanness begin to miss this point, then it is necessary for Our Lord to correct you. He does this out of love, for it is only in growing closer and closer to Him that you have everlasting life.

"We in His Kingdom know this. You in your imperfect humanness lose sight of it. When this happens, He reminds you of it so that you may

---

[Note: The "test" my Guardian Angel refers to here is the one he gave me several years ago. Whenever something of a supernatural nature seems to be occurring, he said I am to pray, "If you (or this) is of my Lord Jesus Christ, then you (it) is welcome in the name of the Father, and of the Son, and of the Holy Spirit (making the sign of the cross.) If you are not of my Lord Jesus Christ, then by His Holy Wounds, His agonizing Passion, His cruel death, and His glorious rising you are to be gone now: In the name of the Father, and of the Son, and of the Holy Spirit (making the sign of the cross.)]

be blessed. It is His love and mercy which keep guiding you towards Him until at last you are united with Him and us in complete love.

"Do not despair. All shall be made clear. You are His beloved ones, and He sees your sincere efforts always and respects them. Pray with all your heart to be kept close within His wisdom. Pray for His wisdom to be given to you. Pray never to stray from the path He has set for you. Pray for all who stray from His path, and pray for mercy for yourself and others when you do wander from His way.

"All things that are good are brought into the light of the Lord. Nothing need be hidden which is of God. The simple ones among you are those who know most clearly what the great ones believe to be unfathomable mysteries. All of you must come to this simplicity of love; the simplicity and purity of the love which Our Blessed Lord has for you in order that you may see clearly.

"All that truly matters is very simple, and is so clear it cannot be and will not be hidden, especially will it not be hidden by those of good intent. They will see clearly the beauty and simplicity of what was thought to be secret. This is the great wisdom of which Our Lord taught, and which He teaches you now.

"Be at peace."

July 20, 1992

My Blessed Angel spoke to me once again concerning Opus Angelorum and other devotions, "As long as you are centered in the Sacraments and in Our Lord, then all devotions to the angels and Our Lady are centered in the Sacraments. All devotions are purified with the sole and exclusive purpose of bringing human beings to their Creator. Any controversy is worth the salvation of one soul. Souls come to God by different routes, and as long as these routes are approved and sanctified by the Church established to bring about Our Lord's Kingdom on earth, they are to be respected.

It is not the devotion to the holy angels which Mother Church objects to. It is an over–emphasis in this devotion with an element of esoteric knowledge and cliquishness as in being privy to this unavailable knowledge.

The devotion to the holy angels is one which is special for your time. This is the time of the angels and of our Beloved Queen. This devotion will be spread because it is necessary in bringing souls to God. It should be spread. It has been necessary to make this purpose for the devotion clear.

It is not for our sake that you become aware of us. It is not for us to be honored. Our greatest honor is your praise and trust in the Creator of all things, of all love. This is our greatest joy. Your sincere praise and love for our Creator will bring you, with our assistance, to the feet of God."

My patient Guardian Angel said that the word "dedication" rather than "consecration" would be more apt in explaining this commitment. We are dedicated to working with our guardian angels for the purpose of helping them bring our souls to God.

# THE LIGHT OF LOVE

# Chapter 50
# ANOTHER JUDAS

July 8, 1992

I had been speaking to my Lord in prayer when I felt His presence with me, His actual presence. I heard again that beautiful voice, so firm but yet totally loving, incapable of being harsh with those trembling within themselves and wishing to do right. I had said, "Lord Jesus, my dearest Lord, please help me to be a saint. I want to be a pure reflection of You. You have given me free will. My free will is that I should do nothing apart from You, and do everything in You and for You. That is my freely given wish. But I am weak and human. I know that everything that is not grace from You is weakness."

He said, "I do give you My strength and My love. I will teach you to be gentle in My way."

"But what about being firm?"

"True gentleness is firmness. It takes much more strength to be gentle than it does to fight or to be hard."

"I see. Yes. But what, then, is gentleness that is weak and does not take responsibility?"

"It is self-convenience, nothing more. True gentleness is peace of soul. But mainly it is trust in God. That trust is not complacent. It knows that God loves the soul which trusts Him. So, of course, I will work through that soul which trusts Me. I will bring about all things which are good and necessary in that soul and in other souls through that soul. That is why you can be gentle, but it is a gentleness which acts and is not complacent or looking to self-convenience and using gentleness or non-action as an excuse not to act. When you are gentle in My way, you have already conquered adversity, sorrow, deception, and all else that is not of Me.

"Be at peace, my dear little one. I will speak with you again, and yet again. I will teach you, my little one, of the things which are being forgotten so that they may not be forgotten. My peace is with you, my little love."

"Thank You, Lord. I love You. I Love You."

July 11, 1992

Miriam is moving out of our home. I know children can't stay children forever, but, oh, how I miss her already.

July 12, 1992

I was asked by my Guardian Angel to offer. I began to feel the sickness in my body, the feeling I have come to know as a preparation for what is to come. It is, as best I can describe it, a sensitivity to sin — a physical, emotional and spiritual sense of sickness in myself for sin itself.

As D. and I prayed the Sorrowful Mysteries, I began to see an old man. I knew he was not the soul for whom I was to offer. My blessed Guardian Angel said to me, "You are offering for another Judas." His words made me sick at heart, but I knew I would go on. Have I not been another Judas at one time or another?

I saw the old man praying. He had a crucifix in his hand. He was preparing false papers. I saw that he had helped someone very dear to leave their country, a country where he was in great danger.

The old man's son, out of fear for himself because his father was under suspicion, betrayed him to cruel authorities. He was angry at the danger his father had put him in and justified his betrayal in this way. The old man has suffered great physical and emotional torture and has been imprisoned. He is still alive. I think the son of the old man is about thirty years old.

Then I saw the young man, the son who had betrayed his father. He was dying after being shot. I don't know the circumstances of the shooting.

The pain for me grew greater and greater, and there seemed no openness in the young man's soul. His evil and hardness made me very sick. He had no regret for the agony of his father, no shame at all.

Then my Blessed Angel told me, "He damns himself." The pain of my offering had not lasted long.

Then I heard a voice speaking in great sorrow but strong and firm. I knew my Lord's voice. He said, "let his evil go where it deserves."

My Blessed Angel then said to me, "You understand now why it is so important that you pray for — (person's name omitted), that you love him, that you point out his errors to him?"

"Yes."

"More souls condemn themselves to hell because of their pride, their self-justification, their refusal to let go of themselves and their reasons for doing evil, than for any other reason. Nothing is more important to them than to prove they are justified in their evil. And so, while justifying themselves to themselves, for they cannot justify any longer to anyone else, they are absorbed by the laughing King of hell and then spat out, as you have seen, to suffer for eternity, for always and for always.

"Do not justify what you know to be wrong. Do not excuse yourself for anything. Be relentless with yourself in uprooting what you know is evil in yourself. It is truly better for you to tear out your very self than that you should go to the place where there is no chance, no mercy, no love where you yourself become the evil you have embraced.

"Our Blessed Lord will cultivate the good in you if you give Him even a small chance to do so. Trust Him. He has not created you for nothing. He has created you for joy, for peace. He has made you to be a mirror of His love, to increase His love in this world and the next. Even the smallest good in you He will increase to a great good, to the supreme good, to the eternal good.

"But do not forget. It is you who decide. If you hold fast to yourself, to your reasons, to your small, selfish selves which care nothing for the pain of others, He will pass by you because of your own refusal to allow Him into your souls.

"There is nothing more that can be done for the soul you saw condemned by its own pride. Please pray for this young man's father who is a good and devout man. He is already near to the gate of Heaven, but his sorrow will be great when he learns of the fate of his son."

I knew my Guardian Angel was not referring to the young man's bodily death, but to his eternal spiritual death. I said, "I will pray."

"Bless you, little one. Your pain will be used, as it was before, for another soul. Be at peace now."

The pain and sorrow over this soul has been great for me and for D. All he had to do was say, and feel, "I'm sorry." He only had to feel a little sorrow for such a great sin. That would have been enough. And he had a father who loves him and who was praying for him. But he chose. Why do people choose hell? All of us have been like this young man, but some of us are sorry and will be sorry. Some of us suffer over our painful regrets. Why did not this young man feel even a little regret?

# Chapter 51
# STRUGGLING TOWARD HUMILITY

Saturday, July 25, 1992

Morning: I awoke after a dream in the wee hours of the morning. In the dream, I was kneeling before Our Blessed Lord in the Holy Eucharist. He spoke to me from the Eucharist, saying with infinite tenderness, "Consume Me that I may give you life."

After I awoke, I thought, "Yes, Lord. And please consume me in a different way that I might give others Your life." I was thinking of the souls for whom I offer. My wish to be completely used up by my Lord does not come from heroism or magnanimity. No, not at all. It is there because I have seen my Blessed Lord gently place a soul nearly damned into the bottom of Purgatory to begin its purification through His love expressed and given to us in His Life, Passion, Death and Resurrection. I have felt a small part of His inexpressible joy knowing that one more of His beloved people will eventually be with Him.

10:30 p m:

The Angelic Guardian of my soul spoke to me, gently reproving me over my lack of charity for a soul who seems always to be hurting others and bungling human relationships. He said, "Do not blame those of Our Lord's children who do not know how to be His true sons and daughters as well as you know. Treat them as younger brothers and sisters. Do you blame a four-year-old for not knowing how to set an elaborate table? Do you blame a three-year-old for not knowing how to make a bed perfectly?

Thank God for the experiences and blessings you have received which have taught you how to be more pleasing to the Lord of Love. Teach those younger in spirit than you are by your example.

Do not be afraid of your younger brothers and sisters. What can they do to you if you are older in spirit?

Our Lord's peace is with you."

With these kind words, he warned me also against pride and ceased speaking.

Monday, July 27

I have come across a phrase in a book about the last seven phrases of Jesus. The author says of Jesus, "His heroism is not stoic resistance, not clenched toothed defiance of pain. He reflects a deeper power. He concentrates on the spiritual uses of pain in the cause of restoring the primacy of love." I will read this over and over.

Today is Kelly's seventeenth birthday. D. and I are both sick, and Scott is coming down with the sore throat from which we have been suffering. Kelly is spared so far.

And yesterday, my dear Eileen got engaged to be married to Ed Hester, a young man she met at Christendom College. Lord, please, please bless them and help them.

July 28, In the wee hours of the morning.

Dearest Lord, please allow me by Your infinite grace to love You above all familial and other human and earthly affections. May I love all others through, with, for and in You alone. May it be for You and because of You and for Your sake that I love them. Amen.

Wednesday, August 12, 1992

I miss my girls so much. This is their nineteenth birthday. Miriam is visiting Eileen in Virginia at Christendom. Do other parents ache in loneliness for their children who are off living their lives, forgetting us so completely as it seems? I tried to call but could not reach them. I am sad tonight.

# Chapter 52
# SCENES FROM OUR
# BLESSED LORD'S PASSION

Thursday, August 13

Two weekends ago, our house was filled with about 25 kids from a youth group from Iowa and the adults with them who had traveled down here on pilgrimage. Thank God for the pasties in the freezer, made by Kelly and Scott over the last month! They and D. have worked so hard to accommodate the kids, their gear, their sleeping bags and all. If we could not have quickly prepared the pasties to feed them, life would have been impossible. We are all quite sick with fevers and colds, and are hoping none of our guests will take our germs back home with them.

Mike Slate spoke to them, and it was a joy to hear him speak of Our Lady. We then came back home and, after finally being able to borrow a TV from our neighbors and renting a VCR, they watched the film about the Feast of the Assumption here in Lubbock at Saint John Neumann Church in 1988 called "Love Lights", done in 1988 by Catholic Television from San Antonio. Many of the kids saw the sun spinning on the film, and some saw Our Lady and other figures.

One young man who had been very heart-sick since his arrival the night before seemed so changed that at first I thought he was someone else, not realizing it was the same young man I and one of the adults with the group had prayed for earlier that day. I was so very moved by his unhappiness. He said he was going through the worst pain he had ever felt in his life. He did not want to talk about it so we just prayed, though I think his group leader knew the cause of his pain. I did not need to know what was causing him so much pain to care deeply about his heartache. I felt so desperate to help him and knew I could not except through prayer. I asked to be allowed to go before the throne of God in prayer with all the angels and saints and our dear Blessed Mother to intercede for this young man.

"Please, Lord," I prayed, "give him whatever he needs to know that you are there and you love him. I don't know what is wrong, but I do know he needs you." I prayed with all my heart because of his deep grief.

Later, as I have said, he was so changed that I did not realize he was the same young man. He kindly got me a dinner plate after we had prepared supper for everyone. He came and sat next to me and began talking. Then he said quietly, "God heard your prayer and answered it right away."

I was embarrassed and asked about what, then he told me who he was and I explained I had not known because of the great change in him.

"God heard you," he said again.

"What happened?" I asked.

"My rosary turned gold," he said. He did not want anyone but his group leaders to know right away. It was a joy he wanted to keep to himself for a while to savor the amazement and wonder of it. I think also he was still trying to grasp it. Our Dear Lord is so kind, so beautifully kind. That is one of the things about Our Blessed Lord I love the most.

I had received permission from Father to talk to the kids. We went outside in our big back yard, and I told them about some of the most painful and yet most beautiful experiences with which I have been blessed. I will recount here two different experiences I had with my Guardian Angel by my side, as he took me in spirit to the scene of Our Blessed Lord's Passion.

My Guardian Angel and I were standing in a courtyard of some kind, with cobblestone paving. It was surrounded by trees and bushes, not well kept. There was a crowd there of about 30 or 40 men, some soldiers, and other tough hangers-on. They surrounded Our Blessed Lord, mocking Him and jeering at him.

They taunted Him most with the words, "King of the Jews!" They struck Him as He was blindfolded. Then someone yelled, "The King needs a crown! The king needs a crown!"

One rough soldier ripped a cloth of some sort, a head covering I think, into strips. He ran over to the side of the courtyard where a large thorn tree grew. He wrapped the strips of cloth around his hands and arms. Then he broke dried branches off the thorn tree. The thorns were not little. They were about four inches long, very sharp at the tips and gnarled and thick at the base. I have never felt anything like them in Hawaii or the mainland. They were horrible things. The man twisted the branches into a rough cap. He ran back to Jesus with the cap in his hand.

The others tore off Jesus's blindfold, one saying in such cruel mockery, "It might get in the way of the noble king's crown!"

They forced Him to kneel. The man with the cloths wrapped around his hands and arms stood in front of Our Dear Lord. He pressed the cap of thorns far over His head and towards His eyes. Another man came up behind Jesus and smashed the crown into the back of His head with a stone.

The crown was a solid cap of thorns, not a circlet at all. It was so clumsily twisted together that it would have fallen off were it not for the buffeting the men began to give Our Blessed Lord. They hit Him with sticks and clubs and the butts of spears. They knocked the crown down into His head and hit Him on the sides and back of the head, driving the crown deeply into His poor skull. I got the impression that the crown was being held on his head by the sticky blood from His wounds and the skin and flesh of His head as the thorns were driven in.

"Only two of those you see here repented of their cruelty to the Savior of the world, and to others whom they had treated brutally," my Dear Angel told me sadly.

It was horrible. I had never realized that when the Scriptures say He was buffeted around the head that the crown of thorns was in place.

Finally, they pulled Him to His feet. He was hardly able to stand, and I wondered how He could be expected to carry a cross and walk the long way to Golgotha. His poor body was a bloody mess from the scourging, and the paving stones were slippery with His precious blood.

I felt sick to my stomach and ashamed that I had so underestimated His pain. I felt so sick with nausea at what was being done to Our Lord, and my own inability to help Him at all, that I almost fainted.

The scene faded and my Dear Angel comforted me. I surely was not the one who needed comforting most.

One night I was feeling sorry for myself, worrying about my work, the pain which has prevented my studying and especially writing papers. "It is bad enough being a blind person and being slow that way,"

I complained to God and whoever else was listening. "But on top of that, this pain is so limiting. I do want to offer the pain and my difficulties but, well but..."

My Dear Angel spoke to me. "Our Lord and King has experienced all of the pain you and all other people have ever suffered, both through you and because of His love for you, and directly in some way during His Passion which was not only a Passion caused by what was done to Him by those who tortured Him, but a suffering caused by all the evil ever done, all the pain ever experienced through sins of cruelty or neglect."

I was still in my moribund mood. I had the nerve to answer him, "but He doesn't know what it is like to be blind." I am not proud of this answer, nor of my attitude. I am ashamed, very ashamed. But there it is.

Suddenly, I was standing in a street with my loving Angel beside me. It was a dusty road full of stones, debris, filth, and holes. It was crowded with noisy people. Down the center of the road came Our Blessed Lord. I had read somewhere and believed that He carried only the cross beam of His cross.

But no. His arms were tied behind Him. Around His body and through His arms the thick ropes were wrapped cruelly, tying the cross to His back. The cross was long and heavy, about one and a half times taller than Our Blessed Lord, and the bottom of it stuck out at an angle to His side, quite far out. The bottom of the cross dragged on the ground behind Him and to His left side. Jesus carried the cross beam at an angle over His torn back with the upper part of the cross sticking up in the air on the other side. His face was covered with fresh and dried blood.

Suddenly, He stumbled. I understood from a wordless communication from my Guardian Angel that He had stumbled because He had not seen a hole in His path. He had not seen the hole because there was so much blood dripping from the crown of thorns and into His eyes. It was hard for Him to keep His eyes open because of the sticky blood which He could not, of course, wipe away. He was literally blinded by His own blood. I wanted to scream in shame for my self-centered words, and I cried aloud in pain for Him.

As He stumbled, the cross, which was sticking up as I have said, banged hard against the back of His head, smashing the crown of thorns in from the back. He fell to the ground. The heavy cross lay over Him. He could not move because of the ropes tying His arms behind His back. He could not in any way break His fall because of His arms being tied behind Him to the cross on His back.

He fell flat on His face in the mud and filth in the road, the crown of thorns in front slipping over His forehead and, I think, falling over His upper nose and eyes and gouging into His face. He lay there unable to move, even if He had tried to do so. The soldiers had to pull Him to His feet with agonizing jerks, some pulling on the cross from behind while others forced Him to stand up. One of the soldiers "readjusted" the crown of thorns.

This was apparently not the first time He had fallen, for the soldiers exclaimed in exasperation. They were shouting and cursing vilely. There was no pity for Him whatsoever from them, or at least it did not seem to me that any of them pitied Him. Their only emotion was impatience to get a job over.

It was then that they grabbed Simon of Cyrene, a big fellow with broad shoulders. I had always pictured from the Scriptural passages that Simon, "took up the cross and carried it behind Jesus." I thought He took the cross and walked behind Jesus, carrying the cross, and that Jesus no longer carried it. Now I saw what the Scriptures meant. The cross was not untied from Jesus. Simon took up the heavy end of the cross which, as I have said, dragged as Our Blessed Lord carried the cross at an angle. Simon carried the cross walking slightly behind Jesus and to His left. He steadied the cross and was strong enough so as to prevent our Blessed Lord from falling flat again and delaying the annoyed soldiers. Our Blessed Lord was not untied from the cross nor relieved of carrying it. This act of the soldiers of forcing Simon of Cyrene to help Jesus carry His cross was simply done for expedience. There was no mercy for the bloody Man blinded by His own blood and in agony too great to describe.

The scene in the street faded. I cry as I think of this, and I cannot retell it without feeling sick with shame at my own words and contribution to this misery. I remember something my Blessed Angel told me during the week of the Passion in 1991. "Longinus," he said, "the centurion in charge of murdering our Lord is in Heaven. By grace, he became a Christian after our Lord's death and rising. Longinus left the army and returned to Rome where he was one of the first to die there for our Lord God. He wants people to know that he is waiting to intercede for them. He says to them, "I murdered Christ and there is forgiveness for me. There is love and forgiveness for you too, no matter what you have done, if you have even a little remorse over your sins. If I have been forgiven as I have, you also will be if you are not hardened, and feel sorrow over your sins. I want to pray for you."" My Dear Angel said Longinus wanted to pray especially for us in our time, and for all people who believe they can never be forgiven. After telling the kids this, we went back into the house to pray. I did not understand why some of them began to cry even harder than we all had done outside as I told them of these scenes I had been privileged to live of Our Blessed Lord's Passion.

Then one by one, three or four of them came quietly up to me and handed me the crucifixes of their rosaries. The figures were moving. They did not get excited or tell their friends loudly. They quietly showed the people around them what was happening and then began to cry. Then they came up to me and wordlessly put the crucifixes into my hands. They cried quietly from their hearts to witness this miracle, given to them as a special gift which will bear fruit until we are together again in Heaven.

---

[Note: In researching the question as to whether historically Christ would have carried the entire cross or the horizontal bar of the cross, I discovered that it was customary for condemned prisoners to carry the horizontal section of the cross. When they reached the place of execution, this horizontal section of the cross was nailed or tied to the permanently placed vertical cross piece which stood in the earth and was used many times.

However, when the Romans wished to inflict added agony to their prisoners, they would force their victim to carry the entire cross. This was especially done in cases in which the prisoner was seen to be an enemy of the Empire.]

# Chapter 53
# A RESPONSE OF LOVE

August 17, 1992

The Feast of the Assumption this year brought about four thousand people to Saint John Neumann, plus many from other parishes in Lubbock to give thanks. I wish those from Lubbock came more to the Monday night rosaries, but I am grateful that they do not forget entirely. I go to Saint Elizabeth's Church whenever I can because the Mass is more traditional and I enjoy Father Mike O'Dwyer and his special sermons so. Also, we are getting to know Father James, the priest from Viet Nam, more. He is also a priest at Saint Elizabeth's. He has asked us if we would like him to come and pray the rosary with us every evening! What a blessing. When he prays with us, he prays very quickly but with great fervor. He slows down a little to accommodate us, and our hearts are opened to God through his holiness, which I suspect many people are not aware of because of Father's being a foreigner and not speaking English very well. But love is not limited by these sorts of restrictions.

As usual, we became hoarse leading rosaries for the pilgrims this year. But, again this year, I was fortunate. Our Lord sent us unexpected help. A group of pilgrims were delighted to wear their throats out with us and help lead.

Every year, the crowds become more and more quiet. A young girl put her rosary in the fountain, and when she took it out the crucifix was noticeably bleeding. The people around her were very quiet. Most of them cried. There was no outburst of sensationalism. They go home with a greater love and trust for Our Lord, and so it is as it should be. They tell me they will share with others what they know is true. I believe more and more that these signs are given to us because God knows we need encouragement. If we had the faith and love of former times, we would not need them. But He loves us as we are, in our crazy world, and gives us these unusual signs of His active presence and love among us. Perhaps we are more spiritually asleep than other people of other times have been, and so we need to be startled awake with these signs. I am afraid, however, that we have become so used to sensationalism that many of us may turn away from these indications of Our Lord's presence among us and the truth of the Gospels because, God help us, we may become inured to what God is trying to show us in these outward signs, and the necessity He is trying to illustrate to us of the importance to Him that we change our lives and draw our souls closer to Him, ever closer. But there are some who do wake up, who want to awaken from their torpor of unreality to the deepest reality of all, and for those who are struggling to awaken He does everything to help.

My dear Father John Walch came from Oklahoma City again to hear confessions all day. It is in the confessional that the true miracles occur, he tells me. But it didn't help matters much when I told him (about 11 o'clock at night I think it was) that several bus loads of people were coming for Mass at our house at 8:30 the next morning. It is indicative of the special love between us that he is still speaking to me.

August 23, 1992

My Dear Angel spoke to me before I received Our Blessed Lord in the Holy Eucharist, "Please repeat the glory be as often as you can, especially before you enter into Holy Communion with Our Blessed Lord, and when you pray Our Lord's Prayer and the Hail Mary as you do now in every day prayers and in the holy rosary. It is a special prayer of belief and affirmation for your time. Before it, pray, "I believe no matter what the circumstances of my life or the appearance of this world may be that My Lord, Jesus Christ, is King over all forever and ever."

The Glory Be, "Glory be to the Father, and to the Son, and to the Holy Spirit, as it was in the beginning, is now, and ever shall be; world without end. Amen."

September 1, 1992

My Guardian Angel said, "Our Blessed Lord wishes all of His people to follow Him willingly.

"As you ask that His active will be done, so He wishes you to actively want His will to be done. He does not want passivity, which is the same as lukewarmness. As His heart is on fire, burning with love for you, He wants a response of love from you which is as great as your heart can give. He longs for your heart to be on fire with love for Him. In this way, love is increased. His Kingdom on earth draws nearer with each heart burning with love and wishing to do His will, His will which is love only."

Saturday, September 5, in the wee hours of the morning.

These days have been very painful in an emotional sense, though blessed in a physical one. I am finally getting help with the headaches which are almost continuous since my surgery four years ago. More physical therapy to come. Doctor A. gave me a medication which will help in the condition I have which he is able to treat. After trying the medication for a day or two, I have slept better and am more truly rested than I can remember in four years. I had forgotten what it is like to rise in the morning with a smile. Mornings are when my headaches are most regular. I used to be able to bless God and sing for joy most in the morning. Perhaps I will again.

We started a novena to Saint Therese, the Little Flower, asking for her special prayers for Scott and Kelly, D.'s children. On Thursday night, D. , Scott, Kelly and Father James (our beautiful, saintly Viet Namese priest) all smelled roses. D. and her children were comforted. She believes it was an answer from Saint Therese of the little flower. I did not smell the roses. I had been praying D. would receive comfort. It was not for me. Thanks be to God that she has received this kindness from God, Our Blessed Mother, and the Little Flower Therese.

In the meantime, I am using this new physical strength to work long hours, praying the strength and relief from the worst of the pain will continue. The faculty have given me so much leeway, but this underhandedness is not uncommon in our department: being warm and supportive to one's face and slipping "confidential" memorandums into boxes without a word. One is expected to go on as if everything were wonderful in order that the facade of warm support can continue.

## Monday, September 7

I was praying very deeply for D. and the kids today, praying that Our Lord's will, as expressed by my Guardian Angel, would be accomplished and they might remain in Lubbock and their family be fully reunited according to Our Lord's plan. We had turned the Saint Michael chaplet into a novena. As I offered the Lord's Prayer and the three Hail Marys to the choir of archangels, I suddenly heard many beautiful voices: thousands of them, perhaps millions, praying with me.

They were waiting for me to lead them in prayer! They stopped when I stopped in amazement at hearing their voices, and began when I falteringly began to pray again. Yes. You would have had shivers of incredulity running up your back too. I realized the angels were joining with me in prayer for God's will to be done and for the good of everyone concerned. They really do want to pray with us for our Lord's gracious will to be done in our lives!

They do pray with us, especially when we ask them. Their voices are so beautiful, and their love so extraordinary. What a gift to us from God. I still hear the multitude of their beautiful voices in my inner ear as I remember listening to it. May I be given the gift to never forget the sound of their prayers for us. And to think they are waiting at any moment to join us in prayer for what troubles us! They pray for "the channels of grace to be opened that Our Blessed Lord's Will will be done."

# Chapter 54
# CHRIST'S LAMENT

September 13, 1992

After our prayer group meeting this evening, I was holding a crucifix which had broken off a rosary given to me by Father John Walch. The figure began to move. D. and Scott saw it. Scott told me later that he did not actually see the figure move because the movement was slow. He said, however, that the change in position was unmistakable and, as he said in his wonderful factual way, if he had been able to take good camera pictures at intervals, the change in the position of the figure would have been unquestionable.

Then I was shocked to hear my Lord's voice. He was singing in a way I have never heard. I have read of songs of lamentation in the Scriptures and I love the Psalms, but I have never heard anything like this. The song was one of such heartbreak that I got the impression the only way such a deep sorrow could be expressed was in this way: through a song of lamentation. I copied the words as I heard Our Blessed Lord Jesus sing them,

"I have tried to save you
And you would not.
I have called you to be My love
And you would not.
I cry for you!
I am Your God,
And you have allowed other gods before Me.
I created you in love
And you have forgotten Me.
All other things of your life
You have put before Me,
Though I gave you life
And the gift of all the things you have.
And yet you discount Me and My wishes,
Giving yourself many reasons why you are disregarding Me.
I will do nothing now but mourn for you.

It is you who must return to Me now
Because all of those I love are free to choose Me,
Or a false lord of their own choosing.

(The cadence of the song changed here.)

I will hold fast now to those who have chosen Me,
To protect them from the storm of hatred and death
Which is to come.
I will shield their hearts and souls.
Though many will lose their lives,
Their souls are in My keeping
And My mark is upon their foreheads.
The mark of the Beast cannot come near them

For I have already claimed them.
Please, My dearest little ones of My Heart,
Please believe.
Please believe.
Please repent
And believe.
It is because of My love for you
That I ask this,
And because My Heart,
My Heart which has bled for you,
Bleeds for You again now.
I could be aloof from you,
Apart from you.
But You are Mine,
Made from the essence of My Heart.
Can you not understand and know that I LOVE YOU!
I would not be in this grief over you
If I did not love you.
Do I ask so very much of you?
Can you not look at My crucifixion
And feel My pain in your hearts?
It is the pain I have and still feel for you
Because I love you and will not,

Cannot,
Abandon you to your fate of selfishness
And self-destruction;
Your fate built on your own needs and wishes
Which my adversary tries to tell you
Can be fulfilled by hatred and rejection of Me.
Please look at Me!
Please see Me!
Please, please know Me
And put all else aside for Me
So that you may be with Me in My Kingdom forever.
The other way,
The way of selfishness and hardness of heart,
Is so easy for you,
But it leads you only to pain,
Emptiness,
And eternal damnation.
Can you not understand what I say
And believe?
Can you not hear Me speaking to you?
Listen to your heart,
The heart which I created.
Listen to the voice inside your own soul
Which is My voice
Pleading with you.
You cry out for help to Me
And when I answer
You ignore Me.
Then you reproach Me.
What else can I do?
You are free to choose.
You are choosing.
Do you know what you are choosing?
Do you know?
I love you.
For you, I will do
Much more than I have already done.

But will it matter to you?
Does My love matter to you?
It is My decision and will
To open My Sacred Heart to you.
I have become as small and frail as you
So that I can let you know of My love.
Please do nothing to separate us,
And do everything you can
To be with Me, your Lord and your God.
You matter to Me.
You are My love."

He says to me, "Courage and peace to you, little one. You doubt so much. Do you not know I can use anyone with an open heart? Yes, you have an open heart, though a fearful one. I love you, and I will remain with you forever. You are truly Mine, and I am truly Yours. Be at peace. Amen."

Later. My Guardian Angel told me to keep my note taker near by. I am restless tonight after this copying out of my Blessed Lord's lament. The painful strains of this song of grief echo and reecho in my mind, and tomorrow is a full day. It all seems so irrelevant when I think of my Blessed Lord's sorrow for His people. The last line of His song was sung with such heartbreak, "You are my LOVE!"

# Chapter 55
# PERSPECTIVES

Friday, September 25, 1992

12:40 p m. I had been very sad tonight, thanking God for the many blessings He has given me and yet hurting over the gossip and slander of someone I once believed was a friend. I felt like a sad little girl needing her Mother.

I woke from a deep sleep with these verses of love to my Heavenly Mother running in my mind like a song:

O gentle Mother,
Tender and small,
Bore God become flesh
Now she carries us all.

A virgin unspotted
And yet not divine
Brought forth her Child:
The prophesied Sign.

She, created by God
But in her holy womb,
God was made Man
That a Savior might come.

Virgin and Mother,
Daughter and spouse,
Related to God
As is no one else.

Mother not only
Of the Everlasting Word,
But of those who keep God's commandments
And acclaim her Son, "Lord."

Greeted "Full Of Grace"
As if by a new name,
Now a channel of grace,
For the Spirit's new flame.

Please be with me always
Your wise counsel give;
Teach me your Son's Way
Every moment I live.

Monday, October 5

Again, for the third MONDAY in a row, I have not gone to the Monday night rosary because of headache. Friday night was one of the worst ones so far. Yet it is at these times that I am most close to my Lord and God. Somehow it is brought home to me more clearly when I am in intense pain that He is all I need. Even as I reach for pain killers, I know this. I am saddened by my weakness not to be able to offer more, and amazed that I am still asked to do so with such a track record. But my inability to offer more pain for the souls by refraining from taking pain killers is indicative of my total and complete humanness, and great distance from any appearance of sanctity.

As I knelt to receive Our Blessed Lord in the Holy Eucharist tonight, my Angel said to me, "All who are present, whether receiving Our Lord or not, are to show reverence for the infinite miracle that is happening. God is uniting with human beings. That is a greater miracle than any other you have witnessed. There is no greater miracle in Earth or in Heaven than this."

I asked if this meant we should kneel. All over the country now, we are told not to kneel during the Consecration, or at all during the Mass for that matter. After Vatican II, the Communion rails were removed and we stood in line to receive the Lord. Now we are not to kneel even in the pews during preparation for the Consecration. We are "encouraged" to stand even during the consecration itself.

"You are to show reverence in the way you know best," my Angel answered me. I was somewhat confused at this reply.

He said with his wonderful humor, "You stand in line for everything. Are you showing reverence then?"

So the question is not what we do but that we show reverence, and an outward sign of reverence surely helps us ordinary mortals to feel more reverent. Otherwise, why show any respect for anyone or anything if one could always argue, "But I am reverent in my heart" while actions contradict this? But I think with all the arguing over this it is so easy to lose sight of the miracle of which my Dear Angel spoke: that God should unite in any way, and in such a special way, with us ordinary people!

Tuesday, October 20, 1992

As the pain from my headaches gets worse, it becomes a miracle to do bare essentials; to go to class, to cook a meal. I have tried to hide the fact of the intensity of my pain for so long. I may not be able to keep it hidden much longer. But, conversely, my appreciation for being able to do these every day things increases, and my understanding that there are many types of courage in the world, most going unrecognized, becomes sharper.

I would be in the deepest depression now because of my physical limitations if it were not for my certain knowledge, not faith but knowledge, that my Lord has a purpose, a plan, and an unshakable love for me and every single one of us. My sense of who I am has been so very based on my success at accomplishing: getting papers in on time, doing well in my grades, helping my clients, doing the best I can to care for my girls.

I have had to ask for more leeway in these past four years than at any time in my life, and the pile of incompletes still daunts me. By the yardstick used in the world, I would be considered a failure, with not much I can do about it.

But I am never a failure to my Lord. I have thought a great deal about the loving wisdom of my beloved Creator in giving me through these special experiences the sure knowledge of the worth and importance my physical and spiritual pain can have as an offering, the fruits in eternity these prayers and offerings bring. The greatest cry of my heart all my life has been that I could make a difference in the world, that my existence would somehow matter for good, that I might bring

---

[Note: Though headaches caused by a build-up of scar tissue still plague me, there has been no reoccurrence whatsoever of tumors or any other serious problems. Thanks be to God.]

even a little joy to God and His people in return for His bountiful gifts to me of life and His love. This desire is not born of great dreams or idealistic wishes, but comes from the fear that I might not be able to make a difference, to be of use in the world.

And in response to my yearning, what has He done but given me another gift: the gift of being able to give the treasure of my pain for the salvation of the souls He loves so devotedly. I am allowed to participate with Him in a work He could easily do alone, and by that participation my soul becomes deeper and stronger, and I am united more and more closely with Him through our mutual love and efforts. How grandiose all this might seem if I did not know that all of it is a gift to me of His love. Glory, glory, glory to my Lord.

I think of what my Blessed Angel said when I asked him why handicaps are permitted. I have puzzled over Jesus's answer to the Apostles when they asked Him about a blind man. Did he sin or did his parents sin, they wanted to know. Neither, He told them. He said the man's blindness had been allowed in order that the glory of God might become apparent. My beloved Guardian Angel told me when I asked about my own blindness, that my disability had been permitted, among other reasons, as a gift to my Mother that she have the opportunity to grow greatly in her ability to love. It is given to me as a gift that I may have the opportunity, not the certainty because that is a choice, but the opportunity to grow in spirit. I remember one of the angels telling me, "all life is an opportunity for love."

As I offer for souls, I realize more and more that this special love of Our Lord's is very simple, and my participation in it is not as extraordinary as it seemed to me at first. I do not in any way mean to diminish the gift I have been given. I mean only to say that everyone has the opportunity to love and offer for others. My awareness in every day life grows deeper. I look at other people as souls God loves. I think of God's mercy extended to try to save each soul from itself, coupled with His justice which is an inseparable aspect of His mercy. "God's justice IS His mercy, and His mercy IS His justice," one of the angels told me.

In loving us, whenever Our Lord asks for something He always gives so much more back in return. His request to us opens our hearts so He can give us more. So it has been with me.

# Chapter 56
# HELL

October 31, 1992

The light grew bright this afternoon as I sat in my living room. I tested the presence twice because of my shakiness and surprise that it should happen at a moment I least expected. I was reassured, and the gentle angel began, "I am 'Gentle Wisdom of God.'"

"O! I am glad you are here again! Bless you."

"Thank you, little one. I have come to tell you, as your blessed Guardian Angel promised, about a subject which has caused controversy and misunderstanding in your time. The question is asked by those who do not understand either their own world or the next how our Lord God could have created a place of everlasting torment for souls who have chosen against Him. As you have been told, Our Lord God did not create hell in the strict sense. Lucifer's hatred formed hell. Lucifer, if I may put it to you this way, created hell by his hatred of our Almighty Lord and by his wish to be totally separated from Him except insofar as he could do Him hurt. This animosity and hatred which is greater than anything you know boiled in the being of Lucifer. Those who joined him also joined in this total rejection of their Creator and their hatred of all that is good and loving. Their hatred creates and sustains hell. Their hatred and the total absence of God except to the degree that it is necessary for them to still exist is the Kingdom of Evil and Darkness.

Just as your love and your loyalty to your Creator, the Lord Who made you and sustains you, brings about His Kingdom in your hearts, so this absence of love for God creates a terrible void. Hatred ultimately feeds on itself and devours itself, needing more of good to hate in order to remain in existence. Do you understand?"

"No, I really don't. How does Lucifer get more to feed on? I don't really know what you mean."

"Lucifer and those in his Kingdom of Darkness feed on the souls of those who wish to join them in their total rejection and hatred of

God and those who love Him and who, by their love, cause the Kingdom of the Lord of the Universe to grow strong and beautiful, a true home for all loving and sincere hearts. In their perversity, Lucifer and his underlings hate more as they draw more souls to them. They revile God more and hate Jesus Christ especially, the Word made flesh, because He is Love in the flesh, Love Itself. They receive a vile nourishment from their hatred, and thus are able to continue hating the more they draw souls into their Kingdom of Darkness. The more they wound God because of His pain over the loss of these souls, the more they are filled with a vile elation which is a horrible mimicry of eternal life. But they are more and more dead in reality as they hate with greater ferocity and abandonment. Their shrieks and curses against the Almighty Lord increase their torment, and they do not understand that they are the cause of this increase in agony so they blame Almighty God and curse Him more, increasing their torment even more.

You also may be caught in this entrapping downward spiral of hate. The more you hate, the less you see of the love of God around you. How can you hate even one of your brothers or sisters on earth, and yet say you love God or another of your human family members? Hatred is all encompassing, just as love is all encompassing. You cannot belong to one kingdom and then to another. You must, ultimately, choose forever to whom you belong, and the lives you live here are the process of that choice.

Whether you choose to join Lucifer in eternal hatred forever or strive towards the Kingdom of God in the merciful purification He has provided for all who wish it, or whether your soul is purified by love and grace here on earth, you are His beloved ones. As you have seen, little one, He does everything He can to bring all of His precious souls to Himself. You will see the truth of this more clearly and beautifully and in different ways, and you will be a witness to those with open hearts to the great mercy and love of the One Who IS Mercy and IS Love.

His peace and the love of those in His Kingdom are with you. We pray for you, and for all others seeking Our Almighty Lord's Kingdom. Be at peace."

"Thank you. My Lord's mercy amazes me and gives me such joy."

"And you will see again and yet again that this mercy of Our Lord's and this everlasting love is always there except for those who have rejected His love AFTER understanding what they are doing. He does not allow one soul to condemn itself unknowingly. How could this ever have been thought of Him? It was thought by those who do not even begin to know their Lord and His mercy. Peace now, little one, peace.

Please pray for those who are being sucked into the maelstrom of Lucifer's evil this day and this night which he and his followers claim as their own. But the only possession they have is hatred, and hatred is nothing because it is an absence of Love, an absence of our Almighty Lord. Our Lord is beside you, little one. Be at peace."

Because Lucifer is desperate and his time is short, he has come out of hiding from behind the myth he has perpetuated that he does not exist. He is especially angered when God's little people, His weak people, His unlikely people, His very ordinary people are used to bring about a greater love and knowledge of Him and become vehicles, by His grace, for His glory.

We ourselves in our home have had experiences to let us know how petty and churlish, spiteful and uncouth, not to mention cruel, Lucifer is.

One night as I lay sleeping, I was having deeply troubled dreams. I awoke and rose to use the rest room. When I came back into the room, the smell of human excrement was so strong I nearly fainted from it. At first I thought it might be my little cat Abbie or my guide girl Gia, but the smell was undoubtedly that of human excrement.

I went into the next room and awoke my house mate D. We prayed using holy water, calling on the Saving Blood of Our Beloved Lord Christ and His army of the holy angels lead by Saint Michael to get rid of the evil presence. Within moments, the air was completely clear of any odor (something impossible if the source had been a natural one), and there was a feeling of deep peace in the room.

Another time when Father Walch was visiting us, a woman friend, D. and I went into my computer room to run something off for Father. D.turned on the main switch for the computer. There is a sound system in my computer, along with other programs which are automatically loaded.

Before *any* of the programs were loaded and a second after the power had been turned on, a gruff and unpleasant voice yelled, "Six, six, six!"

We yelled in chorus, "Father!!!"

When the computer itself was fully loaded without anyone having touched it, "666" was written on the screen. We erased it, and Father prayed an exorcism prayer.

We have had many other experiences to make it abundantly clear to us that Lucifer and his hatred is very real. May we all know this clearly, and give our lives entirely to Our Blessed Lord.

# Chapter 57
# LOVE COVERS A
# MULTITUDE OF SINS

My mind, heart, and thinking are being reorganized by listening to the beautiful angels, and by intense reading of Scriptures in the light of what they have told me. I realize that God's anger against us because of our sin is present because of His immeasurable love for us, as He sang in His lament. My prayer now is that He will not hold back His hand a moment longer than necessary, that His mercy towards us will not cause the loss of one soul.

There is talk now that our newly elected President Clinton will allow young girls, minors, to have abortions without the knowledge or consent of their parents. I wonder if very many people have thought of the ramifications of this. Besides the horror of the murders which will be committed, the state is in effect saying, "The government is really the legal guardian of your children. We decide what is right and wrong for them to do or not do. We take responsibility for them, to do as we wish with them." If the state can take guardianship away from parents like this, can it not take my guardianship over myself as an adult away from me, and then do with me whatever it wishes? I believe a horrible precedent has been set.

One night in early November, Father John Walch and I were talking on the phone. My Guardian Angel suddenly joined the conversation. I tested as always, and was reassured.

Father took the opportunity to ask a question. He asked if our guardian angels come from the choirs of angels and archangels, the two of the nine choirs which are most active on earth, as Father has told me.

My Guardian Angel said, "Yes, most of our guardian angels do come from these two choirs. But," he went on, "sometimes a soul has a particular need or is created by God for a purpose which requires an angel from another choir."

As an example, he said that when a little one is to be aborted by his or her mother, very often Our Lord will assign a cherubim or seraphim

THE LIGHT OF LOVE

to that poor little soul. When the baby is destroyed, his or her guardian angel takes that little soul straight to Heaven where it is purified of the consequences of original sin.

My Guardian Angel said that the little one is then taken into the full Presence of God, in the inner circles of the cherubim and seraphim right before Our Lord's great Majesty, and there that little soul becomes one of the purest and most cherished souls in Heaven.

"These little souls are so dearly loved because they have no concept at all of evil," my Guardian Angel told us. "We, the angels of Heaven, know of evil because we have seen Lucifer's disaffection and we had to choose. We also witness you human beings doing evil. But these little ones do not even begin to know what evil is, and therefore are precious beyond words to the Father." He went on to say that though they are not angels (because angels and created human souls are distinct and completely separate, human beings not being able to become angels or vice versa though angels may temporarily take on human form to be of assistance to us if God wills it), still they are angelic souls in their unblemished purity. Both Father and I were quite choked up by all this.

In late November, Father and I went to San Antonio to meet a special priest who has been talking to (and being answered by) the angels. He is a young priest and very dear. That God should allow such things to be happening! Who, fifteen years ago, could have dreamed of this?

While we were there someone, reputed to be a holy and just man, called me "a liar and a fake" without knowing anything about me. This hurt me to the bone. Being painfully aware of the loving trust which has been shown me in these blessings, I have tried to be strictly accurate and truthful in everything I have said or written, for the sake of others but also for the sake of my own soul. I beg Our Lord that I will never be a channel for error. I know my Lord will hold me to account, and I beg Him for His grace to help me.

I prayed for my accuser day and night. I prayed for my hurt, asking God to bring good out of this calumny as He does out of all wrongs which are brought to Him by His people. I realized after going through a great amount of spiritual pain that whenever anyone hurts me or another, this is in a sense God's way of asking us to pray for the person responsible for the hurt. Who knows? Perhaps no one else is praying for that individual. The greater the hurt, the greater I believe is the appeal from Our Blessed Lord.

Our King loves all His people and wants us all to be with Him eventually in His Kingdom. Is the pain He allows His followers to bear a sign to us, a way of indicating to us who needs help? Is allowing the pain a way God has of asking us to pray for the inflicters of it? Who else but true followers of Jesus would react in this unworldly and fool-ish seeming way? He asks us not to do what would seem sensible, what would be the natural reaction, but He asks us to respond with incred-ible, amazing love.

I begin to look at each person who hurts me as a gift, as a request from the One I love most to pray for that individual. Though their in-tention in causing me pain is not honorable of course, my Lord asks me to pray for them an He deepens my heart's ability to love and bear pain and thus I grow stronger through their actions. So Jesus brings good out of what was meant only to wound.

I also came to realize that this sincere prayer for someone who has wronged me is the beginning of my forgiveness for that person, and certainly is the beginning of my being forgiven of my own sins by God. I had always believed that some one wronging me would have to ac-cept my forgiveness before I could give it. No. I may give my forgive-ness, and in that giving my own heart is cleansed and purified. But, whether the other can benefit and be healed also by accepting my for-giveness is not up to me or within my control. That I have forgiven regardless of whether the other accepts my forgiveness or not frees me, joyously frees me.

True loyalty, then, is doing or saying whatever is necessary to help another soul towards God. Anything other than this under the guise of love or loyalty is a betrayal. It is a betrayal because it is not true love based on a wish for the true happiness of the person one professes to love. Anything that does not lead others closer to God, may in fact lead them farther away from God, is a betrayal of those I claim to love. If I pretend no wrong is being done or that everything is all right when it is not, then I am at least partly responsible for others continuing to do wrong, and therefore am partly responsible for their descent towards perdition. Beautifully, the opposite is also true. Small efforts can bring about such great good. Glory be to God.

Another lovely discovery — it is impossible to hate or wish ill towards a person for whom one is in deep prayer, especially when offering. I see the soul of such a one for whom I offer as infinitely precious to God. What the person is doing to hurt me or others, the circumstances of the matter, the events, or the personality of the individual become unimportant. Everything slips away except the love which God has for all of His souls, without exception. So by God's grace this gift of being able to offer which is available to everyone makes me in time begin to see the soul for whom I am praying as dearly loved and precious.

As prayers for them, I offer a headache, a cold. Offering the very hurt they have inflicted on me as prayers for them is wonderfully healing. The more this is done, the more precious I see their souls to be, and the more impossible it becomes not to love them.

In his first letter, chapter 4, (verse 1), Saint Peter says, "Since therefore Christ suffered in the flesh, arm yourselves with the same thought. For whoever has suffered in the flesh has broken with sin." I pondered over this verse for a long time, then realized that when I am in pain and that pain is offered as a prayer (as of course all of life can be offered to Jesus as a prayer), that prayer of pain — a sacrificial gift of love — prevents me from sinning in deed OR thought. In other words, I am too busy hurting and offering the pain to sin.

As Saint Peter says in verse 8, "Above all, let your love for one another be intense, because love covers a multitude of sins." How well Saint Peter knew the truth of that, and could promise us it is so.

# Chapter 58
# TOO HIGH ABOVE MY HEAD

My Dear Angel spoke to me briefly two or three times about things not of deep concern to me. Painfully, I was going through a time when I felt in desperate need of his love, his counsel, his presence reminding me of the love of God for me. I cried many a tear begging God to relent and allow him to speak to me. How frail and human I am, and how God in His mercy continually reminds me of this.

One of the brief exchanges we did have was over a question raised in a conversation. It was this, "If every soul on earth has a guardian angel, then who was Jesus Christ's guardian angel?"

My Dear Angel courteously broke into the conversation. After I had tested, he explained that the Holy Spirit is Christ's guardian angel. "None of us could have been a guardian angel for God," he exclaimed.

I was puzzled at this reference to the Holy Spirit as an angel. I am still not at all sure about this, not having any sort of theological background. My Dear Angel said that often references in the Scriptures are made to "the angel of the Lord." This may refer to the Holy Spirit. "For instance," he said, "when in the Mass the priest says, 'and may Your angel take this sacrifice to Your altar in Heaven,' this is a reference to Christ's guardian angel, the Holy Spirit." He warned that we must be careful not to try to assign roles to the Father, the Son, and the Holy Spirit. "God is one, God is three," he said. This, he said, was no contradiction, a mystery beyond us. Then he said,

"God guarding God,
God presenting God,
God loving God."

My Blessed Angel said, "No angel could ever be equated with our Creator, nor can our Creator ever be an angel. The singular honor of God becoming one of His creatures occurred once and for all when the Lord of Love became man through the consent and submission of His holy Mother.

But please understand that the action of God, the work of God both in Heaven and on earth through those who have given Him their free will — the Breath upon the waters which gave life — is the Holy Spirit which is the outpouring of love between the Father and the Son. This outpouring of love is the creative life which makes all life possible, all love possible.

Our Lord God works in this way of love through all His creatures, both angels and man.

It was through the love of the Father and the Son united with the faith of the three in the fiery furnace through which deliverance came.

No mediating angel could come between God and God, and so Our Lord God did not have a guardian angel in the same way you and all other people have. But because you are in the flesh of humanity, though sanctified by Jesus Christ, the mediating angel, serving your One and only Mediator, Jesus Christ, takes His supreme offering to His Father as initiated by the priestly power of the Son through His servants.

THIS ACTION OF LOVE MUST BE ACCOMPLISHED THROUGH THE HOLY SPIRIT. That is why the whole of the Trinity is totally involved in Holy Mass, and the Angel of the Lord a Holy Server."

The theological discussion which ensued between Father John and Father George after I read them the above paragraphs was too high above my head. Glory be to God.

# Chapter 59
# LET THE CHILDREN COME

Despite my growing weakness and increased pain, Father and I have done a good deal of speaking. On these occasions I am constantly reminded of what the Blessed Mother told me four and a half years ago, "You will be given grace to do what is necessary." God graciously adds to this grace another: my definition of what is necessary is more and more left up to the discretion of my Blessed Lord.

I am thus relieved of the burden of worrying so much about not being able to do what I believe is important, while at the same time experiencing more fully the amazement when it is obvious I am being given grace far and above my own natural strength. How many times now have I faced the prospect of speaking to hundreds of people while hurting abominably, and yet have done so purely by God's grace and with the crowd being completely unaware of my pain?

One of the most touching experiences I have is the joy and belief of the crowds. For the most part, they are faith-filled — far more faith-filled than I. The world completely contradicts the truth of my experiences, and the people and I have been taught to believe only what is tangible and "provable." Yet they, by God's grace, do believe.

Another blessing for me is the people who line up to speak with me after the talks. They share their hearts, and ask for my prayers. One night a lovely lady said to me, "I am disturbed by something you said."

"Oh, dear," I thought, "God, please help!" I was worried that I might have hurt her in some way.

"I am disturbed that you said the Blessed Mother told you that you would face ridicule. Please, when that happens, remember I am praying for you. I will pray for you every day." I said to this lovely lady, "God bless you. I beg God to remember your kindness to me for the rest of eternity."

A friend told me that, after one of my talks, a young lady in her teens got the impression that "we can do anything we like and then when we are about to die God saves us." No! No! God's mercy is also His justice, and He is not to be deceived. It is only in extenuating circumstances that He chooses to save one at the last. Most of us have made our choices by the way we have lived at the time we reach our last moment here on earth. But with the gift of the Sacraments and our free will, sincere repentance is always possible. But we must always be sincere. Our Creator knows us through and through.

It is amazing to me how many people have had experiences with angels. They are hesitant to share these experiences lest others think both they and the experiences odd. One night, the mother of a little four–year–old girl told me her daughter's story. From the time she was a tiny baby, the little girl had looked intently at what appeared to her parents to be nothing — and babbled away.

When she was old enough to talk, she told her parents she could see her guardian angel. She is now dying of leukemia. She says that the Mother of God has taught her how to pray and to offer pain as a prayer.

One day her parents came to see her in the hospital. "You know that mean man in the room next to me," she said to them. "He died today. The Blessed Mother told me he went to Heaven because I offered my pain for him." Because of her pending death and her unusual maturity and wisdom of spirit, she was given permission to receive Our Blessed Lord in the Holy Eucharist.

One night I spent time with a mother. Both her children had been brutally murdered. As she trusted me with the terrible grief of her poor heart, she explained that one of the things which tore at her most was that the youngest girl, Serena, a three–year–old, had never been baptized. She had delayed the baptism, hoping it could be performed in the town from which the family came, among their relatives.

In tears, she asked me, "Could I baptize her now?"

"I don't know," I said. "I do know there is such a thing as baptism by desire. But let's go ask Father about it."

We went out into the living room of the house where Father John and a dear mutual friend of ours were talking. The mother asked her question again.

Father said, "If it makes you feel better."

The mother was given some holy water and went to the other end of the room. As she poured the water out saying, "I baptize you, Serena, in the name of the Father, and of the Son, and of the Holy Spirit," the room was filled with light.

To my amazement, angels began to enter the room in solemn procession. They sang with a deep, vibrant joy. Their song was so beautiful that, Father told me later, I had a look of wondrous rapture on my face.

"Tell them to turn up the volume so we can hear too," Father said. The song broke off for a moment as the angels burst into lovely laughter. Then they began singing once again.

"What is this?" I asked aloud.

The angel nearest me stopped singing for a moment and replied, "The angels and saints of Heaven are rejoicing because, though Serena has been in the arms of Jesus Christ through grace, she is now declared a Christian on earth." Our belief in the Communion of Saints took on a new meaning for me that night.

The angels processed out of the room, but their joy was so great that I am sure that they and the Saints of Heaven continued the celebration of the little girl's baptism by desire in Heaven.

Later, because the question arose as to whether Serena's mother might have been performing a baptism, something contrary to Church teaching and therefore in error, I asked my Guardian Angel about it for clarity's sake. He said, "Please understand that the pouring on of water in the ceremony which was to soothe the heart of the mother of Serena was not, and is in no way, to be construed as a baptism. Let it be clearly known now and forever that this ceremony was for the purpose merely of soothing the torn and ravaged heart of a poor mother. However, it is not the wish of Our Lord Christ that any of His people, especially His little ones, should be lost. He does not forget any of His children, His created darlings, and wherever you are you are known to Him. He is aware of you in everything, and though there are times in your lives when it seems to you He must have forgotten you, it is only because you do not know of His love for you that you could believe this for a moment.

"The wish of Serena's mother that she be baptized, not the pouring on of water which cannot be done for a person already in Heaven, is what caused the rejoicing in Heaven. There are many joys in Heaven for those who are there, and Our Lord God in His love and mercy, and His wish to give delight to His children, gives the diverse peoples of the world joy in different ways according to what has given them loving joy on earth. But for one who has been baptized a Christian, or for one who has been baptized a Christian through the desire of those Our Almighty Lord has placed over them, there is a special place and a special joy. This is because they are truly redeemed with the Blood of

THE LIGHT OF LOVE

the Lamb, the Blood shed in Our Lord's Agony in the Garden, the Blood shed in the sufferings which followed, and the Blood and Agony on Calvary.

"The Lord of all Love honors the wishes of those who have been put over His little ones in authority. Remember what I and the other angels have taught you about hierarchy. If parents or others in authority wish children to be baptized, because God has placed them in authority over His little ones, He honors their wish. This is true in all cases. Do not doubt this, my little chronicler. God's love cannot be contained, and His mercy is expressed whenever and wherever that is possible without the violation of your free will.

"He, the Lord of all Love, is with you, especially in your pain, fear and uncertainty."

# Chapter 60
# "CAN YOU GIVE ME EVERYTHING?"

My Blessed Angel spoke to me in a lengthy conversation, giving me en-couragement and words of love and advice. I will not record it here because of the need for respecting the privacy of others. But his last words to me in this conversation have sung in my heart, and I pray will sing in yours, whatever your circumstances or state of life might be. He said with the tenderest kindness and love:

"Be of good cheer and gladness of spirit, for the God of the Universe loves you and is concerned with all that concerns you. He untangles even the most complicated and painful of all webs of pain, lies, anger and unforgiveness for those who truly seek Him and His will. Be at peace."

One morning as I prayed deeply for a friend who, up till now, has had little understanding (my lack as well) about the beauty and usefulness of Christian suffering, Our Lord Jesus spoke to me. Because of Jesus's suffering, all human suffering (especially that which is offered in union with Christ's Passion) becomes a living sacrifice to God. When Jesus spoke to me for my friend, I knew His beautiful words were not just for my friend but for me as well, and all of us who are hungry for His Kingdom. He said, "I am calling you to a deeper faith than you have had in the past because your deeper faith and love for Me will be sorely needed in the future. The test of faith and depth of your love through which I am putting you now, though an agony for you, is necessary, my beloved soul. Without it you would not be strengthened for the time to come, and you would not be able to serve as I wish you to serve.

Please understand that what you see as pain and death are very often the beginnings of new life. When I said, "A grain of wheat must fall to the earth, die, and then grow once more," I was not just referring to Myself. As a follower of Mine, you also must die to all that you hold dear. You do this by trusting everything to Me, giving everything to Me.

Do you not trust My wisdom in everything? If I withhold a miracle from you, it is only because I have a greater miracle waiting for you.

You are faith-filled. But do not allow your faith to be based on things seen, on the outcomes of this world. I want a faith from you which stands everything, which endures everything. Can you praise Me and bless My name no matter what happens to you and those you love, knowing that I will not allow anything to befall you that I cannot turn to your good?

This is what I call you to: a faith unshakable by what the world does or what circumstances bring you; a hope rooted solely in Me, not in what I can do for you; a love which will enable you to serve the most cruelly crushed of My beloved people.

Can you trust Me to bring about My good purposes in you in the way in which I know is best? Can you give Me everything?"

I think of the story of the rich young man who asked Jesus how he might gain eternal life. When Jesus told him to keep the commandments, he answered that he had done so from his youth. Jesus, looking at him with love, said, "Sell all you have, give the money to the poor, and follow Me." The young man looked at Jesus sadly and went away.

Jesus had shown that particular soul what its next step towards Him, towards perfect union with Him, was. What is mine? What is it that might cause me to walk away from Him sadly if He asked, either that I give or that I do? Whatever that might be, from giving him my life to forgiving someone, that is what lies between us. That is what I must overcome with His help in order to be in perfect union with Him.

O Lord, please grant me the grace to trust You with everything, to give You everything. May nothing be more important to me than You and Your will. Please grant me this grace that we may be together both here on earth and forever in Heaven.

# APPENDICES
## APPENDIX A

### A SCRIPTURAL ROSARY

You need not be a Catholic to pray this beautiful prayer which is one of the two weapons which can bind the demons of hell! It combines meditation on the lives of Jesus and His Mother with personal petitions. It is repetitious only when worshippers make it so. Expressing love is never repetitious.

Intentions may be offered for each decade, especially when praying in a group. People may be encouraged to join in the entire Hail Mary since the scriptural verses may be considered too long for the reader when added to the first part of the Hail Mary. If you do not already know The Lord's prayer, the Hail Mary, The Glory Be, the Fatima prayers and the Apostles' Creed by heart, memorize them before you begin.

All the Scriptural verses may be read at the beginning of each decade rather than interspersed between the prayers if this helps you to make the rosary a wonderful combination of deep personal prayer and a walk through the lives of Our Lord Jesus and His Mother.

The Joyful Mysteries are traditionally prayed on Mondays and Thursdays, the Sorrowful on Tuesdays and Fridays, and the Glorious on Wednesdays and Saturdays. The Glorious Mysteries are also prayed on Sundays.

When ending each set of five Mysteries, if praying only these for the day, with the prayers at the end of the rosary beginning with the SALVE REGINA (Hail Holy Queen). If praying the entire rosary, continue with the next group of mysteries with any break for prayer you wish.

### THE BEGINNING OF THE ROSARY

The Sign of the Cross: In the name of the Father, and of the Son, and of the Holy Spirit, Amen.

## THE APOSTLES' CREED

I believe in God, the Father Almighty, Creator of Heaven and Earth,
And in Jesus Christ, His only Son, Our Lord,
Who was conceived by the Holy Spirit,
Born of the Virgin Mary,
Suffered under Pontius Pilate,
Was crucified, died, and was buried.
He descended to the dead.
On the third day, He arose again.
He ascended into Heaven,
And sits at the right hand of God, the Father Almighty,
From thence He shall come to judge the living and the dead.
I believe in the Holy Spirit,
The Holy Catholic Church,
The communion of saints,
The forgiveness of sins,
The Resurrection of the Body,
And life everlasting. Amen.

## THE LORD'S PRAYER

Our Father, Who art in Heaven,
Hallowed be Thy name.
Thy Kingdom come,
Thy will be done
On Earth as it is in Heaven.
Give us this day
Our daily bread
And forgive us our trespasses
As we forgive those who trespass against us.
And lead us not into temptation,
But deliver us from evil. Amen.

Continue with three HAIL MARYS, each one offered as a request to Our Lady for her intercession that faith, hope and love be increased in our own hearts and in the world.

## HAIL MARY

Hail Mary, full of grace, the Lord is with thee. Blessed art thou among women, and blessed is the fruit of thy womb, Jesus. Holy Mary, Mother of God, pray for us sinners now, and at the hour of our death. Amen.*

## GLORY BE

(While making the sign of the cross)
Glory be to the Father,
And to the Son,
And to the Holy Spirit,
As it was in the beginning,
Is now,
And ever shall be,
World without end. Amen.

## FIRST FATIMA PRAYER

O my sweet Jesus, forgive us our sins.
Save us from the fires of hell.
Lead all our souls to Heaven,
Especially those in most need of Thy mercy. Amen.**

---

*[Note: The first part of the Hail Mary is directly from Scripture Luke 1:28; Luke 1:42. The second part is a request added by the Church to Our Lady to please pray for each of us "now, and at the hour of our death."]
**[Note: My Dear Angel asked me if I would please add the prayer given to the children at Fatima by the angel of peace. It is to be prayed after each decade of the rosary after the first Fatima prayer usually prayed. This was a personal request to me and others may add it or not as they wish. My Angel told me that this simple prayer gives comfort to Our Heavenly Father, that when prayed lovingly it consoles His heart.]

## SECOND FATIMA PRAYER

Lord, I believe in Thee,
I adore Thee,
I hope in Thee,
And I love Thee.
I beg pardon for all those
Who do not believe in thee,
Who do not adore Thee,
Who do not hope in Thee,
And who do not love Thee. Amen.

## THE JOYFUL MYSTERIES

### THE FIRST JOYFUL MYSTERY
### THE ANNUNCIATION OF THE ANGEL
### GABRIEL TO THE MOTHER OF GOD

(personal intention)

We cannot know how it was for the most Blessed Mother of all time to be so filled with the amazing grace of the Lord that God became a physical being in her womb. But please Lord Jesus, grant that we, too, may be so filled with the Holy Spirit, that You will be fully present in all that we do, think, and say — in all that we are. Amen.

THE LORD'S PRAYER.

1. The angel Gabriel was sent from God into a town of Galilee called Nazareth, to a virgin betrothed to a man named Joseph of the House of David, and the virgin's name was Mary.
HAIL MARY.

2. And when the angel came to her he said, "Hail, full of grace, the Lord is with thee. Blessed art thou among women."
HAIL MARY.

3. When she had heard him, she was troubled at his words and pondered what manner of greeting this might be.
HAIL MARY.

4. And the angel said to her, "Do not be afraid, Mary, for thou hast found grace with God. Behold, thou shalt conceive in thy womb and shalt bring forth a Son, and thou shalt call His name Jesus.
HAIL MARY.

5. He shall be great and shall be called Son of the Most High, and the Lord God will give Him the throne of David, His father; and He shall be King over the house of Jacob forever, and of His Kingdom there shall be no end."
HAIL MARY.

6. Mary said to the angel, "How shall this happen since I do not know man?"
HAIL MARY.

7. The angel answered and said to her, "The Holy Spirit shall come upon thee, and the power of the Most High shall overshadow thee; and therefore, the Holy One to be born shall be called the Son of God.
HAIL MARY.

8. And behold, Elizabeth thy kinswoman also has conceived a son in her old age, and she who was called barren is now in her sixth month, for nothing shall be impossible with God."
HAIL MARY.

9. Mary said, "Behold, the handmaid of the Lord. Be it done unto me according to thy word."
HAIL MARY.

10. And the angel departed from her.
HAIL MARY.

GLORY BE.

FATIMA PRAYERS.

Luke 1: 26–38.

## THE SECOND JOYFUL MYSTERY
THE VISITATION OF OUR LADY TO SAINT ELIZABETH

We have not deserved that the Mother of Our Lord should come to us, should pray for us, should plead for mercy for us before the throne of Our Almighty Lord. Glory, glory to God that He should give us such a one to pray for and with us. Amen.

THE LORD'S PRAYER.

1. Now in those days, Mary arose and went with haste into the hill country to a town of Judah, and she entered the house of Zachariah and saluted Elizabeth.
HAIL MARY.

2. And it came to pass when Elizabeth heard the greeting of Mary that the babe in her womb leapt.
HAIL MARY.

3. And Elizabeth was filled with the Holy Spirit and cried out with a loud voice saying, "Blessed art thou among women, and blessed is the fruit of thy womb!
HAIL MARY.

4. And how have I deserved that the Mother of my Lord should come to me?
HAIL MARY.

5. For behold, the moment that the sound of thy greeting came to my ears, the babe in my womb leapt for joy. And blessed is she who has believed, because the things promised her by the Lord shall be accomplished."
HAIL MARY.

6. And Mary said, "My soul magnifies the Lord, and my spirit rejoices in God, my Savior, because He has regarded the lowliness of His handmaid.
HAIL MARY.

7. For behold, henceforth all generations shall call me blessed because He who is mighty has done great things for me.
HAIL MARY.

8. And Holy is His name. His mercy is from generation to generation on those who fear Him.
HAIL MARY.

9. He has shown might with His arm. He has scattered the proud in the conceit of their hearts. He has put down the mighty from their thrones and exalted the lowly.
HAIL MARY.

10. He has filled the hungry with good things, and the rich He has sent away empty. He has given help to Israel His servant, mindful of His mercy, even as He spoke to our fathers, to Abraham and to his posterity forever."
HAIL MARY.

GLORY BE.

FATIMA PRAYERS.

Luke 1: 39–55.

## THE THIRD JOYFUL MYSTERY
### THE NATIVITY OF OUR LORD

Lord, in the moments in our lives when we feel most forsaken, help us to remember that You, the Creator of the universe, were born a human child in a stable, lived, suffered, died, and rose from the dead among us. You remain ever with us in the Comforter, the Holy Spirit, and in the Holy Eucharist. We are never alone. Amen.

THE LORD'S PRAYER.

1. A decree went out from Caesar Augustus that the whole world should be enrolled...
HAIL MARY.

2. And Joseph too went up from Galilee...to the City of David that is called Bethlehem, because he was of the House...of David.
HAIL MARY.

3. With him went Mary, his betrothed, who was with child. While they were there, the time came for her to have her child, and she gave birth to her first–born Son.
HAIL MARY.

4. She wrapped Him in swaddling clothes and laid Him in a manger, because there was no room for them in the inn.
HAIL MARY.

5. Now there were shepherds in that region living in the fields and keeping the night watch over their flock. The angel of the Lord appeared to them, and the glory of the Lord shown around them, and they were struck with great fear.
HAIL MARY.

6. The angel said to them, "Do not be afraid; for behold, I proclaim to you good news of great joy that will be for all the people. For today in the City of David, a Savior has been born for you who is Messiah and Lord.
HAIL MARY.

7. And this will be a sign for you: you will find an infant wrapped in swaddling clothes and lying in a manger."
HAIL MARY.

8. And suddenly there was a multitude of the Heavenly host with the angel, praising God and saying, "Glory to God in the highest, and on earth peace to those on whom His favor rests."
HAIL MARY.

9. ...So they went in haste and found Mary and Joseph, and the babe lying in the manger. When they saw this, they made known the message that had been told them about this child. All who heard it were amazed by what had been told them by the shepherds.
HAIL MARY.

10. And Mary kept all these things, reflecting on them in her heart.
HAIL MARY.

GLORY BE.

FATIMA PRAYERS.

Luke 2: 1–19.

## THE FOURTH JOYFUL MYSTERY
### THE PRESENTATION OF OUR LORD
### JESUS CHRIST IN THE TEMPLE

Almighty God, the Father, as Your Son Jesus Christ was presented to
You in the temple, please accept my heart. Please do not consider my
unworthiness; but, in Your kind graciousness, grant that I may serve
You. Amen.

THE LORD'S PRAYER.

1. When the days for their purification were completed according to
the Law of Moses, they took Jesus up to Jerusalem to present Him to
the Lord.
HAIL MARY.

2. Now there was a man in Jerusalem named Simeon. This man was
righteous and devout, awaiting the consolation of Israel, and the Holy
Spirit was upon him.
HAIL MARY.

3. It had been revealed to him by the Holy Spirit that he should not see
death before he had seen the Messiah of the Lord.
HAIL MARY.

4. Guided by the Spirit he came into the temple, and when the parents
brought in the child Jesus to do for Him what was customary under the

Law, he took Him in his arms, praised God and said, "This day, Thou givest Thy servant his discharge in peace, now Thy promise is fulfilled. HAIL MARY.

5. For I have seen with my own eyes the deliverance which Thou hast made ready in full view of all the nations, a light that will be a revelation to the heathen, and glory to Thy people, Israel." The child's father and mother were full of wonder over what was being said of Him. HAIL MARY.

6. Simeon blessed them and said to Mary, His mother, "This child is destined to be a sign which men reject, and you too shall be pierced to the heart so that the secret thoughts of many may be laid bare. Many in Israel will stand or fall because of Him." HAIL MARY.

7. There was also a prophetess, Anna, a very old woman. She never left the temple but worshipped day and night, fasting and praying. HAIL MARY.

8. Coming up at that very moment, she returned thanks to God and she talked about the child to all who were looking for the liberation of Jerusalem. HAIL MARY.

9. When they had done everything prescribed in the Law of the Lord, they returned to Galilee to their own town of Nazareth. HAIL MARY.

10. The child grew big and strong and full of wisdom, and God's favor was upon Him. HAIL MARY.

GLORY BE.

FATIMA PRAYERS.

Luke 2: 21–40

# THE FIFTH JOYFUL MYSTERY
## THE FINDING OF THE BOY JESUS IN THE TEMPLE

Lord, You are the Lamb of God who takes away the sins of the world. Please help us to grow in our understanding of this mystery of Your foreknowledge as a child of twelve as to the reason You were born, and the purpose for which You came into this world. Amen.

THE LORD'S PRAYER.

1. One of the elders said to me, "Do not weep; for the Lion of the tribe of Judah, the heir of David, has won the right to open the scroll and break its seven seals." Then I saw standing in the very middle of the throne, inside the circle of living creatures and the circle of elders, a lamb with the marks of slaughter upon Him.
HAIL MARY.

2. Jesus's parents went every year to Jerusalem for the solemn day of the Passover Feast. And when He was twelve years old, they went up to Jerusalem according to the custom of the Feast.
HAIL MARY.

3. Having fulfilled all that was required by the Law, they began their journey homeward, but unknown to them the child Jesus remained in Jerusalem. Thinking He was in their company, they traveled on for a day. Then they sought for Him among their kinsfolk and acquaintances.
HAIL MARY.

4. Not finding Him, they returned to Jerusalem to seek Him.
HAIL MARY.

5. On the third day, they found Him in the temple, sitting among the doctors of the Law, listening to them and asking them questions.
HAIL MARY.

6. All who heard Him were astonished at His wisdom and His replies.
HAIL MARY.

7. Seeing Him, they wondered. His mother said to Him, "Son, why have You done this to us? Your father and I have been searching for You, sorrowing."
HAIL MARY.

8. He said to them, "Why were you searching for Me? Did you not know that I must be about My Father's business?"
HAIL MARY.

9. They did not understand what He meant.
HAIL MARY.

10. And He went back with them and came to Nazareth, and lived under their rule.
HAIL MARY.

GLORY BE.

FATIMA PRAYERS.

Revelations 5: 5–6
Luke 2: 41–52

## THE SORROWFUL MYSTERIES

### THE FIRST SORROWFUL MYSTERY
OUR LORD'S AGONY IN THE GARDEN

Lord, please grant me the grace to keep awake with You at least one hour each day, to watch and pray. Amen.

THE LORD'S PRAYER.

1. Then they came to a place named Gethsemane, and He said to His disciples, "Sit here while I pray." He took with Him Peter, James and John, and began to be troubled and distressed.
HAIL MARY.

2. Then He said to them, "My soul is sorrowful even to death. Remain here and keep watch."
HAIL MARY.

3. He advanced a little and fell to the ground and prayed that if it were possible the hour might pass by Him. He said, "Abba, Father, all things are possible to You. Take this cup away from Me, but not what I will, but what You will."
HAIL MARY.

4. And to strengthen Him, an angel from Heaven appeared to Him.
HAIL MARY.

5. He was in such agony and He prayed so fervently that His sweat became as drops of blood falling on the ground.
HAIL MARY.

6. When He returned, He found them asleep. He said to Peter, "Simon, are you asleep? Could you not keep watch for one hour?
HAIL MARY.

7. Watch and pray that you may not undergo the test. The spirit is willing but the flesh is weak."
HAIL MARY.

8. Withdrawing again He prayed, saying the same thing. Then He returned once more and found them asleep, for they could not keep their eyes opened and did not know what to answer Him.
HAIL MARY

9. He returned a third time and said to them, "Are you still sleeping and taking your rest? It is enough. The hour has come.
HAIL MARY.

10. Behold, the Son of Man is to be handed over to sinners. Get up, let us go. See, my betrayer is at hand."
HAIL MARY.

GLORY BE.

FATIMA PRAYERS.

Mark 14: 32-36.
Luke 22: 43-44.
Mark 14: 37-42.

## THE SECOND SORROWFUL MYSTERY
### THE SCOURGING OF OUR LORD AT THE PILLAR

As the Roman multi-lashed, barbed whips tore into Your back and legs, ripping as they went in and came out, Lord, please help me to remember that a love like Yours which would suffer so for my sake will never abandon me unless I wish it. Please give me the grace never to turn my back on You. Amen.

THE LORD'S PRAYER.

1. Then they brought Jesus from Caiaphas to the Praetorium. They themselves did not enter the Praetorium, in order not to be defiled so that they could eat the Passover.
HAIL MARY.

2. So Pilate came out to them and said, "What charge do you bring against this man?" They answered and said to him, "If He were not a criminal, we would not have handed Him over to you."
HAIL MARY.

3. At this, Pilate said to them, "Take Him yourselves and judge Him according to your law." The Jews answered him, "We do not have the right to execute anyone," so Pilate went back into the Praetorium and summoned Jesus and said, "Are You the King of the Jews?"
HAIL MARY.

4. Jesus answered, "Do you say this on your own, or have others told you about Me?" Pilate answered, "I am not a Jew, am I? Your own nation and the chief priests handed You over to me. What have You done?"
HAIL MARY.

5. Jesus answered, "My kingdom does not belong to this world. If My kingdom did belong to this world, My attendants would be fighting to keep Me from being handed over. But as it is, My kingdom is not here."
HAIL MARY.

6. So Pilate said to Him, "Then You are a king?" Jesus answered, "You say I am a king. For this I was born and for this I came into the world, to testify to the truth. Everyone who belongs to the truth listens to my voice."
HAIL MARY.

7. Pilate said to Him, "What is truth?" When he had said this, he again went out to the Jews and said to them, "I find no guilt in Him. But you have a custom that I release one prisoner to you at Passover. Do you want me to release to you the King of the Jews?"
HAIL MARY.

8. They cried out..."Not this one, but Barabbas!" Then Pilate took Jesus and had Him scourged.
HAIL MARY.

9. Despised and the most abject of men, a man of sorrows. We esteemed Him not. Surely He has born our infirmities and carried our sorrows. But we thought of Him as one struck by God and afflicted.
HAIL MARY.

10. But He was wounded for our infirmities, He was bruised for our sins: the chastisement of our peace was upon Him, and by His bruises we are healed.
HAIL MARY.

GLORY BE.

FATIMA PRAYERS.

John 18: 28-40, 19: 1.
Isaiah 53: 3-5.

## THE THIRD SORROWFUL MYSTERY
### OUR LORD IS CROWNED WITH THORNS

Lord, may the anguish I feel that You should have been crowned with cruelty and disrespect, murdered for the sport of it — may this anguish in my heart for You be turned to compassion and awareness for those around me. Amen.

THE LORD'S PRAYER.

1. Then the soldiers of the governor took Jesus inside the Praetorium and gathered the whole cohort around Him.
HAIL MARY.

2. They stripped off His clothes and threw a scarlet military cloak about Him.
HAIL MARY.

3. Weaving a crown of thorns, they placed it on His head, and a reed in His right hand.
HAIL MARY.

4. And kneeling before Him, they mocked Him, saying, "Hail! King of the Jews!"
HAIL MARY.

5. They spat upon Him and took the reed and struck Him on the head, again and again.
HAIL MARY.

6. Then Jesus came out, wearing the crown of thorns and the purple cloak. Pilate said to them, "Behold the man!"
HAIL MARY.

7. When the chief priests and the guards saw Him they cried out, "Crucify Him! Crucify Him!"
HAIL MARY.

8. Pilate said to them, "Take Him yourselves and crucify Him; I find no guilt in Him." The Jews answered, "We have a law, and according to that law He ought to die because He made Himself the Son of God."
HAIL MARY.

9. Pilate said to the Jews, "Behold your king!" They cried out, "Take Him away! Take Him away! Crucify Him!"
HAIL MARY.

10. Pilate said to them, "Shall I crucify your King?" The chief priests answered, "We have no king but Caesar." Then he handed Him over to them to be crucified.
HAIL MARY.

GLORY BE.

FATIMA PRAYERS.

Matthew 27: 27-30.
John 19: 5-7.
John 19: 14-16.


## THE FOURTH SORROWFUL MYSTERY
### OUR LORD CARRIES HIS CROSS

Lord, may I in some small way in my lifetime be allowed to offer suffering as You did — for the salvation of souls. May I imitate You in this also. Please grant me the grace to drink even a small drop from the cup

out of which You drank. May I carry my cross as You carried Yours —
with courage, and ever mindful of others. Amen.

THE LORD'S PRAYER.

1. As they led Him away they took hold of a certain Simon, a Cyrenean,
who was coming in from the country; and, after laying the cross on
him, they made him carry it behind Jesus.
HAIL MARY.

2. A large crowd of people followed Jesus, including many women
who mourned and lamented Him.
HAIL MARY.

3. Jesus turned to them and said, "Daughters of Jerusalem, do not weep
for me; weep instead for yourselves and for your children.
HAIL MARY.

4. For indeed, the days are coming when people will say, 'Blessed are
the barren, the wombs that never bore, and the breasts that never nursed.'
HAIL MARY

5. At that time, people will say to the mountains, 'fall upon us' and to
the hills, 'cover us.'
HAIL MARY.

6. For if these things are done when the wood is green, what will happen when it is dry?"
HAIL MARY.

7. He was afflicted, He submitted to be struck down and did not open
His mouth. He was led like a sheep to the slaughter; like a ewe that is
dumb before the shearers.
HAIL MARY.

8. Without protection, without justice, He was taken away; and who
gave a thought to His fate?
HAIL MARY.

9. He was cut off from the world of living men, stricken to death for our transgressions.
HAIL MARY.

10. He was assigned a grave with the wicked, a burial place among the refuse of mankind, though He had done no violence and spoken no word of treachery.
HAIL MARY.

GLORY BE.

FATIMA PRAYERS.

Luke 23: 26-31.
Isaiah 53: 7-9.

## THE FIFTH SORROWFUL MYSTERY
### OUR LORD'S CRUCIFIXION

Blessed Mother of God, please pray for me that I may have the courage to walk beside you in spirit as Saint John brought you word, and you followed Jesus through the streets of Jerusalem. You stood at the foot of your Son's cross and felt His agony as your own because of your love. May I, too, be granted the courage of love not to run away. Amen.

THE LORD'S PRAYER.

1. They led Him out to what is called the place of the Skull, in Hebrew, Golgotha. There they crucified Him, along with two others, one on either side of Him.
HAIL MARY.

2. Pilate had an inscription written and put on the cross. It read, "Jesus, the Nazarean, the King of the Jews"...The chief priests said to Pilate, "Do not write, 'the King of the Jews' but that He said, 'I am the King of the Jews.'" Pilate answered, "What I have written, I have written."
HAIL MARY.

3. When the soldiers had crucified Jesus, they took His clothes and divided them into shares. They also took His tunic, but the tunic was seamless, woven from the top down. So they cast lots for His tunic that the Scriptures might be fulfilled.
HAIL MARY.

4. Standing by the cross of Jesus were His Mother and His Mother's sister, Mary the wife of Cloepas, and Mary of Magdala. When Jesus saw His Mother and the disciple there whom He loved, He said to His Mother, "Woman, behold your son."
HAIL MARY.

5. Then He said to the disciple, "Behold, your Mother." And from that hour, the disciple took her into his home.
HAIL MARY.

6. By now it was about midday and a darkness fell over the whole land, which lasted until three in the afternoon; the sun's light failed. The curtain of the temple was torn in two.
HAIL MARY.

7. After this, aware that everything was now finished, in order that the Scripture might be fulfilled, Jesus said, "I thirst."...So they put a sponge soaked in wine on a sprig of hyssop and put it up to His mouth.
HAIL MARY.

8. When Jesus had taken the wine He said, "It is finished." And bowing His head, He handed over His spirit.
HAIL MARY.

9. The soldiers came and broke the legs of the two crucified with Jesus. But when they came to Jesus and saw that He was already dead, they did not break His legs. But one soldier thrust his lance into His side, and immediately blood and water flowed out.
HAIL MARY.

10. An eyewitness has testified, and his testimony is true; he knows that he is speaking the truth, so that you also may come to believe.
HAIL MARY.

GLORY BE.

FATIMA PRAYERS.

John 19: 16-27.
Luke 23: 44-45.
John 19: 28-35.

## THE GLORIOUS MYSTERIES

### THE FIRST GLORIOUS MYSTERY
THE RESURRECTION OF OUR LORD, JESUS CHRIST

Blessed Mother of our Lord Jesus Christ and therefore our Mother, please intercede for us that we may know, even in a small way, the joy you knew when you discovered that your Son had risen, just as He said He would. May we also rise with Him in glory. Amen.

THE LORD'S PRAYER.

1. "Amen, amen, I say to you, you will weep and mourn while the world rejoices; you will grieve, but your grief will become joy.
HAIL MARY.

2. For I will see you again, and your hearts shall rejoice, and no one will take your joy away from you. ... On that day, you will not question Me about anything."
HAIL MARY.

3. At daybreak on the first day of the week, they took the spices they had prepared and went to the tomb.
HAIL MARY.

4. And behold, there was a great earthquake; for an angel of the Lord descended from Heaven, approached, rolled back the stone, and sat upon it.
HAIL MARY.

5. The angel said to the women, "Do not be afraid! I know that you are seeking for Jesus who was crucified. He is not here, for He has been raised, just as He said. Come, and see the place where He lay..."
HAIL MARY.

6. Then they went away quickly from the tomb, fearful yet overjoyed, and ran to announce this to His disciples. And behold, Jesus met them on their way and greeted them.
HAIL MARY.

7. Then Jesus said to them, "Do not be afraid. Go tell my brothers to go to Galilee, and there they will see me."
HAIL MARY.

8. Then they returned from the tomb and announced all these things to the eleven and to all the others. Those who had accompanied them also told the apostles, but their story seemed like nonsense and they were not believed.
HAIL MARY.

9. Peter and the other disciple went out and came to the tomb. They both ran, but the other disciple ran faster than Peter and arrived at the tomb first. He bent down and saw the burial cloths there but did not go in.
HAIL MARY.

10. Simon Peter arrived, went into the tomb and saw the burial cloths there. The other disciple also went in, and he saw and believed.
HAIL MARY.

GLORY BE.

FATIMA PRAYERS.

John 16: 20-23.
Luke 24: 1-2.
Matthew 28: 2-10.
Luke 24: 9-11.
John 20: 3-8.

## THE SECOND GLORIOUS MYSTERY
### THE ASCENSION OF OUR LORD INTO HEAVEN

May we, too, O Lord, proclaim Your Gospel to all the nations. Please grant that we may never do this with arrogance, narrow-mindedness or conceit. May we forever recognize that all Your creation is loved by You. May we speak Your words as You did — with nothing but love. Amen.

THE LORD'S PRAYER.

1. While they were speaking about all this, He stood in their midst and said, "Peace be with you." But they were startled and terrified and thought they were seeing a ghost.
HAIL MARY.

2. Then He said to them, "Why are you troubled? Why do questions arise in your hearts? Look at my hands and my feet, that it is I myself..."
HAIL MARY.

3. He said to them, "These are My words that I spoke to you while I was still with you, that everything written about me in the Law of Moses and in the prophets and psalms must be fulfilled." Then He opened their minds to understand the Scriptures.
HAIL MARY.

4. He said to them, "Thus it is written that the Messiah would suffer and rise from the dead on the third day and that repentance, for the forgiveness of sins, would be preached in His name to all the nations, beginning from Jerusalem..."
HAIL MARY.

5. So when they were all together, they asked Him, "Lord, is this the time when You are to establish once again the sovereignty of Israel?"
HAIL MARY.

6. He answered, "It is not for you to know about dates or times which the Father has set within His own control."
HAIL MARY.

7. ...When He had said this, as they watched, He was lifted up, and a cloud removed Him from their sight.
HAIL MARY.

8. As He was going, and as they were gazing intently into the sky, all at once there stood beside them two men in white.
HAIL MARY.

9. They said, "Men of Galilee, why stand there looking up into the sky? This Jesus who has been taken away from you up to Heaven will come in the same way as you have seen Him go."
HAIL MARY.

10. They did Him homage and then returned to Jerusalem with great joy, and they were continually in the temple praising God.
HAIL MARY.

GLORY BE.

FATIMA PRAYERS.

Luke 24: 36-47.
Acts 1: 6-7; 9-11.
Luke 24: 52-53.


### THE THIRD GLORIOUS MYSTERY
THE DESCENT OF THE HOLY SPIRIT

As the Holy Spirit descended upon Your people at Pentecost, Lord, please grant that this same Holy Spirit might descend on us in this time and in whatever way or manner that pleases You. Amen.

## THE LORD'S PRAYER.

1. When the time of Pentecost was fulfilled, they were all in one place together. Suddenly, there came from the sky a noise like a strong driving wind, and it filled the entire house in which they were.
HAIL MARY.

2. Then there appeared to them tongues as of fire, which parted and came to rest on each one of them. They were all filled with the Holy Spirit and began to speak in different tongues, as the Spirit enabled them.
HAIL MARY.

3. Now there were devout Jews from every nation under heaven staying in Jerusalem. At this sound, they gathered in a large crowd, but they were confused because each one heard them speaking in his own language.
HAIL MARY.

4. Then Peter stood up with the eleven, raised his voice and proclaimed to them, "This is what was spoken through the prophet Joel: 'It will come to pass in the last days', God says, 'that I will pour out a portion of My Spirit upon all flesh.
HAIL MARY.

5. Your sons and your daughters shall prophesy, your young men shall see visions, your old men shall dream dreams.
HAIL MARY.

6. And I will work wonders in the heavens above and signs on the earth below: blood, fire, and a cloud of smoke.
HAIL MARY.

7. The sun shall be turned to darkness, and the moon to blood, before the coming of the great and splendid day of the Lord, and it shall be that everyone shall be saved who calls on the name of the Lord.'
HAIL MARY.

8. Let the whole House of Israel know for certain that God has made Him both Lord and Messiah, this Jesus whom you crucified."
HAIL MARY.

9. Now when they heard this, they were cut to the heart, and they asked Peter and the other apostles, "What are we to do, my brothers?" Peter said to them, "Repent and be baptized, every one of you, for the forgiveness of your sins, and you will receive the gift of the Holy Spirit."
HAIL MARY.

10. Those who accepted his message were baptized, and about three thousand persons were added to their number that day.
HAIL MARY.

GLORY BE.

FATIMA PRAYERS.

Acts 2: 1-6.
Acts 2: 14-21.
Acts 2: 36-38.
Acts 2: 41.

## THE FOURTH GLORIOUS MYSTERY
### THE ASSUMPTION OF OUR LADY INTO HEAVEN

Lord Jesus, may I honor and love Your Mother, even just half as much as You do. May I follow the commandments of the Father and adhere to Your teachings to love unconditionally all of my brothers and sisters of humanity so that I may be a member of Your Holy Family forever. Amen.

THE LORD'S PRAYER.

1. The Lord God bestows favor and honor. No good thing does the Lord withhold from those who walk uprightly.
HAIL MARY.

2. Behold my beloved speaketh to me: Arise, make haste, my love, my dove, my beautiful one, and come. For winter is now past, the rain is over and gone.
HAIL MARY.

3. I saw that there was no way to gain possession of her except by gift of God, and it is a mark of understanding to know from whom that gift must come.
HAIL MARY.

4. I went to the Lord and besought Him, and said with all my heart, "God of my Fathers, Lord of mercy, You who have made all things by Your Word, ... give me Wisdom, the attendant at Your throne.
HAIL MARY.

5. Send her forth from Your holy Heavens and from Your glorious throne dispatch her that she may be with me and work with me, that I may know what is Your pleasure."
HAIL MARY.

6. For she knows and understands all things and will guide me prudently in all I do, and safeguard me by her glory.
HAIL MARY.

7. When she opens her lips, it is to speak wisely.
HAIL MARY.

8. Loyalty is the theme of her teaching.
HAIL MARY.

9. She keeps her eye on the doings of her household, and does not eat the bread of idleness.
HAIL MARY.

10. With one accord, her children rise up and call her blessed.
HAIL MARY.

GLORY BE.

FATIMA PRAYERS.

Psalm 84: 12.
Canticle of Canticles 2: 10-11.
Wisdom of Solomon 8: 21—; 9:—11.
Proverbs 31: 26-28.

## THE FIFTH GLORIOUS MYSTERY
### THE CORONATION OF OUR LADY AS
### QUEEN OF HEAVEN AND EARTH

Blessed be Your great mercy, O Lord, that You have allowed the Mother You gave us from the cross to come to us continually, to reach out to us in our pain and sinfulness. May she be blessed and may You forever be thanked for Your kindness. Amen.

THE LORD'S PRAYER.

1. Then God's temple in Heaven was opened, and the ark of His Covenant could be seen in the temple. There were flashes of lightning, rumblings, and peals of thunder, an earthquake, and a violent hailstorm.
HAIL MARY.

2. Then a great sign appeared in the sky, a woman clothed with the sun, with the moon under her feet, and on her head a crown of twelve stars.
HAIL MARY.

3. She was with child and cried aloud in pain as she labored to give birth.
HAIL MARY.

4. Then another sign appeared in the sky; it was a huge red dragon .... Then the dragon stood before the woman about to give birth, in order to devour her child.
HAIL MARY.

5. She gave birth to a son, a male child destined to rule all the nations with an iron rod. Her child was caught up to God and His throne.
HAIL MARY.

6. Then the dragon became angry with the woman and went off to wage war against the rest of her offspring, those who keep God's commandments and bear witness to Jesus.
HAIL MARY.

7. Blessed art thou, O daughter, by the Lord, the Most High God above all women upon the earth. Blessed be the Lord who made heaven and earth who hath directed thee to the cutting off of the head of the prince of our enemies.
HAIL MARY.

8. Because He hath so magnified thy name ... that thy praise shall not depart out of the mouths of men who shall be mindful of the power of the Lord forever.
HAIL MARY.

9. For thou hast not spared thy life by reason of the distress and tribulation of thy people, but hast prevented our ruin in the presence of our God.
HAIL MARY.

10. Hail, Queen of Mercy, protect us from the enemy; and receive us at the hour of death.
HAIL MARY.

GLORY BE.

FATIMA PRAYERS.

Revelations 11: 19; 12: 1-5.
Revelations 12: 17.
Judith 13: 23-25 in Douay from THE GRADUAL

## SALVE REGINA

Hail, Holy Queen, Mother of Mercy,
Our life, our sweetness, and our hope.
To thee do we cry,
poor banished children of Eve.
to thee do we send up our sighs
mourning, and weeping in this valley of tears.
Turn, then, most gracious advocate,
thine eyes of mercy towards us;
and after this, our exile,
show unto us the blessed fruit of thy womb,
Jesus.
O clement, O loving,
O sweet Virgin Mary,
pray for us O Holy Mother of God,
that we may be made worthy of the promises of Christ our Lord.
Amen.

## ROSARY PRAYER

Let us pray. O God, whose only-begotten Son, by His life, death, and resurrection, has purchased for us the rewards of eternal life, grant, we beseech Thee, as meditating on these mysteries of the most Holy Rosary of the Blessed Virgin Mary, we may both imitate what they contain, and obtain what they promise; through the same Christ Our Lord. Amen.

## PETITION TO SAINT MICHAEL

Saint Michael, the Archangel, defend us in battle. Be our protection against the wickedness and snares of the devil. May God rebuke him, we humbly pray, and do Thou, O Prince of the Heavenly Host, by the power of God, cast into hell Satan, and all the evil spirits, who prowl the world seeking the ruin of souls. Amen.

## THE ANGELUS

V. The Angel of the Lord declared unto Mary
R. And she conceived of the Holy Spirit.

HAIL MARY.
V. Behold, the handmaid of the Lord.
R. Be it done unto me according to Thy Word.

HAIL MARY.
V. And the Word was made flesh [genuflect]
R. And dwelt among us.

HAIL MARY.
V. Pray for us, O holy Mother of God,
R. That we may be made worthy of the promises of Christ, Our Lord.
Amen .
V. Let us pray:
R. Pour forth, we beseech Thee, O Lord, Thy grace into our hearts, that we to whom the incarnation of Christ, Thy Son, was made known by the message of an angel, may, by His passion and cross, be brought to the glory of His Resurrection, through the same Christ Our Lord. Amen.

---

[Note: The Petition to Saint Michael and the Angelus are not technically parts of the rosary, though the Saint Michael Prayer has been included in later years. We include the Angelus with every rosary, though it is traditionally prayed at 6 AM, noon, and 6 PM.]

# THE LIGHT OF LOVE

# APPENDIX B

## FAVORITE PRAYERS
## AND MEDITATIONS

### MORNING PRAYER

Thank You, Father, for safely taking us through the dark of night,
And into the light of this morning.
Father, as we face this new day,
We ask that all we do
Bring us closer to You.
May all our actions and thoughts this day be pure,
And filled with Your love and mercy.
Dear Father, send us today those You want us to touch,
Those who need Your words to be spoken to them.
Speak through us, and use us this day
For Your glory and Your honor.
And, Dear Father, when we fall and stumble on our journey today
Send us Your holy angels
To gently lift us
And place us back on the path to You.
And let us live this day as though it were our last.
And if, Dear Father, You call us home today
May we be prepared to meet you
Face to Face. Amen.*

### EVENING PRAYER OF SAINT AUGUSTINE

Watch, O Lord, with those who wake
Or watch,

---

[ Note: This prayer was dictated by Our Lady to Mike Slate, one of the messengers of Lubbock, Texas. She asked that we pray it every morning, and that we pray for the grace to live the prayer.]

Or weep tonight;
And give Your angels and saints
Charge over those who sleep.
Tend Your sick ones, O Lord Christ.
Rest Your weary ones,
Bless Your dying ones,
Soothe Your suffering ones,
Pity Your afflicted ones,
Shield Your joyous ones,
And all for Your love's sake. Amen.

## EVENING PRAYER

Eternal Father,
I offer Thee the Sacred Heart of Jesus,
With all Its Love,
All Its Sufferings,
And all Its Merits;
To expiate all the sins I have committed this day,
And during all my life:
Glory Be to the Father,
And to the Son,
And to the Holy Spirit,
As it was in the beginning,
Is now,
And ever shall be,
World without end, Amen.
To purify the good I have done
In my poor way, this day
And during all my life:
Glory Be, etc.
To make up for the good I aught to have done

------

[Note: A cloistered nun, who had just died, appeared to her superioress who was praying for her, and said, "I went straight to Heaven, for, by means of this prayer, prayed every evening, I paid my debts."]

And that I have neglected, this day
And during all my life:
Glory be, etc.

God be in my head
And in my understanding.
God be in mine eyes,
And in my looking.
God be in my mouth,
And in my speaking.
God be in my heart,
And in my thinking.
God be at mine end,
And my departing.
Sarum Primer, 1527

## MEMORARE

Remember, O most gracious Virgin Mary, that never was it known
that anyone who fled to thy protection, implored thy help, or
sought thy intercession was left unaided.

Inspired by this confidence I fly unto thee, O Virgin of
virgins, my Mother. To thee I come; before thee I stand, sinful
but sorrowful.

O Mother of the Word Incarnate, despise not my petitions but,
in thy mercy, hear and answer me. Amen.

## MARY, IMMACULATE QUEEN

O Mary, Immaculate Queen,
Look down upon this distressed and suffering world.
You know our misery and our weakness.
O you who are our Mother, saving us in the hour of danger,
Have compassion on us in these days of great and heavy trial.
Jesus has confided to you the treasure of His grace,
And through you He wishes to grant us pardon and mercy.

In these hours of anguish, therefore,
Your children come to you as their hope.
We recognize your Queenship, and we ardently desire your triumph.
We need a Mother, and a Mother's heart.
You are for us the bright dawn which scatters the darkness
And points out the way to life.
In your mercy, obtain for us the courage and confidence of which
we have such need.
Most holy and adorable Trinity,
You have crowned with glory in Heaven the Blessed Virgin Mary,
Mother of the Savior.
Grant that all her children on earth may acknowledge her as their
sovereign Queen,
That all hearts, homes and nations
May recognize her rights as Mother and Queen. Amen.

## A PRAYER OF CARDINAL NEWMAN

Dear Jesus,
Help me to spread Your fragrance
Wherever I go.
Flood my soul with Your Spirit and Life.
Penetrate and possess my being so utterly
That my life may only be
A radiance of Yours.
Shine through me, and be so in me
That every soul I come in contact with
May feel Your Presence in my soul.
Let them look up, and see no longer me
But only Jesus.
Stay with me,
And then I will begin to shine as You shine,
So to shine as to be a light to others.
The light, O Jesus,
Will be all from You.
None of it will be mine.
It will be You, shining on others through me.

Let me thus praise You
In the way in which You love best:
By shining on those around me.
Let me preach You without preaching,
Not by words but by example,
By the catching force,
The sympathetic influence of what I do,
The evident fullness of the love
My heart bears for You. Amen.


## A PRAYER OF DEDICATION TO GOD'S WILL

Most merciful Jesus, grant me Your grace.
May it remain with me and sustain me
Until my life's end.
May I always desire and do
Only what You approve and find pleasing.
May Your will be my will.
May my will follow the example of Yours
And agree perfectly with it.
May my will be at one with Yours
In willing and not willing
So that I never act against Your will.
Grant also that I may die to all worldly things
And prefer to be despised and unknown in this life
Because of my love for You.
May it be my highest desire
To rest in You
And find peace of heart in You.
You alone are the heart's peace.
You alone are its rest.
Apart from You,
Every life is difficult and tormented.
In Your peace,
Most High and Everlasting Good,
I shall sleep and take my rest. Amen.

– Saint Thomas a Kempis

Lord, for Your sake I shall cheerfully suffer
Whatever happens to me as coming with Your permission.
I am prepared to accept from Your hand
Both good fortune and bad,
The sweet and the bitter,
The joyful and the sorrowful.
I shall be grateful for whatever happens to me.
If You keep me safe from sin,
I shall fear neither death nor hell.
So long as You do not cast me away from You forever,
Or blot me from the Book of Life,
I shall not be harmed by any distress or suffering. Amen.

– Saint Thomas a Kempis

## A PERFECT ACT OF CONTRITION

O my God,
I am heartily sorry
And beg pardon
For all my sins,
NOT SO MUCH because these sins
Bring suffering and hell to me,
But because they have crucified my loving Savior,
Jesus Christ,
And offended Thy infinite goodness.
I firmly resolve, with the help of Thy grace,
To confess my sins,
To do penance,
And to amend my life. Amen.

or

O my God,
I am heartily sorry
for having offended thee
And I detest all my sins
Because of thy just punishment

But, most of all, because they offend thee
My God Who art all good
And deserving of all my love
And I firmly resolve through the help of Thy grace,
To confess my sins,
To do my penance,
And to amend my life. Amen.


## AN OLD PRAYER

Take, O Lord, from our hearts
All jealousy, indignation, wrath and contention,
And whatsoever may injure charity
And lessen brotherly love.
Have mercy, O Lord!
Have mercy on those that crave Thy mercy.
Give grace to them that stand in need thereof,
And grant that we may be worthy to enjoy Thy grace
And attain to everlasting life. Amen.

"God is not mortal that He should lie, not a man that He should change His mind. Has He not spoken, and will He not make it good? What He has proclaimed, He will surely fulfill."— Numbers 23:19.

"The Lord's true love is surely not spent, nor has His compassion failed; they are new every morning, so great is His constancy." — Lamentations 3: 22-23.

"I took you from the ends of the earth, from its furthest corners I called you. I said, 'you are My servant', I have chosen you and have not rejected you. So do not fear, for I am with you; do not be dismayed, for I am your God. I will strengthen you and help you; I will uphold you with My righteous right hand." — Isaiah 41: 9-10.

## ACT OF CONFIDENCE

Heart of Jesus, I adore Thee;
Heart of Mary, I implore thee;
Heart of Joseph, meek and just,
In these three Hearts I place my trust.

## LITANY OF HUMILITY

V. O Jesus, meek and humble of heart, hear me:
From the desire of being esteemed,
R. Deliver me, Jesus.
V. From the desire of being loved,
R. Deliver me, Jesus.
V. From the desire of being extolled, ...
From the desire of being honored, ...
From the desire of being praised, ...
From the desire of being preferred to others, ...
From the desire of being consulted, ...
From the desire of being approved, ...
From the fear of being humiliated, ...
From the fear of being despised, ...
From the fear of suffering rebukes, ...
From the fear of being gossiped about, ...
From the fear of being forgotten, ...
From the fear of being ridiculed, ...
From the fear of being wronged, ...
V. From the fear of being suspected,
R. Deliver me, Jesus.
V. That others may be loved more than I:
R. Jesus, grant me the grace to desire it.
V. That others may be esteemed more than I:
R. Jesus, grant me the grace to desire it.
That, in the opinion of the world, others may increase and I decrease.
...
That others may be chosen and I set aside: ...
That others may be praised, and I unnoticed: ...
That others may be preferred to me in everything: ...

V. That others may become holier than I, provided that I may become as holy as I should.
R. Jesus, grant me the grace to desire it.
Amen.

## ROSARY OF THE SEVEN SORROWS
## OF THE BLESSED VIRGIN MARY

Sign of the cross. Then three HAIL MARY's are prayed in remembrance of the tears of the Blessed Mother for the sufferings of her Son, prayed in request to obtain true sorrow for our sins.

Seven HAIL MARY's prayed for each of the seven sorrows of Mary (so seven groups of seven). The seven sorrows are: the prophecy of Simeon; the flight into Egypt; the loss of the boy Jesus in Jerusalem; Mary meets Jesus carrying His Cross; Our Lady witnesses her Son's Crucifixion; Mary receives the body of Jesus from the Cross; the body of Jesus is placed in the tomb.
    Prayer to complete this rosary:
Pray for us, O most Sorrowful Virgin,
that we may be made worthy of the promises of Christ. Lord Jesus,
we now implore both for the present and for the hour
of our death the intercession of the most Blessed Virgin Mary,
Thy Mother, whose holy soul was pierced at the time of Thy Passion,
by a sword of grief. Grant us this favor, O Savior of the world,
who lives and reigns with the Father and the
Holy Spirit forever and ever.
Amen.*

## MOST INTIMATE RELATIONSHIP

Mary the dawn, Christ the Perfect Day;
Mary the gate, Christ the Heavenly Way;
Mary the root, Christ the Mystic Vine;
Mary the grape, Christ the Sacred Wine.

Mary the wheat, Christ the Living Bread;
Mary the stem, Christ the Rose, blood red;
Mary the font, Christ the Cleansing Font;
Mary the cup, Christ the Precious Blood.

Mary the temple, Christ the Temple's Lord;
Mary the shrine, Christ the God Adored;
Mary the beacon, Christ the Haven's Rest;
Mary the mirror, Christ the Vision Blessed.

Mary the Mother, Christ the Mother's Son;
By Whom all things are blessed, while endless ages run.

## PETITION TO THE QUEEN OF ANGELS
## TO DEFEAT SATAN

August Queen of Heaven, sovereign mistress of the angels!
Thou who, from the beginning, hast received from God the power and
mission to crush the head of Satan, we humbly beseech thee to send
thy holy legions that, under thy command by thy power, they may
pursue the evil spirits, encounter them on every side, resist their
bold attacks, and drive them into the abyss of eternal woe. Amen.

## SAINT GERTRUDE'S GUARDIAN ANGEL PRAYER

O most holy angel of God, appointed by God to be my guardian,
I give you thanks for all the benefits which you have ever bestowed
on me in body and in soul. I praise and glorify you that you
condescended to assist me with such patient fidelity, and to defend
me against all the assaults of my enemies. Blessed be the hour in
which you were assigned me for my guardian, my defender, and my
patron. In acknowledgement and return for all your loving
ministries to me, I offer you the infinitely precious and noble
heart of Jesus, and firmly purpose to obey you henceforth, and most
faithfully to serve my God. Amen.

## PRAYER FOR ANGELIC HELP

O my Lord Jesus Christ,
As it hath pleased Thee to assign an angel
To wait on me daily and nightly,
With great attendance and diligence,
So I beseech Thee
Through his going betwixt us
That Thou cleanse me from vices,
Clothe me with virtues,
Grant me love and grace to come,
See and have without end Thy bliss,
Before Thy fair face,
That liveth and reigneth after Thy glorious Passion
With the Father of Heaven and with the Holy Ghost,
One God and Persons Three,
Without end in bliss.
Amen.
From the Processional of the nuns of Chester, c. 1425.

## WHAT CALLEST THOU ME?*

Thou callest Me MASTER ...

Yet heedest Me not.
Thou callest Me LIGHT ...

Yet I shine not in thee.
Thou callest Me WAY ...

But dost follow Me not,
Thou callest Me LIFE ...

Yet My Name is forgot.
Thou callest Me TRUTH ...

But play'st a false role.
Thou callest Me GUIDE ...

Yet despisest control.

Thou callest Me LOVING ...

Withholding thy heart.
Thou callest Me RICH,

Yet desirest no part.
Thou callest Me GOOD ...

Yet evil thy ways.
Thou callest Me ETERNAL ...

While wasting thy days.
Thou callest Me NOBLE ...

Yet draggest Me down.
Thou callest Me MIGHTY ...

Not fearing My frown.
Thou callest Me JUST ...

Oh! if just then I be,
When I shall condemn thee,

Reproach thou not Me.

## FOR OUR ENEMIES
### Saint Thomas More

Almighty God, have mercy on N. and N...,
And on all that bear me evil will and would me harm,
And their faults and mine together,
By such easy, tender and merciful means

As thine infinite wisdom best can devise;
Vouchsafe to amend and redress
And make us saved souls in Heaven together,
Where we may ever live and love together with Thee
And Thy blessed saints, O glorious Trinity,
For the bitter Passion of our sweet Saviour, Christ. Amen.
Lord, give me patience in tribulation
And grace in everything to conform my will to Thine,
That I may truly say, "Fiat voluntas tua,
Sicut in caelo et in terra."
The things, good Lord, that I pray for,
Give me Thy grace to labor for. Amen.


## PRAYER FOR WORLD CONVERSION*

Father, all merciful, let those who hear and hear again yet
never understand, hear Your voice this time and understand that it
is You, the Holy of Holies. Open the eyes of those who see and
see, yet never perceive to see with their eyes, let them see this
time Your Holy Face and Your glory. Place Your finger on their
hearts so that their hearts may be open, and understand Your
faithfulness. I pray and ask You all these things, Righteous
Father, so that all nations be converted and be healed through the
wounds of Your beloved Son, Jesus Christ. Amen.


## DAILY GUARDIAN ANGEL PRAYER

Dearest Guardian Angel,
You were given to me as God's special gift
At my very beginning
When my soul was created
By the great love and power
Of the Lord of all things.
Dearest angel,
Please be with me today
In everything I do.

By the power granted to you by my Lord,
To be my protector and champion,
Please shield me from all temptation beyond my strength.
Help me to renounce from this day forward
All things which keep me from my Lord:
All impure thoughts,
All unkind words,
All dishonest actions—
Both actively committed
And committed through omission.
Bring to me all events and people
Which will draw me nearer this day
To my Almighty Creator,
Whether they give me joy or sorrow,
Peace or pain.
And when I come to my last day here on earth,
In your love and loyalty to me
Please remain with me until you lead my soul
Into the full presence of my Lord,
Jesus Christ. Amen.

[Note: Very much with his assistance, I wrote the above guardian angel prayer to my Angel about 3 o'clock one morning.]

## PRAYER OF SAINT FRANCIS

Lord, make me an instrument of Thy peace.
Where there is hatred, let me sow love;
Where there is injury, pardon;
Where there is doubt, faith;
Where there is despair, hope;
Where there is darkness, light;
And where there is sadness, joy.
Oh, Divine Master, grant that I may not so much seek
To be consoled as to console;
To be understood as to understand;

To be loved as to love;
For it is in giving that we receive,
It is in pardoning that we are pardoned,
And it is in dying that we are born to eternal life.


## ACT OF REPARATION*

O good Jesus, in gratitude for Thy many graces,
And in sorrow for many abuses of these graces,
I wish at this moment,
Both for myself, ever ungrateful,
And for the world, ever criminal,
To make an Act of Solemn Reparation.
Listen, then, O Merciful Savior of our souls,
Listen to these Acts of Faith,
To these expressions of sorrow:

For the irreverence we have committed in the House of God,

I wish to make reparation.
For our careless and distracted attendance at Sunday Mass,

I wish to make reparation.
For our lack of preparation before, and our poor thanksgiving after
Holy Communion,

I wish to make reparation.
For our failure to cooperate with Thy daily Graces,

I wish to make reparation.
For our sins of pride, sensuality, and of our entire lives,

I wish to make reparation.
For our bad example and the sins we have caused in others, ...
For the frightful blasphemies uttered against Thee and Thine Immaculate Mother, ...

For the deplorable untruths of heresy, for all deserters and apostates, ...
For the pleasure–seeking and money–mad profaners of the Lord's
Day, ...
For the sacrilegious treatment of Thy Churches and Altars, ...
For the diabolical agents of hell, ever seeking whom they may devour,
...
For the heart–breaking outrages committed by those who should be
Thy greatest consolation, ...
"O Love, neglected!
O Goodness, but too little known!"


## ANONYMOUS

Found scratched on a military prison wall during the Civil War:

I asked God for strength
That I might achieve ...
I was made weak
That I might learn humbly to obey.
I asked for health,
That I might do greater things.
I was given infirmity
That I might do better things.
I asked for riches,
That I might be happy.
I was given poverty
That I might be wise.
I asked for power,
That I might have the praise of men.
I was given weakness
That I might feel the need of God.
I asked for all things,
That I might enjoy life.
I was given life
That I might enjoy all things.
I got nothing that I asked for,
But everything I had hoped for.

Almost despite myself,
My unspoken prayers were answered.
I am among all men most richly blessed!

"One must learn to call upon the name of God more even than breathing — at all times, in all places, in every kind of occupation. The apostle says, "Pray without ceasing", that is, he teaches men to have the remembrance of God in all times and places, and circumstances. If you are making something, you must call to mind the Creator of all things. If you see the light, remember the Giver of it. If you see the heavens and the earth and the sea and all that is in them, wonder and praise the Maker of them. If you put on your clothes, recall whose gift they are and thank Him who provides for your life. In short, let every action be a cause of your remembering and praising God. And lo! You will be praying without ceasing, and therein your soul will always rejoice."

– Saint Peter the Damascene

Prayer to be recited at 3 P.M., given to Sister Faustina by Our Lord Jesus for the conversion of any sinner, "O Blood and Water, which gushes forth from the Heart of Jesus as a fount of mercy for us, I trust in You."

## THE FOUR LAST THINGS

Life is short, and death is sure.
The hour of death remains obscure.
    A soul you have, and only one,
If that be lost, all hope is gone.
Waste not time, while time shall last;
For after death 'tis ever past.
    All–seeing God your judge will be,
And Heaven or Hell your destiny.
All earthly things will speed away,
Eternity, alone, will stay.

    Author Unknown

## HAIL, CHRIST, OUR KING!

Most sweet Jesus!
Come near to us, Thy children.
Remove from our hands that crown
Which those who are but dust of earth
Try to seize from Thee.
Enter now in triumph among us,
Thy fervent followers!
Hail, Christ, Our King!
 Lawmakers may break the table of Thy Law,
But whilst they lose their thrones and are forgotten,
We, Thy subjects, will continue to salute Thee:
Hail, Christ, Our King!
 For some have said that Thy Gospel is out–of–date,
That it hinders progress,
And must no longer be considered.
They who say this soon disappear,
Into obscurity, and are forgotten,
Whilst we, who adore Thee,
Continue to salute Thee:
Hail, Christ, Our King!
 The proud, the worldly,
Those who possess unlawful riches,
Those who thirst for riches,
Honor and pleasures alone,
Declaring Thy moral Law to be for past ages
Will be hurled against the rock of Calvary
And Thy Church and, falling,
Will be reduced to dust,
And sink into oblivion
Whilst we, Thy followers,
Continue to salute:
Hail, Christ, Our King!
 Those who seek the dawn
Of a material civilization,
Divorced from God,

Will surely die,
Poisoned by their own false doctrine,
Deserted and cursed by their own children
Whilst we, who would console Thee,
Will continue to salute Thee:
Hail, Christ, Our King!
 Yes, Hail to Thee,
O Christ Our King!
Put to flight Lucifer,
The fallen angel of darkness,
From our homes, schools, and society;
Force him and his agents into hell;
Chain him there everlastingly
Whilst we, Thy friends,
Continue to salute Thee:
Hail, Christ, Our King!

## TO JESUS CHRIST, KING

O Christ Jesus, I acknowledge Thee
As Universal King.
All that has been made was created for Thee.
Exercise over me all the rights
That Thou hast.
 I renew my baptismal promises,
Renouncing Lucifer, his pomps, and his works,
And I promise to live as a good Christian.
Especially do I pledge myself,
By all the means in my power,
To bring about the triumph of the rights of God
And of Thy Church.
 Divine Heart of Jesus,
I consecrate all my poor actions
To the cause of Thy Kingship,
That all hearts may recognize Thee,
Their ruler,

And thus establish the Kingdom of Thy peace
In all the world. Amen.
(Plenary indulgence, usual conditions: confession, Communion, and
prayers for Holy Father's intentions.)

## RAVENSBROOK DEATH CAMP PRAYER

This prayer was found at the Ravensbrook Death Camp where
92,000 women and children died. It was found scrawled on a piece of
wrapping paper, lying near a dead child.

"Lord, remember not only the men and women of good will, but
also those of ill will. But do not only remember the suffering they have
inflicted on us. Remember the fruits we have brought, thanks to this
suffering: our comradeship, our loyalty, our humility, the courage, the
generosity, the greatness of heart which has grown out of all this. And
when they come to judgment, let all the fruits we have borne be their
forgiveness."

# THE LIGHT OF LOVE